NO REASON TO HIDE

NO REASON TO HIDE

A TRUE, EXTRAORDINARY STORY
OF THE PARENTS' OWN INVESTIGATION OF
THEIR SON'S HIT-AND-RUN VEHICULAR HOMICIDE

ELAINE STARINCHAK

NO REASON TO HIDE
A TRUE, EXTRAORDINARY STORY OF THE PARENTS' OWN INVESTIGATION
OF THEIR SON'S HIT-AND-RUN VEHICULAR HOMICIDE

Windy City Publishers
2118 Plum Grove Road, #349
Rolling Meadows, IL 60008
www.windycitypublishers.com

Published in the United States of America

ISBN:
978-1-941478-41-7

Library of Congress Control Number:
2017946981

WINDY CITY PUBLISHERS
CHICAGO

To Andrew and Betsey,
C.S.F., A.D.Y., and T.Y.,
And to all the families and victims of
Hit-and-Run Crashes

Contents

Illustrations and Documents in Text

Acknowledgements

LIKE MOST PEOPLE WHO WRITE a book, I had help. I want to acknowledge and thank them. Some of those who helped are entrenched in the story, like our brilliant attorney and friend, Mark Adams. Some of them read the manuscript critically like my beloved friend, Mark Miller. And to Mark's wife, Teresa, whose sharp eye proofread each page carefully. Knowing people in high places has its rewards. Ruth Cochrane, whose career as Editor and Vice President of well-known publishing firms, offered me some of the most insightful editing and criticism.

I am grateful to OZ, Andrew's long-time friend who took many of the photos, and to Toni Greetis of Phototronics who provided ideas for the cover. And thank you to Karen Ansary for your courage to offer needed criticism as well as support. I am grateful also to Joje, Louie, Doug, Maureen, Deborah, Luke, and Teresa for their reading of the manuscript. And most especially to Anthony Bouza, former Minneapolis Police Chief and the Bronx Police force commander for his words of wisdom and encouragement.

Joseph, Dean T., and Teresa M., solved my computer problems at various stages as the problems arose with the collection of data.

I mention with gratitude our many remarkable friends in the context of the story. Uppermost on this list are Mark and Patty Adams and Paul Devine. Mark Adams' involvement in what happened to Andrew and to us is central to and at the heart of this story. Paul, Andrew's close friend, continued a relationship with us and gave us the kind of comfort no one else could. I would be remiss not to express my gratitude to The Compassionate Friends organization, the Columbus bicycle community, former students, neighbors, and those we didn't know before Andrew's death who felt our grief and came to help; and to Tina Miller who enlisted her brother to name a street in his development after Andrew.

My husband and Andrew's father took over the daily chores so I could write. And lastly, our daughter's loving spirit of support both nourished and supported us, and in the end, she mightily challenged and inspired me to write her brother's story.

A few words, first...

THE TITLE OF MY BOOK, *No Reason to Hide*, came to me from a friend. Telling him about Andrew's death and investigation, he remarked, "The driver had no reason to hide. No one was looking." At least not the authorities, I thought. Then, ironically, the phrase *"never had any reason to"* was spoken repeatedly during a deposition by the owner of the van that experts identified as the one that killed our son.

In writing about Andrew's death, I put in every single detail I could possibly squeeze in. The manuscript was a massive 200,000 plus words so the detail was preserved. During the process of revision, I felt compelled to write a Supreme Court Memorandum. I'm not a lawyer, but we were out of money, and I either had to write it or do nothing, giving silent affirmation to the lower court's ruling. The clerk told me several times that my chance of moving the Supreme Court of Ohio to select our case for consideration was zero. I knew how to research, find sources, and follow citation guidelines. There's something to be said for ignorance—gross ignorance of the acceptance of any case before the Supreme Court. I did what I needed to do regardless of any ruling.

Not long after, a friend's mother died in an auto accident. As I drove to this friend's house, I was hit head-on by a truck that crossed over into my lane, crushing the bones in both ankles and breaking other bones in my legs. Surgeons held my bones together with metal fixators, placed on the outside of my ankles and legs. That crash set me back more than a year – although I continued to revise when I could.

The idea that the perpetrator of a crime is never charged because the authorities don't investigate was not unique to our case. In Andrew's case, some semblance of an investigation occurred the first several weeks after the crash, but the Sheriff's interest in our son's death quickly waned. Still, many wonderful people in Columbus who were on the lookout for a white van matching the description of the van that killed my son were calling in tips more than a year later. But a tip is good only with follow-up.

When I began to write the story of my family's investigation into our son's death, my thought was to present the evidence as we, with the help of professionals, discovered and what we did and learned in the process of investigating our own tragedy. Instead of writing only a fact-based accounting, I found myself veering off the factual path at times to reveal details about our family and specifically, the human nature side of law enforcement and our legal and judicial systems.

What I discovered, at least in this experience, is a strong need on the part of certain people to protect themselves in situations that might expose them as apathetic, incompetent, careless, even human. Families want only justice—an impartial, truthful presentation of the evidence of an investigation and the perpetrator held accountable. My husband and I could not turn our backs on evidence left at the crash site and on the factual evidence that the Bureau of Criminal Investigation and other professionals helped us to uncover.

In defiance of the obstacles the authorities threw at us, we persevered in our search for the truth. The investigation seemed to expect us to simply mourn and accept whatever they presented as their investigative results. That would never have worked for Andrew had the situation been reversed and we had been killed. He would have stood fiercely for what he believed was right, no matter what the cost. His family and friends will attest to that. His courage and uprightness supported our resolve to do what we trust all loving parents would do. Struggling for relief from a terrible grief drove us to participate in the investigation. If we were to get at the truth, we had to become detached. Like a competent detective, we had to consider the information our attorney and private investigators collected. But at the end of each day, alone in the house where our son grew up and where we now lived without him, our pent-up emotions erupted.

Because deception is a strong thread in our story, the investigation led me to seek experts who have studied and written about deception—serious deception. Of course, the most common deception of all is lying. Our story is about lies that obstruct justice. It's about critical lies dealing with life and death events.

We had to know who took our son from us. We had to know and confront the person who killed him and see that person bear the consequences for his actions. Our search for the truth had to be flawless. We could have no doubt about the soundness of the evidence and facts gathered. As the months passed and no one stepped forward, my disdain for the driver grew with my determination to get answers.

This book, the story of our investigation into our son's death, is based almost exclusively on the evidence found at the scene of the crash, what information that evidence led to, legal documents, and documents gleaned from related sources. Relevant information, ignored by police, was in plain sight—accessible and available—pointing to the guilty van. But the police weren't looking. The driver had no reason to hide.

Where I thought appropriate to discuss egregious omissions in the investigation, I have included copies of public documents in the context of the story or have cited them at the end of the book. All are of public record. Also, where fitting, I changed the names of people who were innocently involved and those whom I had no proof were involved. Those names are marked with an asterisk. Conversations primarily with my husband and our attorneys, private investigators and family I recreated with the help of emails and in tandem with events. Testimony from witnesses, the police and others are a matter of record. I have in safe storage every single important document.

As we undertook this journey to discover what happened to Andrew, I have been harshly candid in describing our gullibility and inexperience. I strongly believed that if my husband and I were to find the van, we would do that by painstakingly tracking down vans. What happened to help us find the van would have been beyond my most creative imagination. If this story were fiction, I would have dismissed it as unrealistic.

After this long, arduous undertaking, when the pieces finally fit and we had some answers, it struck me: A number of unexplainable events just seemed to materialize. The first deputy assigned to our case happened to spot the guilty van not far from his own home several weeks after the crash but didn't suspect it because it had already been repaired. Nearly three years later, through a set of unexpected circumstances, my husband and I were unknowingly led back to that same van—the sample van in all our posters and flyers.

No other person is responsible for the words, for the presentation of evidence and documents or for any other detail. This has been my way, a mother's way, of dealing with an adored son's death. To honor Andrew, I had to hold myself to the highest standards I possibly could in every facet of this investigation.

We really cannot live without truth. We need truth not only in order to understand how to live well, but in order to know how to survive at all.

The notions of truth and of factuality are indispensable, then, for imbuing the exercise of rationality with meaningful substance. We cannot think of ourselves as rational creatures at all unless we think of ourselves as creatures who recognize that facts, and true statements about facts, are indispensable in providing us with reasons for believing (or not believing) various things and for taking (or not taking) various actions.

~Harry G. Frankfurt
On Truth

1998

1

I SLEPT ON THE COUCH that night so I could hear Andrew come in. It's not my habit to wait up for my thirty-one year old son. But this night held signs that this was unusual. In the summer, darkness envelopes our country house after sunset. We live in a small forest with trees hovering over the house. As I dozed on the couch, hundreds of locusts chirped outside the screened windows. Any sound that intruded—a small animal scurrying about—caused me to sit up, listening for the sound of bicycle tires, the crushing sound of tires on a gravel lane.

I must have checked the clock every hour. By three A.M. most restaurants and bars had closed. My stomach churned.

When my husband, Andy, and I arrived home that evening from Picnic at the Pops, a summer concert series for the Columbus Symphony Orchestra, we saw our son's Honda still in the drive. Through the hatchback, we could see that Andrew had packed his duffle bag, cleats, and a stack of Frisbees. The door to the house was unlocked and the television was on. Upon entering, I called out, "Andrew, I thought you were going to Cincinnati." No answer. Andy did a quick check of the house, and from the basement he yelled, "His bike's gone. He must have gone somewhere."

"I don't get it. It's eleven o'clock. He was going to Cincinnati after practice," I said mystified. We saw that his car was packed. He planned to go. Because Andrew was a Miami University graduate, many of his friends lived in Cincinnati, so for him that was a common weekend destination. At some point, he must have decided to take a bicycle ride before heading to Cincinnati. So why didn't he leave as planned?

Months after his death, thinking back to that terrible Saturday, the last day of Andrew's life, I tried to piece together what he did from the time he left the house before noon to the time he was found on Sunday morning. He spent the afternoon at one of Ohio State University's practice fields with his Ultimate Frisbee teammates. After practice, we know he hung out with other players and friends at Paul and Robin's house near campus, came home in the late afternoon, ate some vegetables picked that morning from his uncle's garden and packed his car to go to Cincinnati for a tournament.

The morning light was only a few hours away, and I still hadn't heard from Andrew. Every passing minute intensified my worry. If he was involved in an

1

accident, did he have identification? If not, the authorities wouldn't know who to call. At about four o'clock I slipped on my shoes and went outside to look in Andrew's car. Since our drive is long and private, Andrew often placed his wallet under the driver's seat if he expected to go somewhere later. Stooping down outside his Honda, I felt around under the seat. No wallet. He has identification, I thought, somewhat relieved. "God's in his heaven…"

Why I didn't find the wallet is a mystery to me. It was under the seat—where he always put it. That one bit of carelessness turned out to be a huge oversight—one that perhaps meant the difference between finding him alive or finding him dead.

If I had found the wallet, I would have known that he was without identification and called local police stations and hospitals. Then Andrew's friends. Had I called the police, hospitals, and his friends at four o'clock in the morning, now Sunday, August 2, no one would have had any information about him. The pain of not knowing would have instantly motivated me to climb in my car and try to figure out his route.

But because I didn't find the wallet, I went back into the house, thinking that he left with money and identification. If he had been injured, then someone surely would have witnessed that and helped him. My imagination would not allow me to picture his dying in a ditch on Central College Road, minutes from our house.

At six o'clock that Sunday morning, I clicked on the television to check the early news. By this time my head clanked with alarm bells. As I switched between two local television channels, no one reported a young man on a bicycle having been hit. Nauseated with worry, I woke Andy. "I'm going out to check the roads. I'll go to Central College Road into New Albany and check out by the dam. Something's not right."

"My God, he's a grown man. He can take care of himself. He's okay," Andy responded.

If you turn left out of our lane, you head toward country roads that cyclists prefer. Thinking that's what Andrew would also do, I took a left toward Central College Road. I drove slowly, looking left and right. The early morning light filtered through trees, dappling the road with shadows. What was I looking for? Andrew's body? His bike? I worried far too much about our adult son and daughter. I couldn't totally trust my intuition. Somehow, though, this felt different. We were three adults living in the same house, and out of courtesy or even safety, Andy and I made certain that Andrew knew of our plans if we were going away. We expected the same from him as he traveled most weekends in the spring, summer and fall to Ultimate tournaments on college campuses. He always called if he planned to stay the night at a friend's apartment or pulled an all-nighter at OSU, studying for some graduate test. We never asked for details—just where he was going and when he planned to be home.

Harlem Road intersects Central College Road, not more than a mile from our house. I continued past Harlem Road and Route 605, then made a right onto Route 62. Between Harlem Road and Rte. 605, a section of Central College Road I had just passed, Andrew lay in a ditch, undiscovered, dying.

In 1998 this area was rural. Houses sat back from the roads on fields resembling patchwork, acres of green grass, then acres of brown thatch, separated by long stretches of corn and soybean fields. The coroner placed the time of Andrew's death at seven that morning. Since I left the house at dawn, it was not yet seven.

I couldn't acknowledge my fears. There had to be some logical explanation. Imagining tragedy struck me as illogical. Yet how many times had I worried myself sick when one of our two children was late coming home, only to discover that each was okay, giving an acceptable explanation. Just because I felt that something was wrong didn't mean something *was* wrong. You should have a reason. I did. The whole incident was unusual—contrary to Andrew's predictable habits. To be out on a bike in the dark? No. To be gone all night and not call? No. Few people had cell phones then, but he could walk to a phone. To have already packed his car to go to Cincinnati and not leave? Still, I counted on experience to take the edge off my anxiety.

I didn't expect to find Andrew lying by the side of the road and I didn't. Despite my instincts telling me that something was wrong, I was out to prove myself wrong.

From New Albany I headed to an area around Hoover Dam, traveling up Lee Road, still looking for a clue—something, anything. By the time, Andrew was discovered, I was miles away from where he lay. Had I stayed home, I would have heard the sirens of the fire truck, the rescue squad, the ambulance, and the police cars. A man we met later who lived on Central College had told us that many screaming sirens awakened him. Still sleeping, Andy never heard them. Even if he had, he would not have thought for a second that those sirens had anything to do with Andrew.

I reached home about ten-thirty. Thoroughly puzzled and angered, I wondered where he could have gone and why we hadn't heard from him? Coming through the door and seeing my worried face, he'd say, "Gee mommy, I'm sorry I didn't tell you where I'd be"—his words spoken with a contempt for adult mama's boys. But neither of us ever took offense at the sarcastic remarks we tossed at each other. His sarcasm was always delivered with a dose of lightheartedness. He never wanted to make me feel bad. As we laughed, his real message to me was, "Even though I'm still living at home, I'm not your little boy."

By the time he took that fateful ride, he had owned his bicycle a little more than a month. Our garage was packed with Andrew's sports equipment. If you wanted a metal or wooden baseball bat, you had your pick of five or more. We had fishing poles, lacrosse equipment, and several mountain bikes but not a racing bike. He had been thinking about buying one along with a canoe. One evening as he read over the want ads in our local paper, he spotted an advertisement for a Schwinn ten speed that sounded like a good deal. He bought it. Anything to expand his active lifestyle.

After that, he began cruising bicycle shops for sales on accessories. As a graduate student with money in short supply, he never bought anything that wasn't on sale. He found a pair of clip-in cycling shoes – with purple stripes—the sale price was right so he bought them. He wasn't one to pay attention to fashion. When he took the cycling shoes out of the box to show me, I said, "I don't like the purple stripes." I could not have envisioned that a week later, on Sunday, August 2, those shoes would be one item the police would ask me to describe. When I did, the look on the policeman's face announced the unthinkable.

Several cyclists called us to ask if Andrew was wearing a helmet. He wasn't. I'm positive that a helmet was on his list of cycling gear. Today, with all we know about cycling, a helmet is absolutely the first piece of equipment a cyclist should have. I'm ashamed to say that my husband and I rode our mountain bikes on Central College Road, many, many times without helmets. As kids riding our bikes, we and no one we knew ever wore a helmet.

What Andrew's route was after he crossed onto Central College Road, we can only guess, based on where cyclists usually rode in that area. By the time we arrived home from the concert on Saturday evening, Andrew had already been hit and left to die. The driver didn't stop. He didn't call 911, even anonymously. Most probably, he or she was drunk. And the driver didn't sober up and come forward in the weeks and months following the vehicular homicide.

The coroner placed the time of Andrew's death at seven o'clock that morning, several hours before a couple on their way to church spotted our son, and a half hour after I had passed Andrew, between six and six thirty that morning. Andy's friend, Lou, asked me several weeks later if I had any feelings of guilt. Guilt? Knowing that I was not observant enough to see our son, knowing that I had passed him because I felt that I was overreacting, knowing that I questioned my intuition, and knowing that I could have held my son, been with him and perhaps saved him? Guilt was a permanent part of me.

A caring friend would later remark, "It was a good thing you didn't see him. Can you imagine how terrible that would have been?" No. Knowing that I passed our son and could have been with him is so much worse.

In no way can you prepare yourself for the death of a child—even a young man, thirty-one. Not even in your most creative, compassionate moments can you begin to know the depths of that kind of pain. With sudden death, the victim's family is forced to cope with aberrant circumstances. We became forever linked to the perpetrator who took Andrew's life and then ran and hid. Who was this person?

If the driver suspected that he had hit a person, sobered up, and contacted his lawyer, he would have been charged with a misdemeanor in 1998, even if the victim died. And chances are the driver would not have served jail time. But if the driver, suspecting that he hit a person, repaired his vehicle, he would be guilty of a felony because he tampered with evidence. Killing a person in a hit-and-run crash in 1998 was a misdemeanor and still is, but tampering with evidence was a felony and still is.

The police report marked the point of impact of the vehicle with Andrew's bike. The rubber from the tires painted the road with a thin, black line and then nothing—when the bicycle lifted off the road. The long black tire line was to the right of the white line, as near to the edge of the road as possible. The crash reconstructionists, who we later hired, stated that according to the reconstruction of the crash, the vehicle had to be at least six inches off the road to have hit Andrew. Was this a deliberate hit? Details at the crash support that it could have been. That's murder.

What is it about some people who can kill, walk away, and go about their lives as though they have just swatted a flea? And what is it about those who know what the killer did but choose to protect him? And critically, what is it about those in law enforcement who, despite evidence, fail to act on that evidence? My story is about these people.

Most of us accept whatever the police do or don't do. No one disputes that the job is a dangerous one, and our family feels grateful to them. When Andrew was killed, we respected and believed without question that law enforcement would do its job. Yet, *the Franklin County Sheriff's Office (FCSO) would ignore the piece of evidence left at the scene of the crash that held all the answers, pointing to the vehicle and driver.*

2

WHEN MY MOTHER DIED, MY sisters and I met with the funeral director and selected her casket. It was an awful thing to have to do. To select a parent's casket and clothes for burial. Clothes we will never again see her wear. To plan her funeral—our goodbye. Imagine doing that for a son. I don't know how our daughter, Betsey, Andy and I managed to get through those days. Shock and denial are cousins. I got through it because I couldn't fathom that our lives with Andrew were over. Finished.

The day after Andrew's funeral, August 7, the phone rang. On this morning, this warm, sunny summer morning, I couldn't grasp what had happened to our family. I just did not get it. In a daze, I answered the phone.

"Mrs. Starinchak?" said a male voice.

"Yes."

"This is the Franklin County Sheriff's office. We set up a media conference here at the traffic office on Mound Street at 2:30. Can you and your husband be there? We've contacted television stations and the *Columbus Dispatch*."

Grabbing a pencil and paper to take down the details, I replied that, of course, we'd be there.

While I was talking, Betsey, with Scott, our son-in-law, Susan, our niece, and her boyfriend, John, along with our nephew, Michael, were making breakfast. My husband looked up from his coffee. "What was that about?" he asked.

Repeating the details of the conversation, I gave thanks that we had something to do to occupy our time and minds. Since Andrew's body had been discovered six days earlier, friends, family and the media were nonstop. Being surrounded by loving people mercifully helped, at least for a time, to alleviate a suffering, a longing that would define the rest of our lives. A time would come when we had to be alone. When we couldn't answer the phone or the doorbell.

Before that morning phone call, we had had no contact with anyone from the Franklin County Sheriff. Seven days had passed since our son's hit-and-run death, and this was our first contact with the agency that was to investigate our son's homicide. Unknown to us at the time, the lead investigator, Deputy David McMannis, had been out of the office for training and didn't begin his work on our case until Thursday, August 6, five days after our son's body was discovered and six days after he had been hit.

This valuable bit of information didn't become known until this lead investigator's second deposition, taken in November 2003, five years after the crash as we prepared for a civil trial. Thus, for five years we were unaware that the Sheriff's Office was doing nothing during those first crucial days after the crash. Competent law enforcement practice dictated that the FCSO's traffic investigators should have interviewed us immediately after Andrew's identity was known and swung into action. They didn't.

But on this summer morning, the kind of day that Andrew loved, we had every reason to believe that the Sheriff's department was committed to doing its job. After all, critical physical evidence had been dropped in its lap at the scene of the crash.

Scott volunteered to drive so that Andy, Betsey, and I could collect our thoughts en route to the media conference. Michael followed us in Susan's Jeep. Earlier, we had talked about what we wanted to say. Andy believed that we had to send a strong message to the driver who killed Andrew: give yourself up or face the consequences. I agreed. The truth was I didn't know how to word that warning so the driver would cooperate. The longer the driver stayed hidden, the easier it would become to remain hidden.

When we arrived at the traffic division of the Sheriff's Office, camera crews were setting up in the parking lot next to the building, and a small group of deputies stood together, talking. As we approached them, Sheriff Jim Karnes stepped forward and introduced himself. He said that it was time to call upon the public to help with information. A wave of gratitude washed over me. I reached up and hugged Sheriff Karnes, just as a *Columbus Dispatch* photographer snapped a photo. That photo was to appear the next day on the first page of the Metro section of the *Dispatch*.

One of the reporters placed a microphone on a stand in the middle of the lot and motioned to Andy and me. Positioning ourselves in front of the microphone, we braced ourselves for questions. Betsey, Scott, Susan, John, and Michael came up behind us. A *Columbus Dispatch* reporter, Liz Sidoti, called out to us, "What do you have to say to the driver who killed your son and left?"

I answered, "Accidents happen and if the person who killed our son would have stopped at the scene, we would be home with that person, embracing that person, grieving with that person. If the person who did this is suffering or in anguish now, we still would grieve with them and hold them." *(Columbus Dispatch*, August 8, 1998)

Looking back at those words today, I can't understand how I could have been so—what is the word—naïve, stupid? I had no insight into what had happened to us. My only excuse is that on some level I felt the terrible enormity of taking a life. I mightily regret those words. The driver who hits a human being and hides has no reverence for life. He doesn't feel the enormity.

I wanted to say something that would resonate with my son's killer. I could not imagine that any driver, having killed a person, would not be in agony. I envisioned an elderly person with poor eyesight or a teen who had been drinking. One was too old and the other too young to be held totally responsible. In truth, our killer was middle-aged. I was right in the drinking part—as drugs or alcohol impair most hit-and-run drivers.

Deputy McMannis chose not to introduce himself to us at the media conference. We met him the following week. When a tragedy happens to a family, when a beloved member is killed suddenly, the family goes into shock. We walked around dazed. To others, we probably seemed okay, but we weren't. Thank God, Scott set the timer on the VCR to record the meeting. Without our knowing it, Scott taped most of those early television interviews. Those tapes would become invaluable.

The tape of the first media conference showed a deputy explaining that two fiberglass pieces, somewhat like a running board but without a step, were found at the crash scene—one piece on top of Andrew's bike and the other nearby. These two pieces made up the front third of a passenger side part termed a *ground effect*. The part, a long piece of molding, covers the rocker panel at the bottom of a van. As plain and as generic as it looked, it wasn't. More substantial evidence could not have been left at the crash. A deputy, possibly McMannis, held up the two pieces, showing how the one vertical piece fit like a puzzle into the other horizontal piece. The deputy placed the pieces against a new 1998 Chevy Astro van borrowed from a dealership—showing where they would be installed with screws. Seven days after the crash, we had no idea how vital, how critical these pieces would be to solving our son's homicide.

That tape would eventually be used at trial five years later to confirm exactly what did and did not happen at the media conference. The tape was in direct contrast to the lead investigator's truthfulness. The story was yet to play out.

That evening we watched the local news of the media session to see what was selected from all the comments we made. Were we effective? Was the Sheriff effective in his call for help from the community? We zeroed in on some footage taken at the scene of the crash. The television clip reported that Andrew was killed between Route 605 and Harlem Road on Central College Road in Plain Township. By looking at the houses in the video background, Betsey was sure that she could pinpoint the crash scene. She also pointed out the black tire marks Andrew's bike made when the van hit it from behind.

We planned to go to the crash site the next morning since Michael had an afternoon flight back to Oregon. At breakfast Betsey, looking puzzled, entered the kitchen.

"Mom, where's Andrew's arrowhead necklace?"

"I don't know." I had forgotten about this necklace that Andrew rarely took off. I hadn't seen Andrew until after the morgue released his body to the funeral home. The memory of my son lying stiff and cold on a gurney in that small, round room lined with stained-glass windows seemed crazy, surreal. The sun struck the stained-glass throwing colored diamond patterns on the walls and floor. The only other detail I remember was Andrew's thick eyelashes, locking his brown eyes shut. I was in hell.

"I tore his room apart, so I'm sure it's not there," she said.

We live in an eight-acre forest and so had plenty of firewood for winter fires. Andy and Andrew spent weekends in the woods, chopping up trees which had fallen because of age or weather. On one of these ventures when Andrew was in high school, while chopping a large tree—probably more than 100 years old—he found an arrowhead embedded in the trunk. The arrowhead, we later discovered, was worth between $200 and $300 because its tool marks are of a Native American tribe not usually found in Ohio. He had taken the arrowhead to a shop where it was entwined with copper wiring and then attached to a leather string—material available to Native Americans more than 100 years ago.

We needed to have that arrowhead. Andrew deeply valued it. He held Native American core beliefs about nature. Betsey insisted that she had searched through all the drawers of his bureau and desk and items in his closet. She suggested that we go with rakes to Central College Road to comb the crash site for the necklace. With rakes from the garage, Betsey, Susan, John, and Michael climbed in Susan's jeep to follow us.

The eastern half of Central College Road in 1998 was a country road, flat, characteristic of central Ohio, with rural pockets of fields and houses situated here and there. The house closest to the crash site sat back off the road—an ordinary ranch painted green. The police never talked to the elderly person who lived there. On that morning, a couple on their way to church had discovered Andrew. They went to the green house and knocked but no one answered. Weeks later, Andy stopped by the house and talked to an elderly lady who said that she was afraid to answer the door that Sunday morning. "Did you talk to the police?" Andy asked. "No," the woman answered.

Walking the stretch of Central College where Betsey thought Andrew had been hit, she yelled to us that she had found the bicycle tire track inside the white line. Dazed, we looked at the thin, black rubber mark. Viewing that black mark and standing in the place our son was hit, I visualized a large vehicle, swerving to the right with its tire off the road, hitting Andrew's bike from behind, and tossing him up into the air. The picture lasted only a second. From that time on, I did everything possible to block out that image. And that I had passed by him while he lay in that ditch. How could I have not sensed where my son was dying?

The August sun, providing plenty of light for us to see into the thick grass, silently we went about our task, but no necklace.

For weeks, Betsey, Andy and I took our rakes back to Central College Road. We had to find that arrowhead. Andrew always wore it. It had to be hidden away some place in those grasses.

In those weeks, my husband and I visited the site, not only to look for the necklace but also to grieve. At first, I had to go every day. Today, I avoid Central College Road. Within that week, Andy built a cross. We wanted people to know that our beloved son was taken from us there.

Having been a Catholic for most of my life despite religious doubts, I was entrenched in religious culture at the time of Andrew's death. That fall, I held on to the belief that my adored son was not dead, that he was alive in a kind of heaven-like place—a good place. Parents have no choice but to hold on to any belief that brings comfort. By Christmas, his death had given me the courage to question my religious beliefs.

Fervently, I prayed that we would find not only our son's killer but also our son's necklace. The necklace was a tangible object and priceless to Andrew. That necklace was not a piece of jewelry—it was a symbol of his admiration of Native American culture.

Repeatedly Betsey scoured his room. In October, I prayed a novena to my patron saint, St. Theresa, the little flower. A skeptic, I found it hard to believe that we would ever find the necklace or Andrew's killer. But each was found unexpectedly, and not at all to planned strategies. Both had a hint of the miraculous.

Is it possible our deceased loved ones find a way to communicate with us? How we came upon the murder weapon, the van, can only be described as the synchronicity of extraordinary events. Events that will lead us *back* three years after the crash to a particular van. But after Andrew's death, we were living mindlessly.

Andy is a creature of habit. Every October, he will take down the screens, wash them and store them for the winter in the garage. On a warm October day removing screens, he was on the ladder outside Andrew's room. He remembered that last October he had put a piece of hardware that had fallen off one of the windows in Andrew's desk drawer. He entered Andrew's room and then made a loud sound—a sound so strange—I went running to the room. In his hand was Andrew's arrowhead necklace.

3

ON MONDAY, AUGUST 10, WE met Deputy David McMannis. He and his partner, Deputy Terry Wassmuth, came to the house. Andrew was hit on August lst; it was now August 10th. And finally, a Sheriff's deputy came to see us. Was the Sheriff's Office aware that each *hour* was precious in a homicide? We stood outside by the cruiser and talked. No one took notes. McMannis never inquired about a chronology of events before the crash. No friends' names. Like nothing official. That was our introduction to McMannis' modus operandi: careless. As in he couldn't care less.

We were to discover through Deputy McMannis' deposition some five years later, that he was in London, Ohio, for training for most of the first week after Andrew's death, which also explained why the media conference was not scheduled until Friday, August 7. No investigative activity occurred for a full six days after Andrew was killed and only then to inquire about the make and model of the vehicle, nothing else. From Sunday to Friday, we had no communication from the FCSO. The only policemen we met early on were officers from the Blendon Township Police Department who came to the house to ascertain Andrew's identity on Sunday, August 2.

When I returned home that Sunday morning after circling Hoover Dam and New Albany and still not having heard from Andrew, I began calling relatives and friends. His friends last saw him about five o'clock on Saturday when he left Paul's house after practice. I tried not to worry. The back-brick patio needed weeding so I released anxiety by pulling weeds. The afternoon was bearing down on us and still no word.

Andy, too, attempted to keep busy by working in the yard. The thought suddenly came to him to check for Andrew's wallet under his car's driver's seat. He had no idea that I had checked the car at four o'clock that morning. In feeling around under the seat, his hand touched the wallet. He called to me from Andrew's car and my heart dropped. At that moment, about two or three o'clock in the afternoon, I retreated into myself. I went numb to protect myself from the worst fear a mother could feel.

Immediately, I called the Westerville police and talked to a dispatcher. Our conversation was somewhat strange. While she asked me questions, she was talking to someone else on a radio. "What's your address?" she asked, evading the answer to my question about a possible bicycle accident. Within minutes two township officers pulled in the drive. We were to discover that because Andrew was killed in an adjacent township, the Franklin County Sheriff's Office had jurisdiction.

Now, nine days after our son had been discovered, deputies from the FCSO visited us. We didn't have the insight to question the delay or McMannis' brand of interview. By now any vehicle could have been destroyed, repaired or hidden miles away.

McMannis exited the squad car while his partner, Deputy Wassmuth, stayed inside. Greeting them, Andy shook McMannis' hand. Betsey and I made our way down the walk to the cruiser. Somewhat tall and burley, McMannis sported a brush mustache and looked stereotypically like a deputy.

Because we found him affable, our first impression would be hard to shake in the months and years ahead. At our most vulnerable, we would have embraced the devil if he had smiled and pretended that he would find our son's killer.

"What needs to be done to get some answers?" Andy asked.

"One way you can help is to get some reward posters printed up and pass them out. Crime Stoppers will offer up to $1,000 for information and if you can, you could add to that amount. 'Billy Bob' will turn in his own mother if he gets mad at her."

McMannis' use of "Billy Bob" hinted at a certain class of people. His assessment hinted at the kind of person who could hit a bicyclist and leave the person to die struck me as insightful. Prior to this conversation, my imagination about the kind of person who would commit this kind of crime had been limited. Andrew was hit on a country road in Plain Township, an area in serious residential transition.

New Albany had long enjoyed a reputation for being inhabited by country folk. But in 1998, with the New Albany Company's procurement of land, the area was changing. Still, in some areas, the countryside was littered with junk and abandoned vehicles.

I asked, "What amount would it take for 'Billy Bob' to make a call?"

"About five thousand dollars," he replied.

Andy responded, "OK, let's do it."

McMannis left saying that he would be in touch if anything came up.

We dreaded the end of the week when Betsey had to return home to tie up some loose ends at work. But it wasn't as if we were alone. Dear friends dropped in at all times. During a terrible crisis, I learned how differently people act. One close friend offered her thoughts, "Andrew would not want you to be sad." It had only been three weeks.

We had not yet fully comprehended the horrific reality that our lives with Andrew were over. These friends sincerely thought that we would be better if we accepted Andrew's death and moved on as quickly as possible. Parents never accept and move on. Part of our lives are forever frozen.

Other friends were curious about what the police were doing. They proved more therapeutic. It offered us a diversion, a kind of escape from our grief while at the same time showing a concern for Andrew's life. Our good friends, Patty, and Mark Adams, called us almost daily to guide us. Unknown to us at the time, Mark, an attorney, would successfully search out critical information pointing to the van that killed Andrew. This remarkable man achieved staggering results—given the obstructions we were to face. He interrupted his practice to help us. Under Mark's sharp leadership, we moved forward, with tangible results, in gathering relevant information, especially about the pieces of the fiberglass ground effects. To us, these were just white pieces of molding. To Mark, the pieces held many more secrets than merely revealing the make, model, and color of a vehicle. His insight paid off. Big time.

4

AS THE FRANKLIN COUNTY SHERIFF'S Office reported to the *Columbus Dispatch*, deputies at the scene discovered two pieces of a white fiberglass ground effect, like a running board without a step, on top of and near Andrew's ten speed bicycle. Crash reconstructionists later reasoned that the bicycle flipped over and the handlebars caught the ground effect, tearing part of it off in two pieces. Every conversion company has its own distinctive ground effect design. We saw these pieces for the first time at the media conference on August 7, when the Sheriff's investigator held them up to the television cameras.

It was fortuitous that these particular moldings or fiberglass pieces were unique and installed only on a white, Chevy Gladiator van. On August 6, six days after Andrew's death, Deputy McMannis took the pieces around to Columbus auto dealerships and conversion shops to find out what he could. He discovered then that the Glaval Corporation out of Elkhart, Indiana, manufactured and installed that ground effect exclusively only on their converted vans. One of the dealers gave him Glaval's address, and when he called Glaval and talked to the customer service manager, he received the next most important bit of information helpful in solving this case: a listing of about 700 Glaval vans with this kind of ground effect sold to dealerships across the state of Ohio. Afterward we were to learn that Glaval vans were in relatively short supply in the Columbus area in 1998. Great news for McMannis. Right? Not so much. He claimed he didn't have access to updating Glaval vans' ownerships.

Armed now with physical evidence from the vehicle involved in the crash, Deputy McMannis learned that the vehicle was a white, Chevy, Gladiator minivan and that the Glaval Corporation handled its conversion. And as a huge boost to the investigation, the Glaval Corporation sent to the FCSO a listing of 700 vans sold to Ohio dealerships with that ground effect. Common knowledge among experts held that the van was a central Ohio van.

On Friday, August 14, McMannis and Wassmuth paid us a visit at the house. They came together twice in August and McMannis by himself once in October. Three visits in all.

Later, when we were recreating an August timeline to get an accurate idea of what happened during those early weeks including our interaction with the Sheriff's Office, Andy remembered that at one of the two August visits he had been dealing with the garbage cans. "I had driven up the lane to pick up the empty garbage cans on Friday and as I was bringing them down the lane, I saw a Sheriff's car in my rearview behind me."

Looking at the calendar, we knew that no one from the Sheriff's Office interviewed us the first week. Andrew's funeral was on Thursday. We put no garbage out on that day before pickup on Friday. We didn't formally meet McMannis or his partner at the press conference on Friday, August 7th. By looking at emails and the calendar, we concluded that McMannis gave Andy the van photos on Friday, August 14. The contact we made with my niece, Susan, confirmed the deputies' visit at the end of the second week, August 14. The desire to get a handle on events and when they happened helped us to pinpoint the date that McMannis stopped by with photos of a Glaval van that he suggested we use in our flyers. This seemingly insignificant detail about the garbage—along with information *from McMannis' sworn testimony, himself, as to his whereabouts that entire first week—would put us squarely at odds with what McMannis would later claim he did.*

Although we always invited the deputies to come into the house, they refused. Our two meetings took place outside our house near the squad car. Terry Wassmuth, listening with the window rolled down, as we talked to McMannis, sat in the passenger seat. I don't remember his ever saying anything.

"Did you think any more about offering a reward?" McMannis asked Andy.

"Absolutely. Elaine's niece who owns a printing company is coming this weekend. We want to get started printing posters."

"I have something that may help," and with that he handed Andy a Polaroid photo of a van and one of him holding the ground effect pieces, found at the crash.

"Is this what we're looking for?" Andy asked, scrutinizing the photo.

"It's a white Chevy van converted by Glaval and has their pony board [ground effect]," he answered.

"How'd you get this?" Andy asked.

"I happened to spot this van and saw the pony board. I asked the driver if I could take a picture of it." Apparently, the van owner consented. McMannis referred to the ground effect as a "pony board," a term apparently synonymous with ground effect and running board.

In thinking back to that meeting, we never asked about the photos and the owner of the van—where he or she lived or any other detail. We merely accepted the photos and thanked McMannis. That Andrew's handlebars tore off the ground effect in two pieces proved to be a huge stroke of luck. But we wouldn't fully understand how important that evidence was until we talked to the Glaval manufacturer, ourselves, almost two years later.

Nearing the last week in August, we met with McMannis at the Mound Street traffic office about the van list. We invited Rick, a private investigator, recently retired from the Columbus Police Department to go with us. The rivalry and animosity that oftentimes existed between the FCSO and the CPD weren't in evidence.

At the time, the investigation seemed active—all indications pointed to McMannis working our son's homicide. But we weren't getting the full picture. Unknown to us, the investigation hadn't begun until McMannis returned from training on Thursday, August 6th. Other errors occurred in procedure that we didn't know about. The bike and Andrew's clothes *were not* examined or tested. In the case of a homicide, time is on the side of the perpetrator. As in our case, time gives the offender the opportunity to repair damage and destroy evidence.

Leading us to an upstairs desk situated in a hallway, McMannis showed us the list that he had printed from the 700 plus Glaval vans on Glaval's computer disk. Arranged in columns, the most important information was the VIN, or 17-character vehicle identification number, then the van's year, followed by the original owner, address and the dealership from which it was purchased and its address. The disk also contained the exterior color of each van, but not displayed on our list. The exterior color was crucial in eliminating vans that could not have been involved. Red, blue, and tan vans could immediately be excluded. We were looking for a white van.

McMannis used a green marker to highlight local vans and announced that he would check those vans. We learned that a conversion company, like Glaval, takes a basic van and customizes it. It installs its own seats, compartments, anything to make it more comfortable. On the outside are Glaval's luggage racks, striping, and moldings.

"When can we get started looking at these vans?" Andy asked Rick.

"I'll run a check with the Bureau of Motor Vehicle (BMV) to update the owners highlighted in green."

In 1998, anyone could request information from the BMV. But then early in 2000, my BMV requests were denied. A change in the law? I don't know.

Still, by this time we had two strikes against us. First, the driver and/or owner could have repaired the van. Second, the owner could have destroyed the van, perhaps setting it on fire, as one psychic predicted. Yet the list provided us with a starting point to track the whereabouts of vans on August 1, 1998.

Any suspicious event involving a van would tell us to take a closer look. We weren't out of the game. Not by a long shot.

Then we had McMannis. The law. He was checking the list he had highlighted on page one. Or so we thought.

Every weekend in August, our niece Susan and her boyfriend, John, made the three-hour trip to Columbus on Saturday mornings and returned home on Sunday afternoon. Owning a printing business, she and John printed the reward flyers and posters. We loved them and cherished their compassion and devotion to us. Both in their early thirties, one beautiful, the other handsome. Susan, with a mass of dark curly hair and flawless skin stood in contrast to John, fair-skinned and blonde. I return to those days when we needed them most and if I could have given them the world, I would have.

After McMannis' visit the day before, Andy pulled out the Polaroid photos of the Glaval van and ground effect pieces to show Susan and John.

"Could we take these photos home with us? They should be the focus of the poster," Susan reasoned.

We agreed.

"The message should be visible to someone in a car. We should use bold black letters. And put the important words in red," she said. "Like the reward money."

"I think we should offer $10,000," Andy said.

"People who know something might hesitate to get involved so I think we should say something about anonymity," I added.

With only so much room on a piece of paper, the language had to be succinct and clear. A poster nailed onto a telephone pole had to be read quickly by someone driving by or stopping at a traffic light. Today, instead of the Sheriff's number, I'd set up my own hot line. For reasons that will become increasingly obvious, if not already.

Toward the last week in August, Susan sent a box of flyers for my approval. That weekend, Betsey flew home for a two-week stay. On Sunday morning, August 23, climbing in our cars, Betsey, Andy, and I took half of Central College Road and Walnut Street, while Susan and John in her jeep took the eastern half of Central College Road, plus the side streets, to distribute reward flyers. Leaning out the passenger side window, we attached more than 75 flyers to mailboxes.

We began with Central College Road because the crash had happened there. Later we were to learn of a huge party that had taken place the weekend of the crash on the corner of Harlem and Central College Roads. As the months wore on, I became more convinced that the party was involved. The driver was heading in a westerly direction, so wherever the driver was going, it had to be west of Route 605, toward the party.

For the next weeks into September, we went out every day to distribute flyers and posters. Common sense told us to canvas that northeastern part of Franklin County. We approached every gas station, every restaurant, every antique store, every bank, hardware store, dry cleaners in nearby New Albany, Sunbury, and Johnstown, asking if we could put one of our reward posters in their windows. No one denied us.

One afternoon we stopped with our flyers at an Italian restaurant in Sunbury and talked to the owner. He uttered a negative comment about bicycle riders. The owner declared that his father would try to run bicyclists off the road every chance he got. His father drove a pick-up truck—a vehicle real men drive—that or a motorcycle. Obviously, his father was not familiar with the strength and endurance needed to ride a racing bike. Had he heard of the Tour de France?

Leaving the Italian restaurant and reeling with disbelief at what we had just heard, we entered an antique store on the other side of the town square. The Nestle Chocolate plant had not yet closed, and the town smelled like chocolate coffee. I still associate that smell with those awful first months as we raced around, trying to get information. I gave the woman at the counter our flyer and explained to her who we were. She looked at me and said, "How are you able to do this having just lost your son?"

Caught off guard, I had no answer. What she didn't know was that the knots in my stomach caused constant pain. The pressure would build and at the end of the day at home, my face, contorted with pain, released the tears.

No matter where we went, we carried those flyers. People were responding to them, and to newspaper articles and television stories. When we finally received copies of the Sheriff's file in 2000, we were shocked to learn the number of people who called Crime Stoppers with tips. I'm in awe of those people. I want them to know how grateful we are for their involvement and courage. *No evidence exists that the tips were ever utilized.* A call comes in and it's thrown in a box. What I did know is that tests had not been performed on Andrew's clothes, shoes, his bike, or the ground effect pieces. Nothing. So McMannis was checking tips? Checking tips, checking the van list…what was this poor man supposed to do?

When August ended, we had no idea if the FCSO had any viable leads. Then in the first week in September, McMannis called the house and talked to Andy.

"I've set up a television Crime Stoppers' interview for tomorrow. Are you available?" McMannis asked.

"Yes, sure. Where do we go?"

"I'll give you directions. Channel 6 is doing the interview," he responded. "The guy who owns the Glaval van in the photo is allowing us to use his van. The van'll be parked on the street. Can you be there around ten o'clock?"

"Yes, and our daughter's home so she'll be coming with us."

Betsey, nearing the end of her graduate program, needed every available minute to prepare her thesis. Besides having a career and being married only a year, she provided our link to life and to Andrew. Since she was scheduled for a business trip to Amsterdam at the end of October, she spent every spare second with us. On the morning of the interview, we followed McMannis' directions to Oldbury Court in Reynoldsburg. When we arrived at the address, we saw WSYX's truck, a sheriff's patrol car and a Glaval van parked on the street. The court had only four houses—with the van parked between two of them.

At the time, we never thought to ask about the van owner. We merely accepted the information that McMannis offered and asked no further questions. Three years later when this same van would resurface at Metro Chevrolet, we were surprised to realize how little McMannis told us and we never thought to ask. My usual way would have been to thank the owner for "helping" us.

Jon Griener, a distinguished television personality with a voice any Columbusite could identify, and Deputy McMannis approached us as we exited our car. After Griener introduced himself and his videographer, he briefed us on how he would conduct the interview.

First, he needed to establish the details of Andrew's death. Then Griener would ask McMannis to explain the evidence found at the crash site. McMannis had the two pieces of the ground effect with him. When he held them up to the camera, he demonstrated how and where the two pieces fit together on the passenger side of a Chevy Astro Gladiator [Glaval's model].

At the media conference a week after the crash and now at the Crime Stoppers interview in September, both Andy and I thought that Deputy McMannis handled himself with confidence and clearly articulated what he knew about those ground effect pieces.

Griener's last question, "What do you want people to know?"

Andy and Betsey looked to me to answer. "Someone knows who did this. The van that killed our son sustained enough damage for someone to notice. If you have any suspicion at all about someone's vehicle, please call Crime Stoppers." During that interview, five weeks after our son was killed, I was stuck on the idea that the van was still in need of repair. Nothing could have been further from the truth.

Not even in our wildest dreams could we have imagined that on that day, five weeks after our son's death, we were standing beside the weapon that took Andrew's life. And unknown to us, the day after the Crime Stoppers' interview aired on TV and publicity appeared in the *Columbus Dispatch*, the owner would sell this van.

5

ONE WARM SEPTEMBER AFTERNOON SEVERAL weeks after the Crime Stoppers' interview, I called the Sheriff's Office to ask if the Crime Stoppers' publicity that had aired earlier provided any valuable information. For most of September, we had had little contact with Deputy McMannis. We made calls to the FCSO, but because the calls were not returned, we began to think that we had become bothersome. Our calls were few, but we did want updates.

The calls went something like this: "Hello, may I speak to Deputy McMannis, please?"

The receptionist, "Yes, may I tell him who's calling?"

"This is Elaine Starinchak."

A minute later, the receptionist would return with, "Deputy McMannis is not in the office. May I take a message?"

Was he hiding from us? More than a month had passed and our son's clothes and bike went untested for paint and other materials. The Bureau of Criminal Investigation who handled such tests for the Franklin County Sheriff had never heard of us! Testing a victim's clothes—those walking, jogging, cycling—in a hit-and-run homicide—is so basic, so elementary, we could not have fathomed such an egregious omission.

In August and September, we assumed that the police remained interested in solving our case. Unlike most hit-and-runs, they had evidence and valuable information. Glaval had provided a list of vans sold to Ohio dealerships. How was McMannis handling that list? Before he handed Rick, our PI, the list, he had highlighted the vans sold out of central Ohio dealerships and said that he would check those.

Approximately seven hundred vans were listed on fourteen pages. McMannis had information we didn't. The van that killed Andrew had to have been white, and the ground effect had to have been gel-coated—on vans from 1990-1994. Our Xeroxed copy didn't show van color. Deleting the red, blue, and tan vans would have easily eliminated more than two hundred vans. From 1990 through 1994, Ohio dealerships across the state, in total bought about two hundred vans a year from Glaval. Some of those went to Central Ohio dealers.

We had no experience in investigating hit-and-run vehicular homicides, but even in our grief-stricken state we understood how invaluable the list of

Glaval vans was. The VIN that killed Andrew was on that list. What vans had the highest probability of involvement?

Our attorney and friend, Mark Adams, verbalized the significance of that list. One evening as we sat after dinner discussing the case, he remarked, "If you want to find out who killed Andrew, the first thing you have to do is find the van."

And how do we do that? "By a process of elimination," Don Corbin, a friend in law enforcement, told us. After a long career with the Columbus Police Department, he had just been named the Police Chief of Johnstown, a community not far from New Albany.

"Did you happen to read about Don Corbin?" Andy asked me one morning as he was reading the *Suburban News*. The Corbins had been the neighbors everyone liked because they were young, fun, had horses and an in-ground pool.

"Don Corbin, Chris Corbin's father?" Chris and Andrew were friends in elementary school. The family lived near us on Ulry Road, but they moved when the boys were in middle school. Chris' father, Don, was a member of the SWAT team with the Columbus Police Department and now was Johnstown's police chief.

"Yeah, we should go see him." Johnstown is close to Plain Township where Andrew was hit. It was possible that Don could know something. Many of the merchants in Johnstown allowed us to post reward posters in their stores.

"Give him a call," I said in total agreement. "If nothing else, we can ask him to help."

Before noon that morning we were sitting in the Johnstown police station, waiting to meet with Chief Don Corbin. When Andy called, Don consented to see us as soon as we could get there. His no-frills office, sparsely furnished with a desk, several chairs, and a file cabinet, was what you would expect to see in an outlying community with lots of acres given over to farming.

Tall, blonde and movie-star handsome, Johnstown's new police chief invited us into his office. After we shared family details, "How's Chris and what's he doing now?" the conversation turned to Andrew.

"I read about Andrew. Who has the case?"

"Franklin County Sheriff," Andy answered.

"Has there been an arrest?" he asked.

"No, or at least we haven't heard. We haven't talked to the investigator for some weeks now. He's always out of the office when we call. Can you help us?"

"What would you want me to do?" Don responded.

"Get involved in the investigation," I said.

Don looked at us several seconds. "I'm afraid I can't. It's Franklin County's jurisdiction. If they requested my help, I could. But the request must come from them, not from me. That's the way things are done."

"Is it okay if we tell Deputy McMannis that you would be willing to help him if he asked?" I questioned. We didn't understand, then, that police agencies don't have to work together. To us, they acted like competing entities — a kind of turf war. I can't presume to speak for every agency, but generally, the police whose jurisdiction may be involved in a crime don't communicate, crosscheck or share information with other agencies. In this state, they don't work together. If anything, they appear territorial.

"Sure. I'd be happy to assist in any way I can. Now exactly where was Andrew hit?" Don asked, reaching for a pen and a legal pad. As he wrote our answers to his questions, he would pose another question. This continued for more than a half hour.

Then, he said, "I think I can tell you something about the driver who hit Andrew."

Andy and I both looked stunned. How was he able to tell us something about the driver? This time, I took out my pen and paper.

"I think I can give you a fairly accurate profile of this person. We're dealing with a male. Someone in his fifties. Probably works construction or a blue-collar job. Chances are he comes from Kentucky or West Virginia. He uses his van to drive his buddies around. Look for a van within a six-mile radius. I'd stake my reputation on that."

"So he's somewhere not far from New Albany," Andy said. "Why do you think that?"

"Central College Road? That's local traffic. He's within that radius."

This was the first time we heard someone who should know say the driver was "local" with such conviction. It made sense to us. Central College Road is a rural country road. The driver most probably lived in the Columbus area. That eliminated a lot of vans.

Johnstown Police Chief Don Corbin listed six items in his profile. The six-mile radius turned out to be ten miles, but he hit everything else exactly right—if you can assume that a divorced person with no family mainly drove his buddies around. This was law enforcement experience at its best.

Surely the FCSO wasn't giving up only six weeks after our son's crash? Were they checking the Glaval list? We had not yet been in touch with the

Glaval Corporation to get some questions answered. When we did a year later, Glaval's answers to a few simple questions disclosed information so important that Andy and I saw it as a miracle.

I had a funny feeling that day late in September when I called the FCSO. The receptionist once again said that McMannis was out and could she take a message. Overhearing my call, Andy suggested that we track down a few of the van owners on the list that McMannis highlighted. "Let's check out the list and see if McMannis was there." We began with the first name McMannis highlighted in green. Just to see if our intuition was playing tricks on us.

The first address on the list was in the Forest Park area near Karl Road in Columbus, not more than twenty minutes from our house.

I knocked on the door and a young woman answered. I met her with a smile. No one could have detected that I felt like the lowest human being on earth. En route to the house I hadn't decided what my reason would be to ask about the van, but somehow I did have the presence to draw a crude chart: the date, time, the VIN of the van we were checking, a description of the person I talked to, and then an assessment of what I thought of the van.

Never having done anything like this before and deciding spontaneously to have a "look see," I didn't anticipate problems. I thought that I would see a van in a drive or parked near the house and take a quick look to see if the van stirred any suspicious notions. No one had to know that I was looking. But vans weren't usually visible. I found myself knocking on doors. With each successive van owner I talked to, I knew what to expect.

The first young woman helped me more than she could ever know. Attractive and in her twenties, she smiled back when she opened the door.

"Hi," I said cheerfully. "Do you own a van?"

"No, but my dad does. Why? Is he selling it?"

"Yes, I believe so. Does he live here with you?"

"No, but if you want I can take your name and number and have him call you." She disappeared into the house to get paper and pen. That gave me a chance to catch my breath and give her a fictitious name and phone number.

I had not anticipated this spur-of-the-moment interaction with people who came to the door and who surely would ask the obvious question: Why was I asking about their van? I could hardly say, "I want to see your van because you might have killed our son."

As we talked briefly about her father's van, she reported that her father's van was red. I had made an incorrect assumption about the Glaval list. I thought that all the vans on the list were white because the van in the Polaroid was white. We didn't have all the information Glaval had given the police. Vans were also red, blue and tan. This narrowed the list even further.

We were to learn that Glaval ground effects always match the predominant color of the van so the first van's ground effects would have been red. Tracking that van down, we saw the red ground effects.

On that hot September day that smelled like school, we drove Andrew's red Honda Civic. Warm air blew in at us through open windows, as his car had no air conditioning. But it seemed fitting that we should use his car.

Reading a street map of Columbus, we found the next address, parked in front, knocked on the door and a high school girl with her dog answered. She called to her mom, the owner, and I gave my impromptu story. Andy stayed in the car. We decided that a woman knocking on doors was much less threatening than a man or even a man and a woman.

Trying not to appear nervous, I said, "I have a list of Glaval vans and your van is one of them." I showed her the Glaval list. "A van in the area was involved in an accident, but we know it wasn't your van. All we need to do is to look at your van and check it off. This is just a formality—something that has to be done for insurance purposes."

Briefly showing the Glaval list was to be my ticket to credibility. Out of the sixty or so vans we checked, only one person wanted to see identification, and luckily, I had one of Rick's PI cards in my bag.

After my explanation, Andy would emerge from the car and the two of us would circle the van, looking at the passenger side for any sign of repaired damage—like something that seemed different from the rest of the van.

And not one van owner mentioned that the Sheriff had been there. We were now into the last week in September, about eight weeks after our son's hit-and-run death, and we could only conclude that the FCSO had ignored the list. And that was to be our experience as we continued down the list. If we had been met with even one van owner who asked, "What's this about? The police were here, too," we would have stopped immediately. And have been grateful.

Not encountering one van owner in September, October and November who mentioned the police, we had no choice but to look at vans ourselves.

6

SINCE OUR COMMUNICATION WITH THE police was almost non-existent by the middle of October, Deputy McMannis' presence at a bicycle memorial ride organized by our long-time friends, Lou, and Jewel, surprised us. Columbus Outdoor Pursuits, Lucent, Westerville Bicycle Club, and others from the Columbus area convened at the back entrance of Hoover Dam one October Sunday morning to honor Andrew's life.

When Andy and I drove up, the sea of black, red, yellow, green, and blue cycling shirts all in helmets amazed us. Most of the cyclists there, we learned later, had many of close encounters with motorists and knew a cyclist who had been injured or killed by a motorist.

That morning I could think of nothing but Andrew. I must have had a pained look on my face as we approached more than one hundred cyclists. In scanning the faces, we saw Lou and Jewel and then noticed a Franklin County Sheriff's squad car. The four of us watched Deputy McMannis exit the car and make his way toward us. I'll never forget his greeting.

"Smile," he said to me.

"I can't," I answered. Because I couldn't. The memorial ride served as just another dose of reality. Andrew was dead.

Sure, I wasn't impressed with McMannis' investigation, but he had shown up at the memorial ride and was there along with the cyclists who rolled out of bed that morning, put on their cycling gear and rode to offer us comfort and support. Mistakenly, I thought this indicated some renewed interest.

We left Hoover Dam and crossed over to Central College Road, with a stream of bicyclists following. Not more than a mile eastward, a white cross marked where Andrew was hit. Some of Andrew's friends also rode. Robin and her fiancé, Paul—Andrew's close friends—placed flowers at the cross and we held each other as cyclist after cyclist with bouquets of daisies, carnations, roses, and mums knelt to remember Andrew. Today and many days, I think back to the enormity of that gift.

Several days later, we were surprised to see a Sheriff's car pull up in front of the house. Except for two visits at the house in August, a meeting with

McMannis at the traffic office and once at the Crime Stoppers' interview, we had not been in contact with him until the memorial ride. He was alone and accepted our invitation to come into the house. He handed us a handwritten list of vans with VINs and owners' names and he implied that he had checked these vans out. By this time, two and a half months after the crash, I noted vans he listed that we had visited. Not one person ever said that the police had already been there. No notations. Just handwritten names. We should have challenged the list of names. But we would not have confronted the police. Not then.

He added, "Do you have the list of vans I gave you? You'll need to mark one of them." He was referring to the Glaval master list—the one he highlighted in green.

On top of our files, ready for use at any time, lay the Glaval list. Andy handed him the list. McMannis said, "Look to page thirteen. About half way down do you see the VIN 1GBDM19Z0PB...? Mark it 'checked."

Andy did as he was instructed. Neither of us asked any questions. Why that particular VIN? Why only that VIN? It wasn't on that list of his highlighted vans. And no, it wasn't on the handwritten list of VINs that he claimed he checked. And he didn't ask us to mark the vans on the list as "checked". We could not have dreamed of the magnitude of that VIN, and the magnitude of that missed opportunity.

Friends wondered, "How do you have the energy to drive around looking for vans?" It was that or stay home and lie in bed all day. We kept the floors swept, the dishes washed and the bills paid, but beyond that, except for our daughter, we had no interest. Our son was dead and no one else was looking for the van that killed him.

Because we didn't always have updated owner BMV reports, we felt like the proverbial headless chicken. Before we set out usually around ten o'clock, we would map out a course so that our looking didn't seem so frenetic.

On many days, we traveled hundreds of miles on country roads far from home, keeping our eyes constantly on the lookout for landmarks to determine where we were or that we were heading in the right direction. Often, rural road signs were scarce. The people who lived there knew where they were, but we didn't. We realized that Ohio still had plenty of green spaces.

We never stopped for lunch once we left the house. We lost all interest in food and stopped only at the end of the day to assuage hunger pains. Many evenings we found ourselves on a dark strip of road between miles of corn or soy bean fields when suddenly in a clearing we'd spot a roadside restaurant like "Ma's Coffeepot," turn around and go back for a bowl of vegetable soup or chili.

In the days before Andrew's death, I loved to happen upon those kinds of places, imagining a good cup of coffee and an authentic piece of homemade pie. Without realizing it, our lives were turning into Before Andrew and After Andrew. Many of those simple, wonderful little pleasures never return.

Because finding our first destination may take us several hours, often in a rural setting, we knocked on doors in the afternoon, returning later if someone didn't answer. People move, sell their vans, or come home late. At times, we could find ourselves back in the same area the next day. Day after day we arrived home well after dark. Realistically, we believed that this was something that had to be done. On that list was *the van*.

A typical van encounter involved my approaching the house. The more I talked to people the more confidence I gained. If flowers were growing in the yard, I would start with a comment about how nice the yard looked. If someone had a dog, I would ask questions about the dog. A quick observation of the house and its surrounds gave me the ammunition I needed to put the van owners at ease. Only one woman scowled and asked for credentials as I gave my speech. Her porch, decorated for Halloween—white gauze in corners with black spiders, carved pumpkins, orange lights—indicated that kids lived there. The scene set me at ease as I showed the woman my clipboard of Glaval vans and our PI's business card.

Most people accepted my story about having a list of vans and checking them because one of the vans might have been involved in an accident. I said "accident" instead of "crash" and that "we know your van is not involved." I never felt comfortable hiding my identity. I wanted everyone to know that I was Andrew's mom.

Toward the middle of November, when the days grew shorter and van owners often didn't get home until after dark, strangers on the doorstep were not treated with the same courtesy as strangers during daylight. Not all answered the door. Sometimes as I exited the car, I could hear dogs but couldn't see them. We decided that looking for vans in the dark, especially in rural areas, presented too many problems. With the holidays approaching along with wintry weather, we reluctantly interrupted our van search. But we would continue to update the BMV records to be ready to head back out when an opportunity arose.

Why wasn't McMannis out checking vans? After highlighting vans and announcing he would check those, he never went within ten feet of any of those vans. He chose to ignore the list. His excuse will be that the FCSO didn't have access to updated owners. The traffic department had no access to updating vehicle records? I wasn't buying it.

The problem for us entailed our updating the list's addresses through the Bureau of Motor Vehicles. Ten vans might take two weeks or longer to get the latest addresses and we had hundreds. We had no choice but to wait for each updated address or go with the addresses we had. Later we were told by the State Patrol that updating 400 vehicles, eliminating the colored vans, would have taken no more than several hours. Mark Adams' advice, "The first thing you have to do is find the van," echoed through every strategy we devised. The Glaval list held the answer.

It's beyond incomprehensible to think that the Sheriff of Franklin County, home to the state's capital, did not have in-house or out-of-house access to databases dealing with vehicle registration? Updating was never done. *Ever.* As it happened, precious few white Glaval vans belonged to Columbus area owners within a ten-mile radius of the crash. This case could have been closed within weeks with minor expense to tax payers. And the message sent to hit-and-run drivers: you will be caught.

McMannis spent a lot of his time out at the Cop Shop at Westland Mall. We had no idea what the Cop Shop was. Being a curious sort, I drove out to Westland Mall one day to have a look. The "shop" housed several desks and some equipment, sparsely furnished. Two deputies talked in the corner while one deputy talked on the phone, his chair tilted back in a relaxed manner.

I stood near the shop. No activity. No one approached the deputies. I doubled back later. No customers. The mall was deserted. The mall was on the verge of a total shutdown. What was the Cop Shop? I needed to come back. I did. Same thing—no activity. Maybe the presence of several deputies prevented shoplifting at a shopping mall where the shoppers no longer lifted or shopped?

7

THE LONG AFTERNOONS GREW SHORTER. Leaves fell from maple and walnut trees surrounding our house. To deal with his grief Andy raked leaves in the dark on weekends or forced himself to work on projects which he had started before Andrew was killed.

The season I loved the most, I now hated the most. Before, I could count on clear blue skies to make me happy. And the promise of snow. I would give anything to regain that feeling.

On those fall Sundays in September and October when we stayed home to wash clothes, pay bills—the ordinary chores that must be done—I was confronted with the reality that Andrew was not going to come down the lane and walk through the door. The new cast iron kitchen sink he carried from the car to the house the last week in July was still in its box on the counter where he put it.

That fall was hot and humid. I don't know why, but our oak trees produced an abundance of acorns—perhaps Mother Nature was getting ready for an especially hard winter. That summer Andrew had been painting our house and other buildings on our property. Andy needed to finish the painting before cold weather set in. Also, he and Andrew planned to install skylight windows in the large garage. The box for that remained in the corner of the garage until Andy enlisted the help of his close friend, Bill. Working with Bill, pounding and measuring, they installed the skylights. Being with Bill served as therapy for Andy.

One fall day I experienced an anxiety so awful that I ran from the house. I had no place to go. I circled the house, repeatedly, hearing the crunch of acorns. It's strange what a human will do to dispel anxiety, to be released from hell. I was locked in a prison cell, solitary confinement, with no hope.

You have the entire world in front of you, but if you have no hope, if you have the worst kind of despair, you can see no possibilities for life. In anguish, I found a basket in the large garage, returned to the yard and threw in acorns, one by one. When I filled the basket, I got another and did the same. There were moments when I had to do something, anything to release the aching.

The last Thanksgiving and Christmas celebrations with Andrew were in the previous year, 1997. The "before" time when your child is alive and the "after" time when your child is gone don't register right away.

Because Andrew was not our only child, we had to try to recognize the holidays. Our daughter's favorite holiday has always been Thanksgiving. Like most families, we used our best china, which happened to be Havilland, a gift from Andrew to me. He knew nothing about Havilland. I had to drag him out to an antique shop in Clintonville on Christmas Eve. I had had my eye on this set for some time.

I had no energy to set a pretty table. I had no interest in basting a turkey during the early hours of Thanksgiving morning and peeling apples for pies. I wanted no part of Thanksgiving. I wanted to obliterate the holidays from the calendar. Luckily for us, our daughter had no interest either. Several days before she and Scott were due home, we talked on the phone about Thanksgiving plans.

"Mom, let's have pasta. We can make a pan of lasagna or spaghetti and meatballs."

Having pasta on Thanksgiving was so radically different that nothing about the menu would remind me of Thanksgiving. I wanted nothing to remind me of Thanksgiving without Andrew.

"What do you think if the four of us volunteered to serve dinner at a shelter? The newspaper had an article about shelters and church kitchens needing volunteers where people could go for Thanksgiving dinner. Doing something like that would help me get through the day."

I imagined myself washing large aluminum pots used for making mashed potatoes, green beans, sweet potatoes. I'd wait on people and clean the tables after they'd eaten. I'd be busy. I would have to work hard and come home tired.

"I'd like to do that and I know Scott would, too. We should make it a tradition," she answered.

We did and it helped me to get through the day when I wasn't so much in a mood to give thanks. Momentarily, it helped me to forget about the coward who killed our son. The coward who ran and hid.

And Christmas did come and go. Thankfully, our daughter spent as much time as she could with us, giving up all her vacation time and flying home on the weekends. If this caused a strain on her marriage of only a year, Scott gave no indication of that. And if Scott's mom and dad felt shortchanged during the holidays for the next five years, we never detected a hint of resentment.

Before 1998 ended, we had heard from several different people—entirely unrelated and under different circumstances—about a large party that took place on the corner of Harlem and Central College Roads, the weekend that Andrew was killed.

Naturally, we made a mental note of the information, but the significance of that bit of information didn't register, at least not those first few months.

You can gather information but understanding its potential connection to an event is another matter.

Not too long after Andrew's funeral, an acquaintance called the house. Charles and his wife, Eva, wanted to stop by with some information. The man owned a shop on Sunbury Road. He and Andy developed a friendly relationship after Andy bought several mowers from him and Charles kept them in good repair. He was only one of many whom we described as "angels on earth."

Charles and Eva came by one evening after supper. We sat in the living room, barely able to react to what they believed was important enough for them to report to us in person.

Charles was the first to tell us about "the party." He began, "Did anyone mention to you about the big party at the corner of Harlem and Central College Roads the weekend your son was killed?"

"No. We haven't heard anything about a party," Andy said.

"Every year about this time, the people at the corner house have a big party. It's an outdoor thing. Lots of people."

"Are you invited? Do you go to the party?" I asked.

"We don't know them," said Charles. "There are lots of bikers. We've seen packs of them on Central College Road. Typical bikers. The chains, black leather, bandanas. Last year a fire truck ended up over there. The party has a bad reputation."

"Are you sure when the party took place?" I asked. "Andrew was hit on Saturday, August 1. Is that when these people had the party?"

"Yes, we're certain. The party was that weekend. We've seen it."

Charles and Eva had sons of their own. They did for us what they would have wanted someone to do for them. Our conversation turned to talking about Andrew. I'll never forget their compassion and concern for Andrew and us. Obviously, a connection was implied between his death and the party.

During one of our conversations with McMannis, Andy brought up the visit from Charles and Eva and what they said. Apparently, McMannis knew about the party but never mentioned it.

I've recreated his response. "Yeah, there was a party on the corner of Harlem Road the weekend your son was killed. We did go up to the house. The son said that his parents were in Canada on a fishing trip. I believe their names are Thompson*. Later, we went back and talked to them. Could they give us the names of some of the guests? They said many of the people who attend are friends of friends or relatives of friends, out-of-towners, lots of people they just didn't know."

The Thompsons knew the relatives and friends. That was a start. No names, no nothing.

As 1998 ended, we had accumulated some critical information. What facts did we know and what could we logically infer? We prepared a list:

- Glaval gel-coated ground effect pieces matched the dominant color of the van. If the ground effect was white, the van was white.
- Glaval installed those ground effect parts on the passenger and driver sides.
- Glaval was a conversion company in Elkhart, Indiana, that installed custom options/equipment on General Motors vans, like luggage racks, striping, running boards, etc.
- Glaval provided the Sheriff's Office with a list of their customized vans sold to Ohio dealerships from 1990 through 1994.
- Glaval discontinued installing the ground effect after the 1994 models.
- Glaval was the only company through which auto shops and dealerships could order a new Glaval replacement part.
- White Glaval vans had two designations: frost white (vans 1990, 1991 and 1992) and ivory white (latter part of 1992, 1993 and 1994).
- The van that killed Andrew was a white Chevy, GM Glaval converted van.
- The van traveled Central College Road in a westerly direction on August 1, 1998.
- The van's damage included the loss of two pieces broken off the passenger side ground effect.

Looking at the information accumulated, testing Andrew's clothes for paint could tell us if we're looking for a "frost" or "ivory" van. That designation would put us closer to determining the year. Five months later, still no testing.

The holidays passed, the days grew longer, and Andy and I felt determined to make 1999 the year we would get the answers we so desperately sought.

1999

8

THROUGHOUT JANUARY AND FEBRUARY, WE worked diligently updating the Glaval van list. I was determined to look at every van record to see each van's location the previous August. That adage rang in my ears, "…looking for a needle in a haystack." I failed to see that as a metaphor. I pictured myself in front of a large haystack, literally taking out one straw at a time. We had already consumed four months looking at vans. "Whatever it takes," I repeated to myself. Recently, I saw that same phrase in a magazine. I cut it out and put it on the refrigerator as a reminder. *Whatever it takes.*

Then in March on one cold blustery morning, the phone rang. We have caller ID, but the screen came up "private." Usually I don't answer "private" or "unavailable." The caller, a woman, left a message. Her voice had a southern tinge and sounded raspy like a smoker.

"You don't know me. I live in New Albany and I have some information that might help you to solve your son's accident. I'll call you…"

I hurriedly picked up the receiver and said, "Hello?" This was the kind of call I had hoped for. I could barely catch my breath. "I was on my way into the kitchen when I heard part of your message. You said that you have some information about our son's accident?"

"Yes," the woman answered. "This morning I decided to call and tell you what I know."

"Do you think you know who killed our son?"

"I'm not sure, but I have good reason to believe that a man in New Albany could be involved. His mother or someone in his family owns a van and they live in New Albany."

"Is the man this family's son?"

"Yes." Then silence. Later, after several conversations, she regretted calling when I asked questions.

"Why do you think this guy is involved?" I asked.

"He was just released from prison. About three years ago, he was driving his truck, drunk, killing the driver. People say he's driving again."

"Can you tell me his name?"

"Yes, Matt Kolar*."

"And you say he lives in Westerville or New Albany and someone in his family has a van?"

"Yes."

"Do you know what kind of van it is?"

"No. Listen, I have to go. I'll call you again." Not waiting for my response, she hung up.

Those kinds of tips happened to us at times when we had no hope, when we were as full of despair as parents could be. Many times, I resented the hope that these kinds of tips gave us, but in retrospect, even if the tips were only suspicions, someone knew how important it was to come forward with information. The caller later identified herself as Lizzie.

This could be the call that would end our frustration as to whether we would ever find Andrew's killer. At the library, I pulled up the article charging Kolar with aggravated vehicular homicide. When he lost control of his truck and hit a young man's car, beer cans littered the road. Unlucky for Kolar, a state highway trooper witnessed the crash and was on the scene in seconds. No way could Kolar get out of this one. The law was right there.

We never did see a white van at the Kolars. We did see a large, gray van—not anything like a Glaval van. Nothing about it matched a Glaval van. We called the FCSO to inform them of the tip. Lizzie's trepidation was typical of those who called with tips. She wanted to do the right thing—to tell someone of her suspicions, but not one of them wanted us to make her or his identity known to the authorities.

That weekend when Betsey came home, she said. "I don't want to tell you and dad what to do, Mom, but I think you should put this tip on the back-burner and get back to looking at the Glaval list." My sentiments exactly.

❖ ❖ ❖

The little diner on Route 62 always had freshly made coffee, and regulars packed the diner for the breakfast special. If we had to be out that way, we'd stop in for coffee and the homemade biscuits served all day.

The first time we saw it, we had been across the street at the bank.

Andy asked if he could post a reward flyer in the bank's window. When we pulled out of the bank's parking lot, we noticed the diner.

"Let's take a break and get a cup of coffee," Andy said.

The breakfast crowd had gone, and the server directed us to an empty booth. Andy always carried ten or so reward flyers with him. When the server came to take our order, we complimented the coffee, and then Andy asked her his favorite question, "Are you a New Albany girl?" (or whatever the town was, and usually the person hadn't seen girlhood in many years.)

"No. I live in Alexandria. Have all my life."

"I know your head librarian there. Can't think of her name," he said.

"We used to take the bike path through Alexandria," I interjected, trying to get into the conversation. I knew that these were warm-up comments to what we really wanted to talk to her about. Somehow we managed to steer the conversation into details of Andrew's crash.

"I remembered when that happened," she said. "That was your son? I'm so sorry."

Andy pulled out one of the reward posters, "Would you mind posting this flyer somewhere on the door or in the window?"

"You can put it up on the bulletin board over there," she said.

When she returned to refill our cups, she leaned over and said, "Did anyone ever tell you there was a big biker party that weekend?"

9

ON CHILLY DAYS, I SAT next to the kitchen heater in the breakfast nook, which is really a bay window extension. I can work and have a three-windowed view of the woodland. On one of those cool spring afternoons I noticed a car coming down the lane and then saw Paul, a close friend of Andrew, get out of his car. In speaking to other parents who have lost children, I learned that at least one of the child's friends is especially sensitive and stays in close contact with the family. For us, that young man was Paul.

Talking to Paul was like talking to Andrew. Maybe most young men think alike. His unannounced visits were welcomed gifts. Not everyone who came to visit wanted to talk just about Andrew. But we did. And Paul wanted to talk about Andrew and us and our grief. His visits helped me to survive some difficult days.

On this day, Paul came with an idea. He and some of Andrew's friends, Robin, Bob, Mike, Paul H., April, Ryan, and others, discussed organizing a memorial Ultimate Frisbee tournament in Andrew's name to benefit a charity. Friends and family had already established a scholarship fund at Miami University, given yearly to a Westerville North High School graduate. As Paul and I talked, we both agreed that the proceeds of this event should go to the Salesian Boys and Girls Club in Columbus. If Andrew had known about such a club when he was a teen, he would have joined.

Under Paul's direction that spring day eight months after Andrew's death, ANDY/24 emerged. Paul shared that he and Andrew had wanted to organize an event in Columbus whereby players could participate in Ultimate for twenty-four straight hours. Paul was determined to see his and Andrew's vision realized. Through Paul's contact with the director of club sports at Ohio State, Paul reserved Beekman Field on Ohio State University's campus for the first tournament. Last year was the eighteenth tournament held at Beekman Field.

Paul suggested that if the media were interested, we could talk about Andrew's death and hit-and-run fatalities. The media were interested. All three local TV stations showed up at the first tournament and interviewed us. The tournament raised several thousand dollars as Frisbees flew around the clock and players ate meatball sandwiches at three in the morning. Since 1999, yearly tournaments have brought in Ultimate players from all over the Midwest and beyond. The organizers of the event are Andrew's friends, and if friends are an indication of who you are, we couldn't be more proud of our son.

For the first six years or so, I was solely in charge of feeding this horde of Ultimate athletes, mainly young men with a good share of young women. Within twenty-four hours they would have cleaned out two large crock-pots, constantly being replenished, of one thousand meatballs, on bread donated by Great Harvest Bread store in Upper Arlington. Add to that dozens of pizzas, countless wraps from the university area Chipotle, sandwiches, cookies, veggies, and fruit. Then early on Saturday morning, Shari, a player and co-organizer of the Tenth Anniversary Tournament, plugged in her two-foot long griddle, and flipped pancakes, made from scratch, with fresh blueberries, until the batter and butter ran out.

Arranged under the pavilion, ten or so round metal tables provided places for the players to eat and to put their equipment. On one of these tables, I would stake out an area for my notebook, candles, camera, and cell phone. During one of these later tournaments, some papers appeared atop my notebook. Curious, I picked up a half sheet and read:

Most did not know him.
The loss his family's, his friends,
Not ours.
Yet, *they* take care of *us,* sustain *us:*
Meatballs through the night,
Blueberries in our morning pancakes.

~Casey, the Night Geezer

Every moment of those twenty-four hours takes on a special significance. Every effort, every conversation, every player we meet, every comment, every gift of poetry—we see as a connection to Andrew. The tournament is the most momentous occasion of the year for Andy and me. Betsey mentioned, after the third tournament, that when she drove up and saw Andrew's red Honda in the parking lot, she knew that Andrew was there.

That first year, the ANDY/24 tournament promised something good would happen. As we heard someone say, "We felt the love." Some might interpret that as overly sentimental, but for us that tournament is forever a bond with us, Andrew's friends and all the players.

Late in the afternoon of the first tournament, play on the field stopped. Andy, Betsey, Scott, and I watched as players formed a circle around Kevin, a descendant of the Lakota, a Native American tribe. He came at Paul's request to bless the field. A present-day representative of his ancestors, his ash blonde hair tied back, Kevin turned his blue eyes upward to Father Sky and then down to Mother Earth, chanting in Lakota. Holding short stalks of sticks and herbs tied together, he lit the ends and invoked the winds from all four directions to protect the earth and the players. The similarity struck me as similar to organized religion's use of a censer to carry prayers heavenward. But it was another of Casey's poems that succinctly expressed the essence of this tradition:

Good Bid

Now years later
We gather each summer
To redeem a day long ago, and
Playing for joy of the game,
Each year we briefly bid
Make this field holy.

After the last play, we joined the participants on the field. Many had stayed the entire twenty-four hours, right up to the last minute. That June evening was perfect. Earlier in the day an unexpected rain shower had come, but at the close of the tournament the lush green of the grass met the blue, clear horizon. Becky, a young friend of mine, pointed to the sky, "Look, there's a rainbow!" As we all turned to look, she snapped a photo. Could that be Father Sky's promise of something good to happen? Automatically, I connected the rainbow to an astonishing conversation we had earlier with one of the players—another reason the first tournament was memorable.

That incidental conversation was to play a huge part in our strategy in dealing with the Franklin County Sheriff, and in the Franklin County Sheriff's traffic office's dealing with us. At the time, Bob was an assistant to Governor Bob Taft. He approached us with a citation, commending ANDY/24 organizers and the event, signed by Taft.

As Bob handed the navy-blue folder trimmed in gold to us, he asked, "Do you guys have any information about who killed Andrew?"

Shaking his head, Andy said, "No. In fact, we haven't heard from the Sheriff's Office in months. And when we call, no one calls back."

"I'll bet they're frustrated. Not having any evidence. It's hard to pin down a driver," Bob responded.

"That's just it. Evidence was left at the crash," I said.

"I didn't know that. What kind of evidence?" Bob inquired.

"Two pieces of a ground effect were found on and near Andrew's bike," I answered.

"What's a ground effect?"

"It's fiberglass molding. They take the place of running boards but with this model there's no step," Andy said.

"Andrew's bike somehow tore off part of the passenger side and it broke off in two pieces. The sheriff's investigator discovered that Glaval, a van conversion company, manufactured the part. From there, the investigator narrowed the van down to a white Gladiator van. So they know what kind of vehicle did this," I said.

"And here's the best part. Glaval gave the sheriff a list of their Ohio vans with that part," Andy added.

"Oh yeah? And what happened?" Bob asked.

"Nothing. The investigator was supposed to check some vans on the first page, but didn't," I said.

"We started checking and not one van owner said that the sheriff had been there," Andy interjected.

"Why wouldn't they check those vans?" Bob asked.

"Yeah, it's strange. The deputy in charge highlights the vans he intends to check. We wait a month, hear nothing, and decide to see what's been done. One day we checked the first four vans on the list. No one said anything about the Sheriff's Office already checking them out. The investigator said he would but he didn't," Andy explained.

Puzzled, Bob said, "Know what I think you should do? Try to get the State Highway Patrol to take your case. Why don't you see someone at the Patrol?"

What Bob said made instant sense. Yes, we would do that. Clearly, the Sheriff didn't want our case or someone would have done the common sense basics—like interviewing people living near the crash site, having our son's clothes and shoes tested for paint or other evidence, looking for transference of materials on the bicycle, and checking out the vans highlighted on the Glaval list to see which van owners were living in the Columbus area in August 1998.

The Franklin County Sheriff Office would feel relieved. The case would become someone else's problem. They could rationalize that the request for transfer came from the victim's family not them. That reasoning proved to be incredibly naïve.

The request for a change in law enforcement agencies was without question based on principle. Were we or were we not entitled to have an examination of the evidence and the information at hand to discover who took Andrew's life? The paint chips in his clothes remained undisturbed, stuck to bloodstains, in a garbage bag on a shelf in the sheriff's evidence room, and we were heading into the second year after his death.

After the tournament, we loaded up our cars with my cooking equipment but before heading home, we decided to stop at the Old Bag of Nails Restaurant in Worthington to recap with Betsey and Scott our conversation with Bob. Immediately, they saw Bob's idea as an option to get out from under the FCSO.

That night I didn't sleep well. The call to the State Highway Patrol marched in and out of my consciousness. At one point, I had a particularly vivid dream. I was sitting in the back seat of a car. No one was at the wheel. I was the only person in the car and it was careening down a mountainside in reverse. I bounced around inside the car as it hit rocks and trees.

In relating the dream to Betsey the next morning, she made the comment, "You think you have no control over what happens to you. I can completely understand how you would have a dream like that."

I wanted this call to the Patrol to work, to get an investigation. But in my subconscious I must have had some reservations. Andy, too, seemed to be losing hope. Bouts of depression caused him to stay up late and watch television. The only things he looked forward to day after day were *Night Line* and *Charlie Rose*. And on Friday, Bill Moyers.

Why didn't he, Andrew's father, make this call? Man-to-man. Thinking about it now, I realize what Andy's part was. We argued constantly about how to handle the police. His way was stereotypically masculine. "I'm calling the Sheriff and if something's not done, I'm going to a lawyer and to the press."

My reply was stereotypically snide. "That'll scare 'em. They'll get right on it."

Andrew's death revealed a powerlessness that I had never felt before. My husband could call the deputy in charge, get all his anger out about the lack of an investigation into a case that had plenty to go on, and I believed that his anger would only provoke them—not scare them. One of us beating his chest; the other cowering in a corner.

I was just as frustrated as Andy. I wanted to go to the traffic department and throw a crazy, over-the-top tantrum. I visualized kicking over chairs, swiping files from desks, breaking coffee cups, going on a wild-bull rampage. When the tension built up to eruption, instead of a rampage, I cried—privately.

The problem, then, that entire first year became how do we get the help we need to find Andrew's killer? Glaval provided a list of vans. That was a good place to start. Chief Don Corbin said that he would stake his reputation on the van being local, within six miles. What other probabilities could help narrow down the vans?

On a June morning in 1999, I dialed one of the twenty numbers listed under Public Safety for the Ohio State Highway Patrol, entitled "Investigations." As expected, after I had dialed and briefly explained my situation, the operator transferred my call. A woman answered, identifying herself as the assistant who could take a message and pass it on to the proper person. After I repeated my rehearsed story, she acknowledged our son's death with compassion and said that she would pass the message on to Sergeant Tuttle. "Don't get discouraged." We were ready to sever ties with the FCSO. When the case was securely under the Patrol's authority, we sensed our chances of getting justice would increase ten-fold.

I hung up and cried. As promised, Sergeant Tuttle called in July. Our strategy was to get an appointment to see him. We wanted to show him the Glaval list and what vehicles we checked. I wrote up a report for him and wanted to explain it. I asked, "Could we come to see you—like now?" He hesitated but didn't feel he could stop us. In less than fifteen minutes, we were out the door.

Like most government buildings, an ample reception area offered an information desk planted in the middle. We signed in to see Sergeant Tuttle. Brown leather couches and chairs dotted the foyer. We sat in one grouping that faced the elevators. Minutes later, a good-looking, young man in uniform came directly towards us. Extending his hand, Sgt. Tuttle, welcoming and congenial, eased our anxiety.

Tuttle was intrigued by the Glaval list of vans. He said, "We have technology and might be able to do something with vehicles. But you have to understand— we can't do anything unless the Sheriff's Office asks us. Your son's accident is their case. As much as we would like to help, we can't. Only if they ask us."

"If they do ask, is this something you can take on?" Andy asked.

"Yes, if they ask."

Both of us felt lighter. Filled with gratitude, we thanked Sergeant Tuttle. Leaving the building, we headed for the cemetery. Somehow, we believed that Andrew's hand was directing us.

As soon as we arrived home that afternoon, Andy called Chief Deputy Gil Jones, head of the Sheriff's traffic department. As I remember, when he called Chief Jones on that afternoon, Jones promptly picked up the phone. Andy inquired if Jones was available to meet with us—could we stop by his office to talk to him in person?

Surprisingly, Jones responded, "In the morning I'm going to a funeral not far from your house. I could stop by sometime after one o'clock. Is that okay with you?"

Shocked, Andy widened his eyes as he looked at me, standing by. To have the traffic department chief not only available but also accommodating seemed a miracle. "Yes, we'll be home all day. Thanks for agreeing to meet with us."

The plan was working. The Patrol had already agreed to take our case. All we needed from the Sheriff was an official request.

Simple and straightforward and not an earth-shaking request. No finger pointing, just a request based on principle. To the Sheriff: give up our case. To the Patrol: take over our case. We discovered that citizens just don't go around meeting privately with law enforcement officials. But these are public servants. They work for us. Right? In theory. Then what kind of rights do we really have? Do we sit idly by accepting a reprehensible situation, or do we try to solve our problem?

We had no doubt that the Patrol would somehow figure out which Glaval vans were in the Columbus area and put a strategy in place to examine them. They would capitalize on the evidence found at the crash and use the Glaval list.

Also, what kind of information lay concealed in our son's clothes? And the bike—what could the bike tell us? With the Patrol's expertise, one discovery would lead to another. They would connect the dots and bring our son's killer to justice.

Having no experience at negotiation, the second part of our plan was iffy at best—getting the Sheriff's Office to relinquish authority of our case by handing it over to the Patrol. Chief Jones, himself, was a product of the State Highway Patrol, having retired from the Patrol just before assuming his supervisory position with the Sheriff's Office.

Quite frankly, we couldn't see why Jones wouldn't agree to give it up. It was clear, not only to us but to Mark Adams and everyone else following our case, that after the Crime Stoppers interview the first week in September, activity in the investigation stopped. Bob's suggestion to ask the Patrol to take the case seemed our only chance at justice. We didn't want the Patrol to assist the Sheriff. We wanted the Patrol to take our case out of the Sheriff's hands. That was the only way.

We needed Jones's approval to make the transfer happen. That evening we made pasta with shrimp from a recipe that Andrew liked and watched

Rick Steves' travelogue on quaint Italian villages. Some of the tension sub-sided. We had scheduled a meeting with Jones.

How many times was this to happen to us? Many times. We would think through a problem or obstacle. Discuss its details. Argue. Make a list, pros and cons. Talk. Argue. Delete. Add. Revise. Make another list. Think.

The solving of our son's homicide was not rocket science. Some homicides leave no evidence and it takes sharp detectives to generate leads out of what seems to be nothing to the lay person. That wasn't our situation. Our major problem was with the FCSO.

We had no idea, then, that paint chips were stuck to blood on our son's shirt and glass shards hid in his pocket. Our son's shirt, shorts, socks, and bicycle shoes lay in a black, plastic bag on the shelf in the sheriff's evidence room. Would it be fair to say that these items should have been examined within the first week for evidence? For paint chips? If these simple, basic procedures didn't register with the investigator, what else didn't register? Stunning.

What I have learned from our family's tragedy is that a public agency like law enforcement enjoys a wide range of immunity. Our family could have filed a complaint for dereliction of duty and an internal committee would review it. We all know about the fox guarding the hen house. All the clever advice in the world could not have prepared us to deal with certain kinds of people in power over the rest of us. It is an awful truth.

Almost to the day, a year after our son was killed, we sat on the back deck with Chief Deputy Gil Jones. We first met him in the Sheriff's parking lot about three weeks after Andrew's crash. Sheriff Karnes had appointed him the chief deputy of the traffic department. Tall and distinguished and with the persona to match, he quickly put us at ease when he accepted the offer of something to drink.

The August sun beat down on the deck. We moved to sit under the umbrella with our iced tea. We began by telling Jones about our meeting the day before with Sgt. Tuttle, then explaining why we asked the Patrol to get involved. The reason for deputies not checking the van list eluded us. What motivated Jones to make a special visit to us? We were to learn later that the department was afraid we would sue.

Andy told Jones, "We sometimes forget that Deputy McMannis has a lot of other cases he's working. Not just ours."

"He has one other case besides yours. I think we can work something out," Jones responded.

With lightened spirits, we asked Jones about his family. Since he had adult children, I sought his empathy. He said that his daughters were still somewhat dependent on him and his wife and chuckled. We liked his manner. Friendly and engaging, he displayed a relaxed confidence.

When he left our house that afternoon, we harbored no doubts that he would ask the State Highway Patrol for intervention. Yes, it seemed like a good meeting. He gave no indication that our request was out of the question.

Although we wanted to bypass the Sheriff's Office and take care of the arrangements ourselves regarding the take-over by the State Highway Patrol, the system wouldn't allow such efficiency. We thought that the Sheriff's Office would be ecstatic to be rid of us.

McMannis' response to our request through Gil Jones occurred immediately. When the phone rang, the Sheriff's number flashed on caller ID. I answered the phone. Our perfect plan to enlist the aid of the State Highway Patrol was going to backfire in ways I could not have imagined. Should we have sat back, done nothing, and accepted an abysmal situation? Either way, we were going to lose.

"Andy and I have been thinking about our case. We want the State Highway Patrol to take over the investigation. We know that they have more resources than the Sheriff and we think they'll be able to solve this."

His response, "*That's not going to happen*," was delivered in a flat voice, devoid of emotion. He could have easily added, "And I'll see to it that it doesn't." We expected some kind of negative reaction but not an out-and-out, adversarial rejection of the idea. We honestly believed that he would be relieved—the perfect opportunity to get out from under an investigation that he obviously couldn't or wouldn't handle. My blood pressure rose like a candy thermometer thrust into a boiling batch of sugar water.

"Our son was murdered and nothing's being done."

"Well, you can call the State Highway Patrol if you want, but I won't ask them to do my job," he retorted.

I should have answered, "We wouldn't be having this conversation if you had been doing your job." Then, I should have followed the remark up with questions about the van list—like why didn't one person tell us that someone had been there to look at their van?

To confront him, listing gross omissions in this investigation would not have served any purpose. Confrontation, I thought, would only cause a deplorable situation to become worse. Because we knew that protocol or long-standing practices or something else dictated that the Sheriff had to make the first move, the Patrol had to wait until the request came from the Sheriff.

In the middle of this exchange, Deputy McMannis changed the subject. Perhaps he wanted to demonstrate that he was working our case and that our assessment of his investigation was wrong. "For weeks now, we've been working on a tip. A person called Crime Stoppers and it sounds like the best thing we've heard so far. We've been working it for the past two weeks."

When I pressed for details, he said, "I can't tell you anything yet."

Most of the conversation I preserved in an email to Betsey sent right after speaking to McMannis. In it, I tell her that I don't doubt there has been a tip, but by this time I was getting good at detecting BS.

Jones oversaw the department, right? If Jones instructed McMannis to call the Patrol, then something should have happened. Nothing happened.

10

NO MORE THAN SEVERAL WEEKS after Andrew's crash, we began hearing stories about the biker party held that weekend on the corner of Harlem and Central College Roads. The vehicle that hit Andrew was traveling in a westerly direction, as was Andrew, toward the party, not more than a fourth of a mile away from the corner. Charlie, Andy's friend who lived in New Albany, a man at a nearby gas station and a server at a New Albany diner in New Albany all described the party as raucous with a rough crowd. Rumors over the years circulated that the police were frequent visitors along with an occasional fire truck. In fact, everyone we spoke to in New Albany who mentioned that party described it similarly. Person after person confirmed the information we collected about the party.

We learned that the partygoers converged on the first weekend in August every year. Beginning on Friday evening, the party lasted until Sunday afternoon, with Saturday the big day. Andrew was hit on the Saturday of the Harlem Road party. To ignore this or to dismiss this gigantic possibility that this party had some connection to Andrew's death would be in a word, thoughtless. Instinctively, we had to know more about this party. According to McMannis, the host of the party didn't reveal any guests' names, so we had little to go on except what people in New Albany reported.

Since the party was held on the first weekend in August each year, then in 1999, the year after Andrew's death, the first weekend would be Friday, August 6, through Sunday, August 8. We lived less than two miles from the party site. During that first year, we drove past the "party" house numerous times, observing all we could. Located on the corner, the house was easy to see, but the "L"-shaped driveway obscured license plates. Our plan included surveillance of the party that weekend in 1999. If we, Andrew's parents, approached the host and asked for names of guests, we weren't likely to get them. To record license plates was the only way we could think of to discover the identity of guests. That certainly was the goal.

On Friday, August 6, 1999, I awoke with anticipation of what the weekend would bring. Over coffee Andy and I created a plan of action. We would change cars—driving Andrew's car, my car and Andy's car—just in case people became suspicious. We decided to change jackets, wear ball caps or not wear ball caps—anything to appear different. We prepared to observe the house and grounds late in the afternoon on Friday. If the party was as huge as rumored, the driveway could not accommodate all the vehicles. Some would have to park on the road. The plates on those vehicles would be easier to record.

In 1999 anyone could fill out a Bureau of Motor Vehicle (BMV) request for the owner's name of a certain license plate. The people at the BMV must have found it strange that an "Elaine Starinchak" would request the owners' name of more than twenty plates. But it was legal. The BMV had no idea what our situation was.

Later that morning I had to make a stop at the courthouse. I wanted to see if any of the Glaval van owners, those who bought vans from Columbus dealerships, had criminal records or were arrested for OMVI's (operation of a motor vehicle while intoxicated) in Franklin County. As I was standing next to the computer, plugging in the names of van owners, a young man using the next computer said, "Do you do this for a living?"

"No. I'm just checking to see if some of the people on this list have criminal records."

"Could you show me how to use this computer? I restore old houses and I'm interested in this one property, but I need to find out if there are any liens against the property."

He was about Andrew's age and had the same brown eyes. I was hooked. I pointed to the printed instructions and guided him through the steps. The conversation took on a personal note as I asked him about restoring old houses.

"I like doing it but it doesn't pay much. I've had lots of other jobs and I'm still trying to find out what I want to do," he explained.

Then the conversation turned to what I was doing. I showed him my notebooks and told him about Andrew's death and where he was killed. The similarities between him and Andrew were uncanny—the kind, brown eyes, his age, and the searching for a life passion.

"This weekend will be the one-year anniversary of our son's death. There was a party that weekend near the crash. We believe there's a connection."

"You need someone to go to the party," he said, reading my mind.

"We have no idea if they're going to have it. We'd go but we'd stand out like sore thumbs. Maybe, if we had a motorcycle…," I said.

"I have a motorcycle but it's a Honda. My friend, Eli, has a Harley. If there's a party and you drive up on a Harley, you're automatically in. You don't have to know anyone. No one questions you. You're automatically treated as one of them," he said.

An idea flashed across my mind. "Do you want a job this weekend? Do you think that you and Eli could go to this party? It'd be a job."

Looking at me, he processed the question and answered, "Yeah, but I'd have to call her. I haven't talked to her for a long time. Her name is Elizabeth, but I'll call her and see what she says."

"You sound hesitant. Maybe it's not such a good idea to call her?"

"No, I can call her. But I drive a Trans Am and that would fit in, too. Where is this party?" he asked.

"In New Albany on Harlem Road and it might be this weekend. If you're interested, I'll give you $300," I offered.

Because McMannis said the guy who hosted the party couldn't remember the names of any of the guests—that they were friends of friends, relatives of relatives, friends of relatives and so on—a strange face wouldn't attract undue attention. Could we trust that information? As we discovered a year later in 2000, what the host supposedly said was not accurate. Was she protecting people?

At this point, I introduced myself and he said, "I'm Steve Sherman." We moved to sit on a bench outside the research room. I wrote my name and telephone number on a piece of paper and then told him more about Andrew's hit-and-run crash. I explained in more detail why I believed the party was involved and why we wanted someone to go—someone on the inside to get information.

As I talked, he grew more interested. I can visualize his face today and am more grateful to him than words can express.

He had several questions, so as he asked, we worked out a plan.

"What exactly do you want me to do?"

"Get the names of some of the people at the party."

"I'm not good at remembering names, and I can't go around asking for names and then writing them down," he joked.

"Oh, God, no. My husband and I are going to drive around the block and get as many license plates as we can. Maybe, you could take a little notebook and pencil and write down plates when you can—when no one is looking."

"Yeah, I could do that. When do I go to this party?"

"Tomorrow evening. But before you go, you should stop by our house and we'll drive over there and you can follow. I should have your phone number in case there's a change of plans. Are you sure you want to do this?"

He nodded, "Yes, I want to go."

"We're going over there later today to see what's going on. I may have to call you. What time do you think you should go tomorrow?"

"Ten o'clock? I'll come by your house before ten. It'll be dark and a lot of people will already be there."

I couldn't believe my luck. This young man whom I had just met would be attending that biker party. I cautioned him about the kind of people who could be at this party. He smiled. I said these are people you don't want to mess with and you shouldn't drink. Just make believe you are.

"You might find it hard to believe, but I don't drink. I do the bar scene because there isn't much to do in Columbus. I want to go. You never know what you might hear. When people are drinking, they talk and will say anything."

We discussed the danger of drinking and participating in drugs. He assured me that he didn't drink or do drugs. He said that he was good at walking around with the same beer all night. I believed him. And he had the right look and a relaxed way of handling himself. I recognized that he would have no trouble fitting in. I left the courthouse with a slight smile on my face. I couldn't believe it.

I arrived home about five o'clock. Every year without fail on that first Saturday in August, I recreate in my mind hour by hour what happened that day. I'll look at the clock and if it's three in the afternoon, I'll say, "Andrew was alive." If it's five o'clock about the time he came home from Paul and Robin's house, I'll say, "Andrew was alive."

When he called his friends in Cincinnati at seven-thirty, I look at the clock and say, "Andrew was alive." And on that first Saturday in August, I'm keenly aware of the weather. I don't believe it has ever rained. The days are, as the day was then, warm, bright and sunny—his perfect kind of day. I've wondered if we had changed our plans that day, somehow could we have saved our son?

Andy, like always, was either mowing the grass around the house or out sawing up trees in the woods. When a storm toppled a tree, he jumped at the chance to cut it up for firewood. From late October to March, he built roaring fires every evening. I noticed the woodpile growing. The more wood he cut, the more he tried to outwork his grief.

The work outdoors served as his therapy. Five or six hours of physical work, when we weren't chasing down vans, directed his mind elsewhere, and at the end of the day, after a shower and eating supper, he relaxed his tired body in front of the television until he could stay awake no longer. The work helped him to sleep. But this was early August and the days were long and on that late afternoon I had other plans for him.

I was eager to tell him about my encounter with Steve at the courthouse. Before we got too excited, I thought we should ride by the party house to see what was going on, if anything. So far, all we had were some New Albany people talking and some sketchy detail from the deputy who talked briefly to the host. This was the first weekend in August. We had to confirm what we might characterize as gossip. Did a party exist like the one described and held each year on the first weekend in August on Harlem Road?

We climbed into Andrew's car for the first go-round. If the information we heard about the party was accurate—that the festivities started on Friday evening—then we should be able to see some sign of partygoers gathering. We headed north up Lee Road, made a right on Walnut and then another right on Harlem, for a good position to see the yard.

Sure enough, there it was. The metal black barrel, used for grilling or barbecuing, Christmas lights strung from the garage to tree branches, tables, and chairs, two or three tents, and about ten people or so milling about the yard. Preparations were clearly under way for a party. A few vehicles were parked on the grass near the house, too far away for us to get any plates. Since Saturday was the big day, we were prepared to give our full attention to the party house on Harlem Road.

Heading back home, we considered what we knew about this party.

I said, "Remember what Deputy McMannis told us?"

"Yeah, that the Thompsons* couldn't remember the names of the people who came to their party," Andy answered.

"But do you remember what McMannis said about the kind of party it was?" I asked. This wasn't a quiz. I wanted confirmation of what I remembered McMannis said.

"No, refresh my memory."

"He said that he talked to a father whose high school son attended the party, and the father said that it looked like it was well-chaperoned and a nice party. He used the word 'nice' to describe the party."

"Well, we'll have a ring-side seat and see for ourselves tomorrow."

"But that's not what we heard from Charlie and the waitress, and remember that guy at the gas station who stopped us when we were taping the reward posters on the window?" I tried to trigger Andy's memory.

"And what about that man who lived on Harlem Road who stopped when you and Betsey were nailing posters on the telephone pole? Didn't you tell me he said there was a party the weekend Andrew was hit and the police were called?"

"It's incredible. The party is infamous in New Albany, at least on Harlem Road and McMannis reports it's 'nice' and 'well-chaperoned.'"

The next evening could not have arrived too soon. During the day, burning with curiosity, I took a few turns around the block to see what was happening at the Thompsons. The party was not in full swing. On Friday evening and Saturday during the day, I noticed a sparse crowd. I anticipated the party would swell as the afternoon turned into early evening if our information was right. And it was.

Because Steve had arranged to come at ten o'clock, I wanted to survey the party site during daylight hours when we could see license plates. I drove the first go-round at about seven o'clock. People were arriving. Because cars, trucks, and motorcycles were double-parked in the side yard, I could see only a few plates from the road. At first, I went by myself. Five times. Andy thought that getting Steve to go was sufficient. I couldn't trust that. But trying to drive and take down license plates is not smart, and I felt jittery. Surely someone would notice me in this huge truck painted fiery red with white neon signs announcing who I was and what I was doing. I drove my little non-descript gray Honda Civic, and no one in the yard seemed aware of the traffic on Harlem Road. Vehicles at that intersection were slowing down because of the activity at the corner. I was just another interested motorist.

The surveillance was not going smoothly. I was writing down plates on a sheet of paper beside me, but I couldn't look down so numbers and letters overlapped, and oftentimes I would get the first three numbers in my head before writing, and then my attention would move on to the next plate. Something like a hungry teenager at a buffet. This was not working out as I had planned. I needed Andy to go with me. Someone had to give full attention to driving and another person to taking down plates. By eight o'clock, vehicles lined Harlem Road.

When Andy and I came back around to the party scene, we saw what seemed to us to be hundreds of people. The yard, rather large, swarmed with people. Yes, this was a biker party and stereotypical motorcyclists at that. The black leather, sleeveless shirts, headbands, and chains seemed more like Halloween costumes. But we were witnessing a real spectacle. Motorcycles—Harleys—were parked in haphazard rows. Those plates were impossible to see. But the deputy investigator said that this was a "nice" party or at least he claimed some parent of teens who attended the party said as much. If true, I'd seriously question the parent's judgment.

A horde of bikers mingled in the middle of the yard. When we stopped for the traffic light at the corner, I grabbed my disposable camera and took a picture. Over the garage door hung a sign in bold, red letters, "BEER BASH." But this was a nice party, well chaperoned. You could send your high school kid and it'd be okay.

Vehicles, trucks, vans, cars—lined the west side of Harlem Road, for at least a fourth of a mile, and as many vehicles were parked off the road. The plates of the cars lining the road were easier to see than the ones parked off the road. As Andy drove, I caught at least five plates for each "go-round." We didn't use the same car. We'd drive back to the house, change cars, and sometimes put on a ball cap—anything to make us look different in case someone was suspicious. I doubt that anyone took notice.

As the sun settled down behind the trees, we headed home to meet Steve before ten o'clock. He reasoned that many people will show up around that time—after having partied themselves—getting "tanked" and loosened up before the big event. And that would be a good time to crash a party—a bunch of drunks showing up at the same time. We agreed. Good thinking.

Apparently, he hadn't made connections with Eli because he appeared on our lane in his red, sporty Trans Am. After I introduced Steve to Andy, Andy asked, "Are you sure this is okay with you? I mean, you're not having second thoughts, are you? If you are, we understand."

"No, I'm okay. But I have to admit I'm a little nervous. I could crash a party just to have fun but this is different."

"If you have any doubts at all about going through with this, don't hesitate to back out. We won't be angry. We consider your doing this icing on the cake. And we don't want, God forbid, to put you in any kind of dangerous situation. And if anything happens and you're not comfortable," I cautioned, "we want you to leave immediately. I really don't think your life is in danger or anything like that. Tell yourself you're going to have some fun but be aware of what's going on."

"How do I bring up the accident?" he asked. "What should I say?"

"Don't bring up the accident. Unless someone else says something or there is talk about it, don't say anything. The important thing is to get license plates of some of the people at the party."

"That reminds me," he said. "Do you have a small notepad and pencil?"

I handed him the smallest notebook I could buy and a sawed-off pencil, like the kind used in libraries.

I made my last request, "Would you call us tomorrow morning? And I'll have your money. We can't thank you enough for doing this, but don't do one risky thing."

Giving him a last warning about not doing anything risky, we made our way to the cars—Andy and I in his Buick and Steve in his Trans Am. He followed us down Lee Road, over to Walnut and then down Harlem Road where he parked behind the last vehicle lining the road.

Before we left the house, I grabbed a flashlight in case I could safely exit the car and get a few more plates. We swung around the block again, but this time Andy parked well behind the last car. We got out as we were some distance from the party site and no one else was around.

Andy held the flashlight as I took down plates. If a vehicle came down Harlem, we ducked behind a car. This was not fun by any stretch. It was awful. I was a nervous wreck. Anything that I did like this seemed wrong. Spying on people. But I had to. I had to get information. Who else would do this? Moms do what they have to do. Life experience suggested strongly that Andrew's death and the party were connected. We needed to get some names of people who attended.

And I trusted myself explicitly. If we learned something from spying on people, I would use the information discreetly. I am by nature skeptical. I knew that I would have to have a ton of evidence pointing to the guilty person before I would believe in that person's guilt. All the pieces would have to fit. I'm not afraid to ask the obvious or stupid question. This was far too important. The answer to who killed Andrew would have to be the correct one. I could have no doubt. The party was the one event we knew took place that weekend. It deserved surveillance.

We awoke on Sunday morning, decided against church in case Steve called and waited by the phone. I recalled that noon came and went, then midafternoon and still no word from Steve. A dread increased with every passing minute. Something happened. My God, I put Steve's life in jeopardy. I had his phone number and I dialed it. Steve's mother answered.

"Hi," I said. "I'm Elaine Starinchak and I met with your son last night about some work he's to do for me. Is he available?" Barely able to breathe, I managed to get the words out.

"He's in bed. He was out last night and got in early this morning," she answered.

Thank God, I thought. "Could you ask him to call me, please? There's no hurry."

Before the call, all that mattered was that Steve was okay. After the call, my attention turned to anticipating what he was going to tell us.

Sometime later that afternoon, the phone rang. Glancing at caller I.D., I saw Steve's number and answered. I voiced my concern. "When you didn't call this morning, I started to worry so I called."

"Sorry I didn't call earlier. It was late so I fell asleep in one of the tents and didn't get home until Sunday morning. I can come over now and give you what I have."

Sitting at the kitchen table, Steve handed me the note pad and pencil. I saw the pencil scribbling of what looked like license plates. He began, "I fell asleep in one of the tents. Too many people were around to get plates. So I decided to stay and about four o'clock when people had left or passed out, I snuck around in the dark and got about twenty plates."

I leafed through the pad and when I couldn't read a letter or a number, I'd ask him for clarification.

"Oh, yeah, and I have this paper some guy was passing out. Next Sunday there's going to be a bikers' barbecue to benefit a kid who has cancer. They're meeting at some bar in Columbus. It's on that paper."

"Looking at the handwritten copy of the paper, I said, "They can't be all bad. Did you get the name of the guy who gave this to you?"

"No, I didn't ask."

"You didn't run into any trouble, did you?"

"No, but I wasn't sure how I was going to crash this party. Walking up the drive, I came up with a story. I've used this before. I walked over to this guy and asked him if he knew a Lisa. That I'd just met her at the gas station in New Albany and she invited me to this party. He said he didn't know Lisa but would help me find her. He took me around the party, introducing me to people and asking them if they knew Lisa. No one did. At least not at this party."

"At a big party like that you'd think there would be at least one Lisa. And the way the party's been described, someone at a gas station could have invited you," I said.

"I'm not sure if I was lucky or unlucky, but the guy showing me around said that he was a good friend of the son of the guy giving the party. He said that he knew most of the people there but didn't know a Lisa."

"If he knew most of the people there, then the people giving the party probably knew most of the people there. But that's not what the Thompsons told Deputy McMannis."

"I had only one scare. When we didn't find a Lisa, this guy said, 'You aren't lying just to crash this party, are you?'"

"Did you think he knew you were lying?"

"Yeah, for a second I thought he knew, but he didn't. He started laughing like he was pulling my leg and I started laughing and said, no, but maybe I got the name wrong. Then I just started talking to this one girl he introduced me to and the rest of the night went by pretty fast."

"Did you hear anyone talking about Andrew's crash?" Andy interjected.

"No. I hung out mainly with the friends of the son and daughter. But there definitely was another, older crowd."

"Did you get names?"

"Yeah. On the pad, you'll see names of some of the people I met."

I was eager to compare his plate list to my list. And after we had asked every question we could think of, I could see that Steve was tired. He had to work on Monday. We said our goodbyes and promised to stay in touch. He mentioned at the courthouse that he worked in the Carolinas during the colder months. I did call him after Thanksgiving, but his mother said that he had already left.

Eternally grateful for what he did, I thought about him constantly for many months afterward. When winter gave way to spring, I called his house and left my name, but since he didn't return my call, we never talked again after that afternoon.

His writing was as bad as mine. When you're trying to write in the dark and doing something that may upset people if they find out, the numbers and letters don't resemble an accountant's figures. I discovered that he and I had written down some of the same plates. Between us, we had about twenty-five plates. I figured that I would get at least twenty names.

I filled out the forms for the Bureau of Motor Vehicles. With just a license plate, the BMV could provide the name and address of the person owning the vehicle. It would take several weeks to get all the reports back. The plan was to contact these people or send a private investigator. At least we now had names of some people at the party.

If we strongly believed that the party on Harlem Road had some connection to our son's death, then the party people might provide some useful information to the police. I typed up a list to give to the Sheriff.

I wonder what McMannis did with it?

11

A MONTH AFTER THE BIKER party on Harlem Road and our meeting with Chief Deputy Gil Jones, we were no closer to getting answers about Andrew's death than we were a year ago. We had the Matt Kolar tip that didn't pan out, we looked at more than fifty vans and none looked suspicious, we sent Steve to the bikers' party to get names of some of the people who attended and we asked the State Highway Patrol to help us. The Patrol would have helped, but the FCSO refused to give them our case.

We weren't privileged to know exactly what happened between the Sheriff and the State Highway Patrol, but in the end our case wasn't given to the Patrol and the Patrol didn't assist the Sheriff. Clearly, we had been sent two different messages—one from Deputy Chief Gil Jones that "something could be worked out," and one from McMannis, "that's not going to happen." We concluded that a deputy had more power to obstruct an investigation than the chief of the department had to do what was right for the victim and his family.

We believe that the Patrol tried. I called Sergeant Tuttle several times that month. But they couldn't do a damn thing unless the Sheriff's Office agreed to work with them. In Ohio, we have what is called home-rule. Once a law enforcement agency has a case, they own it. No matter what the circumstances are, you can't take it from them. The Patrol had resources that the Sheriff's Office didn't have. That didn't matter.

Several days after we met with Chief Jones, McMannis called us again. This time he tried to explain his remark, "that's not going to happen." He attempted to minimize the remark. If he thought we delighted in his calling us, he was wrong. We didn't want his explanation. Using plain common sense, we knew that certain duties, if performed, would get us closer to justice. But that wasn't happening. We should have filed a complaint against the Sheriff's Office, but I held out hope that someone would do the right thing. No one did. Why didn't they cut us loose and let the Patrol have Andrew's case? Because it would expose McMannis?

Two years after Andrew's death, our thoughts focused on finding the perpetrator. We were trying to problem solve. "Who could help us?" In Ohio, the Patrol is universally respected.

This was an investigation that didn't get started until six days after Andrew was killed. Officially, the Sheriff's Office should have talked to us as soon as Andrew was identified—or at least the next day, Monday. Can you imagine any hit-and-run homicide investigation giving the perpetrator six days of opportunity before identifying a make and model? Inexperienced, we were grateful that on the sixth day after Andrew had been hit, deputies discovered almost immediately—when they went out looking—the make, model, and color of the vehicle, based on the ground effect pieces found at the crash. Then, after the crash, someone thought to call Glaval. Glaval sent to the Sheriff's Office a list of their vans sold in Ohio. McMannis arranged a media conference and a Crime Stopper's television interview. Asking the public for help was good. Then nothing.

When we received the Sheriff's case file, a number of calls or tips that came into Crime Stoppers were passed on to the Sheriff's Office. Written on these—not all—was "C/C." Checked/Called? No record exists about those tips. Not one note on any call slip. I took one of those calls marked C/C and called the person, a young woman who had information about the party on Harlem Rd. No one from the Sheriff's Office ever returned her call. Suspicions confirmed.

Around the middle of September, a little more than a year after Andrew's death, after lunch, the phone rang. Phone calls were the lifeblood of an investigation. We waited for the Sheriff's calls, we waited for someone to call with a tip, we waited for our lawyer to call, we waited for our PI to call, we waited for friends to call with advice and on and on. I looked at the caller ID. The name showed "Howard Marski*. I had no idea who he was when I answered.

"Mrs. Starinchak?" the voice asked.

Only former students call me Mrs. Starinchak. "Yes, this is she."

"You don't know me but you taught my wife, Diane*, at Gahanna. I work for a construction company and some guy—a day laborer—was helping me with a roof in New Albany and we started talking about the reward posters on the telephone poles. He said he knows who killed your son."

"Did he give you a name?"

"He said Barry Snidka*. He says there's a rumor going around that he did it."

"What's the name of the guy telling you this?" I asked.

"I think John something. I don't remember."

"Have you worked with him before?"

"No, I've never seen him before. When I got off work, I took the number of Crime Stoppers off the poster and called, but it was busy. Diane told me to call you. She remembered when your son was killed."

"And this worker said there were rumors about a Barry Snidka being the person who killed Andrew?"

"Yeah."

"I wonder how he knows Snidka?"

"I don't know. He thinks he lives in New Albany."

Howard shared what he remembered of his conversation with the day worker. I voiced a concern that I would probably need to call him back.

After we hung up, I dialed the Crime Stoppers' number. I was disturbed that the line had been busy when Howard called their number. A dispatcher answered. I identified myself and related the details of my conversation with Marski.

Her voice took on a more personal tone. "Look, I'm not supposed to say anything, but I think you're going to get some good news soon."

My next call was to McMannis to see what I could find out.

Despite the encouraging words of the Crime Stoppers' dispatcher, I don't remember being too excited. That tip would carry little weight unless we could tie the killer to a Glaval van. From there, an examination of the van and an investigation of the alleged perpetrator would have to reveal evidence, beyond any doubt—at least for me—that that vehicle and person were involved.

One June morning the telephone rang and from the bedroom we could hear someone leaving a message. We heard a voice say, "Your son on bicycle. Route 605. Maroon van." Immediately, still in my p.j.'s, I jumped in the car and headed for Route 605, several miles from our house and not far from Central College Road where Andrew was hit. I made note of three maroon vans at various addresses. Which one was the caller referring to? We were looking for a white van. Did this person have his van repaired and repainted? Returning to the house, I noticed the number had come up on caller ID. I dialed the number.

The caller's voice was easily recognizable. When I explained my dilemma, the woman dictated an address. Later that afternoon, when Andy and I drove past the Route 605 address, the maroon van was still parked in the drive. We pulled into the drive as though we were turning around and I took down the plates. With plates, I could track the owners. A little more than a week later, I had my answer: the van had always been maroon and not even close to Glaval conversion. Case closed.

The tip from Howard Marski didn't cause my heart to skip, but I had to check it out. When I called the FCSO, McMannis answered. I relayed to him my conversation with Howard Marski and gave him Barry Snidka's name. McMannis knew the name.

"This kid is in his early twenties and lives with his father in New Albany. He likes to party and wreck cars. He has more than twenty driving offenses."

"Have you talked to him?" I asked.

"No, but I talked to his dad. His dad said he hoped we'd lock him up and throw away the key."

"That sounds pretty harsh. Do you think this kid is involved?"

"All I'm hearing is rumors. His dad owns an Astro van but it's not Glaval converted. It's American Road. Several weeks ago, I went to New Albany and stopped at a light near this kid's house. Directly in front of me was this kid in his old man's van. I stuck my head out the window and took a look at the van. It's not a Glaval. I didn't think there was anything there worth pursuing."

Strangely, we humans take a long time to unlearn a particular bias—no matter how much evidence we accumulate that negates that bias. And so it was with the Sheriff's Office. At any time, they could have thrown us a crumb here and there and like hungry chickens we'd run to feed and swallow anything the farmer threw. So as McMannis talked, I accepted his comment about sticking his head out of his cruiser to size up Barry's father's van. I didn't stop to consider the logic of this kind of investigating. He summarily dismissed a tip based on sticking his head out of his cruiser to examine a vehicle.

After I hung up, I forgot about Barry Snidka. I had become skeptical of tips. I called Howard about his tip to let him know that the Sheriff's Office checked it out and didn't think anything was there. And that ended that until Thanksgiving weekend in November when Andy and I returned from Chicago. The name Barry Snidka resurfaced.

A little more than a year after Andrew was killed, we were doing our best to get answers and to find his killer and hold that person responsible. No doubt, part of the discovery lay in our dealing with the vans on the Glaval list. The Sheriff's Office could have enlisted the help of the State Highway Patrol or the Bureau of Motor Vehicles. They could have had in their possession within two or three weeks of the crash, a listing of all Glaval vans owned in and around the Columbus area whether they were bought from local dealers or not.

Two previous tips that came to the house earlier in the year involved vans. Neither was Glaval converted and neither tip had a shred of validity. How would we handle a tip that remained suspicious?

October 1999 came and went and suddenly we faced our second holiday season without Andrew. At about the middle of November, work on our case came to a standstill. As in the previous year, not much happened until after

New Year's. We realized that we were out of "sync" with the rest of the community. Our minds focused on finding the coward who killed our son—not celebrating Thanksgiving or Christmas.

We had no idea that killing human beings with a vehicle was considered different from killing them with a gun. Our son's death was a homicide. Was there a statute of limitations at work here? If Andrew had been deliberately targeted—the thought crossed our minds—that was murder, and murder carries no statute of limitation. Rural areas carry their own brand of prejudice. Riding a bicycle? Not manly. Riding a motorcycle? Manly.

In 1998, the law judged hit-and-run crimes as misdemeanors. We were and are outraged. Surely, some distinction exists in the law between a driver who hits a mailbox and flees and one who hits and kills a person and flees. No, not much. The kicker comes if the driver repairs his damaged vehicle. Only then is he charged with a felony—tampering with evidence. *A death is a misdemeanor; a repair is a felony.* We initially thought that a misdemeanor was confined to vehicle crashes with property, not with people and certainly not with a fatality.

Killing Andrew with a multi-ton vehicle and then running away and hiding was a misdemeanor in 1998, but if the perpetrator repaired the vehicle that killed Andrew, only then was the crime a felony. No matter how you look at it, this law makes no sense. This was the law when our son was hit and killed. This law applied to our case even though some minor changes had been made since August 1998.

Could the fact that our son's homicide, murdered with a vehicle and not a gun or knife, affect an investigator's attitude? Could law enforcement make the mistake of assuming that a death involving a person and a vehicle is accidental and not intentional? To dispel that assumption, ask any ten cyclists what they think.

Ohio laws are extremely soft on hit-and-run drivers involved in fatalities. A lack of public outrage has allowed hit-and-run drivers responsible for deaths not to be charged with murder.

Drivers, who are most probably drunk or impaired in some way, can go off the road and kill a jogger or cyclist—as in our son's case—and then run and hide but show up at an attorney's office the next day, after they have sobered up, claiming that they thought they hit an animal.

The attorney, looking at the vehicle's damage, determines that indeed his client has been in a crash, and because he suspects from his client's story that he might have hit a person, the attorney investigates the client's details of the accident. Sure enough, on the road where his client said he hit something, a person was walking and killed by a driver who ran from the scene. The case is now in the hands of the attorney. He approaches the police, after having advised his client what to say.

In most cases, the driver would be charged with leaving the scene, fined something and, if the police want to believe the driver's story about thinking that an animal was hit, nothing further is done. It is that easy.

The driver of the van that hit Andrew, most probably the van owner himself, could have sobered up, seen a lawyer, paid a fine and the case would have been marked "solved" and "closed" within days.

After I had talked to McMannis about Howard Marski's tip, we heard nothing further. Had I been a little mouse in the Sheriff's traffic office, we would have witnessed trouble brewing. Not long after, McMannis left the traffic office.

In 2003 when McMannis was deposed for the second time in a civil suit we brought against the owner of a van, McMannis testified under oath that he had not written reports—no documentation existed to memorialize his "investigation." In 1998, according to reliable sources, the Sheriff's Office had no protocol in place for report documentation. This was an agency conducting investigations into criminal matters, involving life and death issues. Having no requirement to write reports and no oversight to do that, especially during those early, crucial weeks of the investigation, would hold dire consequences for us, Andrew's family. Not to mention all those other unsolved cases that came before our case and those after.

12

WE PLANNED TO BE WITH Betsey and Scott for Thanksgiving. We left on Wednesday and arrived back home Sunday evening. Dropping my bags in the hallway, I headed to the phone to check messages. One message stood out—a tip from a person we didn't know. He sounded young and earnest. The call came up as "private" on caller ID, having been made at six thirty p.m. I played the message and then grabbed a pencil and paper and played it again to get the details.

As Andy entered the house after parking the car, I yelled from the kitchen, "You'll want to listen to this. Some guy says he knows who killed Andrew. No ifs, ands or buts. He says he's going to call us back."

"Did he say when?" Andy asked.

"No, but sounds like he's going to call back tonight. But listen to this." I played the message for him: "Some dude told me about your son when it happened. I tried to tell the New Albany police and they told me to call the sheriff but no one answered. I know who killed your son. No ifs, ands, or buts. I'll call back."

We left the unpacking to stay by the phone. Andy made a pot of coffee and I opened containers of leftover turkey and pumpkin pie that Betsey had sent home with us. The house was cold so Andy moved to the living room to build a fire. I must confess a tiny sliver of hope shot through my head. Be careful, my skeptical self admonished.

Not long after we arrived home, the phone rang and glancing at the caller ID "private," I answered. "Hello," trying to sound normal.

"Do I have the right number? Was your son on a bike and killed?" the voice asked.

"Yes, you have the right number. Did you call about a half hour ago?"

"Yeah. I dialed your number about twenty times but hung up. I know who killed your son."

The caller spoke those words with such conviction, I could barely get my breath to ask, "Can you give me a name and how do you know?"

"I got it straight from the horse's mouth. Barry Snidka."

"Barry Snidka," I repeated. I had heard that name before. "And this person told you he did it?"

"Yeah. He was dating my cousin and working for me on and off. Charlotte and him comes by the house this past summer. We sat in the living room smokin' pot. Jean and Lotty go to the kitchen to make something to eat and that's when he told me."

"So…you didn't see him kill our son. You weren't with him?"

"No…no, he comes right out and says that he hit some dude on a bike. He said he heard some clanging. So he stops his car, got out and saw this dude and his bike in a ditch."

"Did he say where this happened?" I realized immediately that many newspaper articles and television coverage all mentioned Central College Road.

"He said he was going home after being out all night, drinking. It was dark out, misty, and foggy, and he thought he hit some trash cans. He got scared and jumped back into his car. That's when I asked him why he didn't call 911. He said he was in too much trouble."

"Do you know what kind of trouble?" I asked.

"All kinds. He was arrested for beating up my cousin. He got her started on crack. Before she started hangin' with him, she was beautiful. Owned a car. Paid her own bills. Now she's a skinny mess."

"Where is Barry Snidka now?"

"In jail. Assault, drugs, D.U.I., suspended license, you name it."

"Who else heard what he told you?"

"No one. Charlotte—Lotty – and my girlfriend were in the kitchen. I told Lotty later what he said and asked her if she was in the car with him. She said no."

"What was her reaction when you told her that her boyfriend confessed to killing a person?"

"She said she suspected him."

"Why would she say that?" I asked.

"She said he went around New Albany tearing down the reward posters. He said, 'that looks like my daddy's van.' And he's the type to see if he could hit the dude and run him over."

"Do you know if Snidka owned a van?"

"I know that he drove lots of people's cars. He borrowed his dad's van. Always showed up in a different car."

"Is your cousin still his girlfriend?"

"No. After he beat her up, she started using and sleeping around. I would rather see her in jail than selling her body."

"So do you know the last time she saw him?"

"When he beat her up, about three or four months ago."

"Do you know if Snidka was dating your cousin when she thought he hit our son?"

"I know she was seeing him. That's the dude who did it. I heard it from the horse's mouth."

"When did he tell you this?" I asked.

"Around the time it happened. But I didn't think too much about it. He brags. You can't trust what he says."

"Why are you coming forward now? Why didn't you call the police when he told you?"

"I just finished a job in New Albany and seen a poster. It hit me then. I had to put two and two together."

His words sounded convincing. I asked if he would be willing to talk to the police.

"I come from a tough family. Let's say we're not friends with the police. You're better off dead than being a snitch."

"To get the reward, you have to help us convict this person."

"But the poster said that you would protect the identity of anyone with information."

"If we can put this together without you, based on your information, we won't identify you, but you might have to testify."

"Barry ain't goin' to confess. He'll take it to the grave. The police will have to have picture-perfect evidence. If this could help Lotty, I'll talk to the police. I have a reputation. I fought in the Golden Gloves. I know karate. I work out. I can handle myself."

Before he hung up, he identified himself as Joey Rollison*. I got his address and phone number but he said that he preferred to call me. I asked him to call back in a couple of days. That would give me time to get a private investigator to meet with him and take his statement. Rollison's statement, "I heard it from the horse's mouth," coupled with "no ifs, ands or buts" strengthened his tip—gave it a ring of credibility—but it shouldn't have. Absolutely nothing about those phrases offered any proof; yet, they affected me. I was offered some chocolates but they weren't Godiva.

If I had taken the time to analyze the details of his tip, I might not have been so eager to believe it, but Rollison gave a convincing performance.

The first detail I should have noticed was the date. Rollison's tip said that Snidka confessed to him when the crash happened which would have been a year and four months before Rollison called us. Rollison, however, sounded as though Snidka confessed in the summer, three or four months ago. Apparently, Rollison was not aware that Andrew was killed in 1998, not 1999.

Then Rollison said Snidka told him he was driving down this road late at night on his way home when he hit Andrew. Rollison didn't know that Andrew was traveling in a westerly direction on Central College Road. If Snidka drove on Central College Road toward home, he would have been traveling in an easterly direction.

Also, Rollison gave distinct details about a dark, foggy, misty night. August 1, 1998 was a typical, warm, sunny summer day. Andy and I, with his brother and sister-in-law, picnicked late in the afternoon at Picnic with the Pops, a summer concert. Neither fog nor mist rolled in that evening or even in the early morning hours. The night was clear. I know because I was up most of it waiting for Andrew to come home. I went out to his car at about four in the morning. I would remember fog and mist.

The time of the crash didn't make sense either. Rollison said Snidka had been out late and the accident happened in the wee hours. That didn't square with Andrew's plans to go to Cincinnati. His car was packed—navy blue canvas duffle bag with socks, underwear, shorts, shirts; his cleats attached with a hook to the bag; all his Frisbee disks. He called a friend in Cincinnati around 7:30 that evening. All his friends knew he was going to Cincinnati, and he mentioned to me on the last morning of his life, "Mom, after practice, I'm going to Cincinnati. I'll be back Sunday." It didn't make sense that he would be on his bike until the early morning hours. We're certain that by early morning he had lain for hours, dying in a ditch.

Advising the Sheriff's Office of Rollison's tip wouldn't raise an eyebrow, but Andy called anyway. At the time, blinded by hope, we didn't bother to evaluate the details of Rollison's tip. So much of it didn't fit with the facts. Still, we had to check it out.

We were without a private investigator. Rick, our first PI who retired from the Columbus Police Department, was impossible to reach. Our second investigator, a woman, proved to be too expensive. We didn't have the technology or the skills to do the job ourselves. We longed to say to a professional investigator, "These are the facts. This is what we know and what we have. Now go find the person who killed our son." We could have done that. But we would have to pay for every single thing the investigator did, results or no results, to find the person who killed Andrew. Every PI, no matter how experienced, finds information through trial and error, and you are obligated to pay for your private investigator's time. Investigations aren't linear. We had only so much money, although Andy said, "We'll find it somewhere."

In dealing with a private investigator or any professional when thousands of dollars exchange hands, a client should be comfortable enough to question costs. Working with an investigator who charges by the hour for services that can't often be pinned down requires a savvy client.

After Rollison's call we went looking for a private investigator. One Sunday, several days later, I noticed a newspaper article honoring a trooper for his work with MADD. The article mentioned that the trooper was retired. Retired law enforcement people often work as private investigators. Using the internet to get the trooper's number, I called him. After I had explained the reason for my call, this retired trooper—one of Ohio's best—expressed heartfelt compassion for our situation, but declined the job. Since he lived near Cleveland, he felt that a local person could be a lot more effective. He advised me to call Jack Holland, "one of the best crash reconstructionists at the Patrol."

My call to Jack Holland supported his former colleague's comments. Jack knew of Andrew's crash. He offered to help with the physics and mechanical aspects of the crash itself, but said he would feel more comfortable recommending another retired colleague to do the investigating. He gave me Don Sonney's name and number. I couldn't begin to list here all the help Jack was to give us, and he never sent us a bill.

I didn't know then that Don was to be of immense help in becoming our friend, investigator, and referee. Andy and I were at our wit's end. Desperately frustrated, we were constantly at each other's throats, often yelling at each other in Don's presence.

After one particularly angry exchange of words, Andy turned to me and said, "You know, I miss Andrew, too." I don't know of any parent who doesn't suffer anger and guilt after losing a child. And I'm not talking about all the times I confronted Andrew with, "You're a royal pain in the ass, you know that?" I'm talking about the times I should have been there for him or listened to him but was too busy with my own activities. The love I have for him is unbearable. He had this air of vulnerability. I thought that if anything ever happened to him, I would not live.

13

MY DREAMS ABOUT HIM STARTED when he was about four years old. At first, they included both our children. The dream was always the same. The kids are sick and the doctor prescribes medicine. One of the doses must be given in the early hours of the morning, but I sleep through that dose and they both die. The dreams were not long or detailed, like other dreams I had. These were almost like flashes. I didn't give my children their medicine and they died. And I would let out this "bloodcurdling scream" as Andy described it. Waking—not because I heard the scream, I didn't—my heart raced and I felt horrendous terror.

I taught high school English from the time Andrew was six months and Betsey, a year, and a half. Most moms didn't work in the late sixties. I think some guilt festered in there somewhere.

Then the dreams or flashes of terror changed. They involved Andrew alone. I forgot to give him his medicine and he died. The idea would pop into my head that I failed to give my little boy his medicine. I would scream and wake everyone. To dispel worries, Andy would say to the kids, "It's just crazy Zelda."

The "dreams" continued into Andrew's high school and college years. As Andrew grew older, what I failed to do in the dream became veiled. It wasn't exactly clear. Subconsciously, I was petrified of losing this beloved child. These episodes came on unexpectedly. I would go to bed with no outstanding worry and awake with such terror, an indescribable, terrifying feeling.

I read books on dreams to understand what was going on and put an end to these "night terrors." The last book I read said that a person dreams of the death of a family member when that dreamer is afraid of one's own death. I wanted that to be the reason.

Today, I'm not so certain that was the reason. I did lose a precious child. Before Andrew's death, no one could have convinced me that a mother senses a catastrophe. That I had a premonition. Also, I possessed little faith in intuition as it is commonly understood. I thought that intuition was the result of subconsciously taking in body language, being able to read between the lines and to understand the context of an event, even though the clues are sometimes subliminal. The day Andrew cycled on Central College Road early in the evening and hadn't returned home by 11:00 o'clock with no word from him posed strong indications that something was wrong. I'm tortured by the thought that

I ignored both my concern and the physical signals. For years, my dreams had put me on hyper-alert status—to be aware of unusual situations, especially dealing with my children. But that night I disregarded the unusual.

One consolation, for me, in this grief process is the comforting idea of reincarnation. I have no idea how anything works in the spiritual world—if indeed there is one—but I want to believe that the love we have for each other proves that we are more than just our bodies. Did my dreams come from some former life I had with Andrew? And that I was forewarned in this life—if I noticed?

The evening before we contacted Don Sonney, we pulled our chairs up to the fireplace to talk strategy. As Andy threw more logs on an already roaring fire, we watched the snow piling up around the house. Instead of Christmas, now a painful reminder of happy times, our thoughts were on Andrew's killer.

"If this guy, Don, is interested in helping us, do we tell him about the Sheriff's Office? I asked.

"Yeah, he has to know the details of our relationship and if he's uncomfortable with that, we shouldn't hire him."

"How do we narrow this thing down? There's so much to do." I said.

"What if we ask him to just consider the Snidka tip? He can start with that."

"We should make a list of all the questions we have—like how much he charges an hour, his experience, and make a point about wanting results."

"If we get that far, he'll need to know about the running board pieces, and that a white Glaval Astro van was involved. We can make him a copy of the Glaval list and mark for him the vans that we've checked. "

"He'll have to know about the Thompson party. We can give him the names and addresses of some of the people who went," I added.

"Yeah, but remember we're hiring him to look at Snidka now."

"Okay, but Snidka could be connected to the party."

"Sure. The tip is good or it isn't. Let's find that out," he said.

"We have to put Snidka in a Glaval van. That's an absolute."

We met Don Sonney within hours of Andy's first call to him. A tall, muscular man emerged from a white Buick parked in front of our house.

In his fifties, Don had retired from the Bureau of Criminal Investigation and before that had done undercover work. He was a mixture of someone who could run with the motorcycle crowd in his undercover days and hobnob with local dignitaries. After reviewing the details of his work background, we knew he would be able to deal with the criminal element, if that kind of person killed Andrew. Joey Rollison, obviously, was no choir boy, and he had revealed unashamedly in our conversations that he came from a family with run-ins with the law.

We learned that Don once owned a Harley and loved riding it so much that he could take off on a whim and be gone for days. His build and his almost genteel manner, as well as his vast experience in dealing with criminals, convinced us to ask for his help.

We made the dining room table our command center and the nearby roaring fire in the fireplace kept us comfortable. After we finished an overview of our case, we informed Don of the Rollison tip. As we talked, he drew up a plan to check out Rollison and investigate Barry Snidka.

Before he left that first meeting, he reviewed his thinking. "I'm going to need to meet with Rollison. Give him some warning that I want to talk to him. We need to set up a meeting as soon as possible. You said he works, so I'll get over to his house after five o'clock, and if he's not home, I'll wait for him."

That evening I called Rollison. I had no idea how he would react to our hiring a private detective to check his tip, but if he wanted any reward money, the tip had to be validated. As it turned out, Rollison agreed to meet with Don the following evening as long as his identity would be protected.

"I don't want Barry to know I called you," Rollison said on the phone. "I'm not afraid of him, but why cause trouble for myself? I wrestled in high school and boxed in the service. Barry talks tough but he ain't."

Knowing nothing about Snidka, I made no comment, except to say, "If Snidka finds out that you called, it won't be from us."

14

DECIDING WHAT TO DO ABOUT Joey Rollison's tip dominated our every thought as our second Christmas without Andrew approached. I had just recently picked up Harry Frankfurt's book *On Truth,* and one sentence struck me as applicable to our investigation. Frankfurt wrote, "No one in his right mind would rely on a builder or submit to the care of a physician who does not care about the truth." Or a Sheriff who doesn't care about the truth.

I don't remember much about that Christmas except that I couldn't stand to hear Christmas music. I'd walk into a grocery store and if Christmas music filled the air, I would walk back out and keep going until I found a store with no music. I was more keenly aware that Christmas than ever before of the pain of loss, of the pain of moms not able to give their children gifts, of the pain of ill health, of the pain of remembering a young man's favorite gift—a warm, flannel shirt. I managed to go to a local department store several times to buy toys to donate, but as I navigated through the aisles, I made certain I didn't look at the young men's section.

Betsey and Scott spent Christmas Eve with Scott's family and then on Christmas morning drove the two-hour trip to Columbus. Scott's family had planned a ski trip after Christmas, so he joined them while Betsey stayed on with us. For Scott to miss the ski trip seemed pointless. If we had asked him to stay, he would have. In those awful first years without Andrew, Betsey and we relied on him for support repeatedly.

One evening she and I were lying across her bed talking. Scott had called earlier to say that he planned to leave Boyne, Michigan, in the morning and head back home. Concerned about unfinished projects at work, Betsey also made plans to leave our house after lunch the next day. To maximize our time with her, we decided to drive her home and stay the weekend.

"Mom, I think we should leave about one o'clock tomorrow. That'll give me time to do my wash and get some work done on a project."

"I can do your wash while you work on your project. But I'd like to run an idea by you. It's Deputy McMannis. He's angry with us for asking the State Highway Patrol to take our case. No matter what, we need him on our side. I'd like to take him a basket of fruit or something." Erroneously, I thought we needed the FCSO.

"Let's go out now and get something. Then we won't have to worry about doing it tomorrow. I don't like the idea of fruit. I can't see him peeling an orange. I think some crackers and cheese and maybe some summer sausage, stuff like that."

Grabbing our coats, we headed to a specialty store. Three days after Christmas the selection for cheese and sausage was limited, but we managed to put some food items together.

"Betsey, I think that you should take the basket in to him. We'll pack up the car and head out from there. Dad and I can stay in the car. I just think that would be better."

Andy agreed that we should try, at least, to repair any damage. Our naïve hope and trust were to motivate him to work our case. Part of that attitude came from Betsey's counsel. Used to working with business people with egos, she reminded us on many occasions to try to see our case from the Sheriff's point of view. We tried mightily, but the omissions were too serious.

Despite imagined excuses, I couldn't figure out why the FCSO didn't start with the Glaval list. If the job demanded that they physically check out the list of seven hundred plus vans, we would have understood. Surely the thought crossed their minds to use a data base to narrow down the list. If they didn't have the technology, one solution would be to enlist the State Highway Patrol's help. Or go to the Bureau of Motor Vehicles. We did. Not dealing with that list was as overwhelming in 1998 as it is today.

On that list was the van, only ten miles from the crash site.

In the spirit of working together, we offered an olive branch in the form of a Christmas basket to McMannis. Our calls went unanswered. Activity in our case had stopped. The testing and examination of our son's clothes and bike more than a year later still had not been done. And yet we were hopeful.

After eating lunch and packing the car, we headed for the Sheriff's Office. The yellow brick, two-story structure has those plain, metal encased windows in the front and sits not far from the street. Andy pulled around to a side road and parked. "We'll stay here," he said.

We watched as Betsey, carrying the basket, walked around to the front of the building, and disappeared. The minute she left we visualized what would happen inside. We could not have imagined what did occur. We thought that she would walk in, ask for Deputy McMannis, extend her hand—maybe even hug him—and tell him that we hoped he had a good Christmas and that she brought him something to snack on at work.

We imagined that he would take the basket and thank her and then make some perfunctory remark about hoping for some success in her brother's investigation. In a few minutes, she would then come around the bend, and we would head north to take her home. Almost an hour went by and still we waited. Andy noticed a gas station directly across the street. "While we're waiting, we might as well get gas," he said and I agreed.

We pulled out of the side street and crossed over to the gas station. We had no idea that we could be seen from the Sheriff's Office, or that Betsey and Deputy McMannis were in a front office talking and had spotted us. After we filled the tank, we drove back to our original parking space and waited. Shortly thereafter, Betsey trudged through the snow to the car.

"I thought you guys were going to stay parked. I didn't tell him that you were outside waiting. Then we saw you pull into the gas station across the street. He said he should go outside and say hello but I told him, no, that it's okay. I was embarrassed because I didn't mention that you were outside."

"We needed gas and saw the station across the street," Andy said.

"So, how was it?" I asked.

"Mom, why did you write him that letter?"

"What letter? The one where I explained to him about how we felt about Andrew and that we wanted his killer caught?"

"But you suggested that he wasn't doing his job," she said. "He let me read it. I felt sorry for him."

For the life of me, I could not remember what I had said. Even with incontrovertible evidence that he wasn't doing his job, did I have the courage to say it? I surprised myself.

"When I gave him the basket, he asked if I was wired. What's wired?'

"He asked you that?" Andy said surprised. "He thought that you might be wearing a recording device. Recording your conversation."

"Why would he think that?" Betsey asked.

"I don't know." I said. "What did you say?"

"I didn't understand what that was and just looked confused."

"You were in there for almost an hour. What else did he say?" I asked again.

"Listen to this. He said that he is leaving the traffic department. That he took a voluntary demotion. And then he said it was because of our case. He's had to go to counseling. And he had tears in his eyes."

Andy glanced at me. "What? McMannis is taking a demotion because of our case?"

We had no idea what "voluntary demotion" meant and we completely mis-interpreted his phrase "because of our case." Don Sonney, our PI, told us later that no one takes a voluntary demotion. If you want out of a department, you ask for a *transfer,* not a *demotion.*

When McMannis informed our daughter that he was demoted because of our case and in counseling, we thought perhaps he had become too emotion-ally involved in his job. This last thought exposed our abject ignorance about McMannis.

That winter afternoon McMannis said much more than he should have. At our civil trial four years later, he denied the details of that conversation with Betsey. *Deny* is a nice word. We don't doubt that our case had something to do with his demotion. Exposed. He couldn't care less about us or Andrew. FCSO was afraid of a suit. They knew we had plenty to go on.

Gil Jones, coming from the State Highway Patrol, must have suffered cul-ture shock when he took the reins of the Sheriff's traffic division. When no reports and no documentation exist, where is the accountability? Can you imagine any law enforcement agency in the late 1990s not having a comprehen-sive policy for keeping track of what happens in an investigation? Especially homicide? Jones admitted the FCSO had no protocol in place.

In December, 1999, we had no more insight than a kid asking a store Santa to bring him a bicycle. For the weeks and months and years to come, we would go back to that afternoon and the details of Betsey's visit after Christmas to the Sheriff's Office traffic department. Bit by bit, we realized that the meeting was not what it seemed.

2000

15

AS DON'S INVOLVEMENT WITH OUR case grew, he and I disagreed about keeping all sources confidential. He didn't think that was possible. He said authorities would want to talk to these so-called witnesses. I felt that the information persons provided would lead us to the evidence we needed, and we'd get nothing if any of them thought for a second they'd be labeled snitches. As experience with criminals goes, Don had the edge. I based my opinion on my experience with teaching high school teens. I had to figure out a way to talk to students who might have information. But the consequences can be ugly for the student trying to help the teacher. I went to great lengths to protect good information. Sometimes being a snitch, ratting out someone, is right and the finger pointers need protected.

During a conversation with Joey Rollison after Christmas, I determined that I would do everything possible to protect his identity. Then he divulged that his cousin, Charlotte, Snidka's ex-girlfriend, was in jail, incarcerated at the Jackson Pike facility.

"Lotty's in jail. She was caught shoplifting. Probably for her pimp. She's due to get out on Saturday and has no place to go except back with her pimp."

"Does she have a mom?" I asked.

"Yeah, but she won't take her. The thing I'm worried about," he said, "is that Barry or her pimp will show up."

Writing this book about the investigation into Andrew's crash has necessitated a closer look at details of 1999 events. As we lived these daily events, I took little time to understand what they meant. I cornered anyone polite enough to listen, and I emailed the particulars of events to our daughter, family, and friends—unaware that through these emails I was recording events. Pushed from one event to another, we rarely stopped to grasp cause and effect. Whenever we took some action—like spending the Labor Day weekend in 1999 re-posting reward signs—that action caused something else to happen. This time it was the Barry Snidka tip. Howard Marski saw a posted reward sign and Joey Rollison claimed he did, also.

I had tried to take refuge in Buddhist philosophy. Reading books about Buddhism, I craved wisdom and a way to know truth. Buddhism teaches that answers will come on their own. It's better to cultivate serenity. Attempting to meditate, I desperately sought serenity. For me, that part of Buddhist teaching, especially in my circumstances, didn't seem to be working.

Here we were beginning a new year and because Andy, Betsey and I had rushed around weekend after weekend several months earlier, from September to November, posting signs, we had a lead. So on Tuesday, January 19, 2000, about noon, Andy and I drove to the Jackson Pike Correctional Center to talk to Rollison's cousin, Charlotte.

We arrived a little early. Here and there, couples or groups of people sat together, waiting to hear a name and then a loud buzz to signal their entrance through double doors into yet another hallway fortified by a heavy metal door leading to a room with chairs, Plexiglas, phones, and inmates.

In the waiting rooms of correctional facilities, and we were to be in several of them, eye contact was rare so I remember taking in as much detail about the visitors as my curiosity wanted. No one smiled. No animated conversations. A place of austere silence.

The reception desk was divided into two windows—one for "professional visits." Don Sonney had preregistered me as a private investigator's assistant. I approached the professional visit window. I addressed the man behind the desk as "officer," telling him who I was and who I wanted to see about an accident.

Looking at a clipboard, the officer said, "She has a visitor right now but since you have an appointment, I can terminate the visit." With that he buzzed me into the visitor's room. Seated behind a Plexiglas wall, a row of about five or six inmates talked on phones to visitors seated in front of them. I scanned the inmates. Only one girl. About nineteen and pretty. The officer approached her male, ponytailed visitor, "Sorry, your time's up. She has a visitor who wants to talk to her about an accident."

The young man vacated the chair and I sat down. I could hear the officer repeating to the young man my reason for the visit. If I could hear them, then the young man could hear what I was saying to Charlotte. I didn't like that. I wanted our conversation to be private.

I introduced myself to Charlotte and explained briefly my purpose. She already knew. I said, "Is this a good time to talk?" The officer and the previous visitor stood no more than ten feet behind me.

"No," she answered.

I was not leaving until I talked to her. "Do you want to finish your visit?" I questioned.

"Yes, I'll be a few minutes."

With the officer as an escort, I headed back to the waiting room. Minutes later, the officer called my name and nodded his head to go back through the double doors.

The door buzzed, I entered the hallway and as I did, the young man visiting Charlotte was exiting through the heavy metal door toward me. He looked at me and asked, "You here about an accident?"

"Yes," I answered.

"About Barry Snidka?" he continued.

"No," I lied. For all I knew it was Snidka. It was.

Approaching Charlotte's station, I saw a welcoming smile. She wants to talk, I remember thinking. I was an assistant to a private detective there to ask some questions. That was all.

"Your cousin, Joey, said that you might be able to give us some information about the hit-and-run death of a bicyclist. He cares a lot about you."

When I mentioned Joey caring about her, tears streaked down her cheeks. Fixing her eyes on me, she answered, "Yes."

"All I need today is a 'yes' or 'no' answer. Did you ever live in New Albany?"

"Yes, I lived with my boyfriend, Barry and his dad for two years."

"Do you have any idea as to who might be involved in the accident with the cyclist in August of 1998?"

"Yes."

"Do you know the person or persons involved in this accident?"

"Yes."

"Did this person or persons ever tell you what they did involving this accident?"

"No," she answered.

"Were you in the vehicle at the time that it was involved in the accident?"

"No."

So she wasn't in the vehicle and no one ever confessed to being involved. How does she know who was involved? I had hoped that the answer would come as I continued questioning her.

"Did you attend a party in New Albany on the day of the accident? That would be August 1, 1998."

"No."

"Do you know if Barry attended a party in New Albany on August 1, 1998?"

"He did."

"How was it that you and Barry were living together that summer, but you didn't attend a party and he did?"

"We had an on and off relationship that summer."

"Do you think that Barry had something to do with the accident?"

"Yes," she answered.

"Why do you say that?"

"This one time we were going to his house. He stopped his car, got out and tore a poster off a telephone pole. It was a reward poster about the hit-and-run accident. He looked at the poster and said, 'This looks like my daddy's van'. Then he said that he was going to look for a van with blood on the front and collect the money."

"Why did this seem suspicious to you?" I asked.

"The way he tore down the poster. He ripped it off."

"Was that pretty much it? The way he tore the poster off the telephone pole?"

"The way he drives. He's had lots of accidents."

"Do you think that anyone else was with Barry Snidka when this happened?"

"I'm not sure but I think two guys who are brothers could have been."

I asked for names. She revealed not only their names, but also gave me a brief family history. Months later, we were to discover that she dated one of the brothers. On one occasion while at a motel with him, Barry followed them, and took a hammer to the boyfriend's truck. Apparently, the motel boyfriend dropped her.

After some discussion, the details of this so-called tip just didn't add up. Despite inconsistencies, we plodded on. If the tip had validity, the pieces would fall into place.

Charlotte's timeline didn't square with the details of the crash. The information she gave about when and where the accident occurred, which just happened to be consistent with Joey's information, was wrong. This girl was in jail. Should that have had any bearing on her credibility?

Some details made sense. Barry Snidka's abysmal driving history, living in New Albany, and his father's van looking like the one in the reward poster made him a prime suspect in Charlotte's mind. That and rumors.

We focused our attention on Barry Snidka because he was, for about a year, a person of interest. Some pieces of the puzzle didn't fit; some pieces did. We had all these pieces that looked like the puzzle but didn't interlock. And a big piece, the Glaval van, was glaringly missing.

In interviewing Snidka's friends, we compiled a list of people he knew and the vehicles they drove. Young guys usually don't drive vans—they may borrow the family vehicle, but it's not a vehicle they choose to drive. We checked out the vehicles of Sndka's relatives in town. I found no matches on the Glaval list.

Furthermore, a major reason the rumors swirled around Snidka was that his father owned an Astro van. Don's photos of the father's van showed the American Road conversion logo on the back door. We checked with Glaval. It wasn't one of their vans. When the tips are investigated, people interviewed, and information checked for validity, but the facts don't add up, then it's time to move on. As Snidka's friends revealed details of his personality, two characteristics stood out—he bragged and he lied. Don thought that Barry probably started the rumor himself to gain attention.

16

NEAR THE END OF 1999, little progress had been made in the investigation of our son's death. Mark Adams, our friend and attorney, reasoned that filing a suit against John Doe, the unnamed driver, gave us access to information we could not otherwise legally get. Mark added our auto insurance company as a defendant because the company posed some questions about the policy. *Filing that suit was a stroke of genius.* Under the suit, Mark could subpoena and depose people who might have information about Andrew's crash. If serious information surfaced, we had the legal power to act. We could bypass the FCSO. That suit and Mark's counsel, his gift for knowing the best course of action, would result in our finding the van that killed Andrew. Donating his services pro bono, however, Mark could not have foreseen the enormous cost of time and energy to help us.

When we returned home after New Year's, we relayed to Mark the details of Betsey's visit to the Sheriff's Office several days after Christmas. With McMannis moving to another department, we just had to wait until the new guy came on board.

At the end of February 2000, Mark Adams sent us an email:

> Andy and Elaine,
> I have been ready to take McMannis' deposition but have been waiting to hear from you re [in regard to] Holland's efforts. I think we might want to act now before McMannis leaves. What do you think? When is McMannis leaving? Let me know if you want to go forward now on this.
>
> All the best, Mark.

I hit "reply" and answered:

> We believe McMannis is leaving the first of May. Yes, we want you to take his deposition. We agree that we should act now. We asked Don to call Holland [retired crash reconstructionist with Ohio State Patrol and Don's friend.] We want him there. We're grateful for your support.

The reason to depose Deputy McMannis was to gain information. We had no idea what the FCSO did in investigating Andrew's death. Based on our interactions with them, or lack of, we needed to know what they had learned, if anything. Deposing McMannis represented the first significant action under the John Doe civil case that Mark had filed on our behalf. Suing the FCSO never crossed our minds—at least not until the evidence of its miserable performance physically sickened us.

Generally, the wheels of justice turn slowly. You don't decide one day to take someone's deposition and do it the next. Much thought and preparation go into asking a witness questions. The witness takes an oath to answer truthfully. Those answers may be used in a trial. An attorney will serve notice to a person or witness, directly or indirectly related to a lawsuit, to appear at a certain time and place to answer questions. Sometimes an opposing attorney will also question the witness.

We had a month to put a plan together. What information did we think the Sheriff's Office had that would help us? Mark was not interested in putting McMannis on the defensive. Our goal was to bring the killer to justice. Despite our opinion of McMannis, we retained a level-headed respect for police and their hazardous jobs.

On April 19, 2000, Mark Adams reported in an email that he had sent a subpoena to Deputy McMannis requiring him to appear at Mark's office to have his deposition taken. That was great news. As Mark explained to us, he could subpoena Deputy McMannis to testify under oath as to what he knew and get a look at the sheriff's investigative files. We could proceed from there.

After Deputy McMannis received the subpoena from Mark, McMannis called Don, our private investigator. Once a person is in law enforcement as Don was—with BCI and the Highway Patrol—a kind of bond endures with other law enforcement people. And we knew with certainty that Jack Holland, Don's colleague now retired from the State Highway Patrol, still maintained close ties to the FCSO.

Sounding concerned, McMannis asked Don what the deposition was about. We didn't get it then. Did he think that we were preparing to sue him and the FCSO? The point of the deposition was to get whatever information the FCSO had to add to our investigation. Surprised by McMannis' call, Don seized the opportunity to talk to McMannis about the subpoena and upcoming deposition.

At about the time Don and McMannis were talking on the phone, I called Sheriff Karnes' office to discuss questions about the fiberglass pieces. Because these pieces represented key evidence in the Sheriff's possession, we had to request permission for Don to take them to Elkhart, Indiana, for Glaval's examination. Don used the term "chain of command"—that the fiberglass pieces could be given only to a person with an official designation. Hence, the reason we called the Sheriff himself.

After the receptionist answered, I gave her my name, a summary of the details of Andrew's death and asked to speak to Sheriff Karnes. Although we made repeated attempts to talk directly to Sheriff Karnes, we were never successful, nor did he ever return our calls. I no sooner finished talking to Sheriff Karnes' receptionist, when the phone rang. It was Don.

"Dave McMannis just called. He wanted to know about the subpoena he got from Mark."

"What did he say?"

"He offered excuses why he didn't do this or that. Then he asked what I knew about the civil case. He asked what that was about."

"All he had to do was to read the complaint. What did you tell him?" McMannis was to give his testimony in our John Doe case, and he didn't read the complaint? The case wasn't about the FCSO."

"I told him I met Mark only once at the house, and that the civil case was against the unnamed driver and that's all I knew," Don said.

"Did he say anything else?"

"He wanted to know if he had to bring the bicycle to the deposition. I asked him whether the subpoena spelled that out. He said the subpoena said to bring all the physical evidence. I told him that the bike was physical evidence and he should bring that. Oh, yes, and he mentioned that you hurt him."

"Did he say how I did that? I hurt his feelings? Because we asked the Patrol to take our case?" Unaware of the politics involved, our request for the Patrol's intervention sent a message to McMannis that the Patrol could solve a case that the FCSO couldn't or wouldn't. Are citizens to accept that certain members in law enforcement have the supreme power to ignore evidence, and that justice should be set aside because a deputy's feelings might be hurt?

I have no documentation of how we hurt McMannis. That was never our intent. And the deposition in 2000 proved that. No one could have treated him with more civility than Mark Adams.

After finishing his conversation with McMannis, Don said, "The deputy taking over McMannis' job starts May 1. I told him [McMannis] if he had any further questions, he should talk to Mark. Why didn't he call him in the first place?"

I couldn't give Don an answer. McMannis had misjudged Mark and us. The subpoena to Deputy McMannis noted May 3, 2000, at Mark's office as the time and place for his testimony. Several weeks before the scheduled deposition, however, Mark received a call from McMannis. McMannis asked to change the venue of the deposition from Mark's office to one of the assistant prosecutor's offices.

At the time this struck Andy and me as a strange request. Or maybe this wasn't so unusual. The Franklin County Prosecutor represents the FCSO, exactly like attorney and client. Perhaps McMannis felt "safer" at the Prosecutor's Office. Mark didn't hesitate to grant the request. We would meet at the Prosecutor's Office.

In 2000 we had no real understanding of the relationship of the Prosecutor's Office to the FCSO. I always thought that the Prosecutor would go after anyone who breaks the law, including a policeman. But in the relationship between the two, the Prosecutor protects law enforcement.

In hindsight, looking at that one little detail, the change in venue of the deposition takes on a bit more importance. Fast forward to McMannis' second deposition, taken three years later in November 2003 at Attorney Mark Gams' office, the attorney representing the defendant van owner through his insurance company, State Farm, in our second civil suit. When Deputy McMannis received his subpoena notice from Attorney Gams at Gams' office, McMannis didn't request a change in the deposition site to the Prosecutor's office. He felt "safe" with Gams? Exactly what was the difference in 2003? *By that time, plenty.*

But on that Tuesday morning, in May 2000, Andy and I entered the office of Harland Hale, a Franklin County Assistant Prosecutor. McMannis had arrived and was engaged in a conversation with Jack Holland, our crash reconstructionist whose presence Mark wanted at the deposition. Jack's stellar reputation in Columbus rated him as one of the top crash reconstructionists in Ohio. Although I had spoken to him a few times on the phone, we had not met. With an air of professional dignity, he greeted us warmly as did Deputy McMannis. In fact, McMannis and I hugged.

Behind this hug was my agenda. I wanted him comfortable enough to give us all the pertinent investigative information. By this time, a year and nine months after Andrew was killed, the Sheriff's Office might have something to add. May 3, McMannis' last day in the traffic department, indicated that another deputy would take our case. A new investigator might see the case differently. Both erroneous assumptions.

Propped up in the corner of the office, the mangled Schwinn ten speed bicycle represented tangible evidence of our family's tragedy. Near it lay a large, black plastic bag containing, presumably, Andrew's clothes and shoes. I never asked the FCSO about the shoes that he had bought days before the crash—those shoes with purple stripes that he bought on sale. Today, I remain concerned about those shoes. What happened to them? They have never been mentioned, except on that fateful Sunday when officers from the Blendon Police asked me to describe them. *Somehow those shoes disappeared. Was vehicle paint visible on them?* That common-sense possibility nags at me, even today. I could never fully embrace a conspiracy to protect the perpetrator.

Thankfully, when McMannis and Holland opened the black bag and looked, they didn't pull out any of the clothing. I would have remembered that. Andy and I sat with Don Sonney and Mark Adams at a long conference table too far away to hear much of what they were saying. The only comment we caught was that Jack Holland noticed a smear of white paint on the bike.

In the middle of the conference table, Assistant Prosecutor Harland Hale sat working on a stack of papers. After we introduced ourselves, he went back to his paperwork. Clearly, he showed little interest. His presence was to indicate protection for McMannis—to keep him safe from us?

Holland and McMannis conferred about an hour before McMannis sat down to give his testimony. Although retired but doing consulting work, Holland had to maintain a cordial, working relationship with the FCSO. In the middle of the table lay stacks of files that McMannis had brought. The Sheriff's file looked voluminous. It wasn't. Multiple copies of the same page comprised each of the files.

What we didn't realize then was the omission of investigative reports. Contained in the file was the crash report—the initial report which a deputy, not McMannis, filled out at the crash site—and then another report, written by McMannis, part of it typed and part of it handwritten but not completed. That was the extent of the investigative report.

Also, the files contained notes about calls that came to Crime Stoppers and those directly to the Sheriff's Office. Some were marked with a "C/C"— meaning "checked"? How? No other notations appeared in the file.

Much of what was contained in those multiple-copy stacks commanded scant attention. Later, we attempted to organize those papers. The stacks also included multiple copies of LEADS (Law Enforcement Access Data System) reports of the same vehicles (named in tips), providing police with data. These LEADS reports would become essential information in 2003. We could tell what vehicles McMannis checked and the ones he didn't.

The LEADS reports in the Sheriff's files proved to be puzzling. Even after the investigators knew the make and model of the van that killed Andrew, McMannis and his partner requested LEADS reports on vehicles that weren't General Motors or Glaval converted despite having the Glaval list. These reports didn't even match up to the tips called in about suspicious GM vans. Misfiled or fake reports? Nothing in the file indicated what deputies did, physically or otherwise.

Some details in McMannis' testimony played well to us, as parents. Andrew was never referred to as "the body" but as Andrew. I can tell you I hate hearing someone referred to as "the body." If no one knows who "the body" is, I can accept that, but if the authorities, journalists, etc., refer to a known person as "the body," I'm disgusted. When we die, our bodies—our physical beings—don't lose their personal identities. We have names. We have personal identities.

What was missing from the FCSO files—information that should have been in those files—would become much more important than every single scrap of paper stacked on the desk in front of us. But we had no way of knowing that—not then.

17

DEPUTY MCMANNIS' DEPOSITION WAS A verbal exchange under oath between him and Mark Adams, our attorney. Because the depositions affected what information we were to gather about Andrew's death and could put us closer to solving that mystery, the give and take between attorney and witness held a certain suspense.

Depositions often contain riveting dialogue, especially when a victim's family is looking for clues to a loved one's death. On the face of it, Deputy McMannis' first deposition seemed unremarkable until we compared what he said in 2000 with his testimony in a second deposition in 2003. The differences in those two depositions helped us finally to understand how the pieces fit, and how and why the owner of the van that killed Andrew had escaped detection.

Crucial to our understanding of the Sheriff's information, we had to depose Deputy McMannis, the lead investigator. He was forced to talk to us under the auspices of our civil case against John Doe, the unknown driver. With training in crash investigation, what was the disconnect between his training and performance? Would a person receive a certificate for showing up?

Mark began his questioning by ascertaining that two pieces of a running board (fiberglass ground effect), were found at the scene of the accident. McMannis concurred. Along with the fiberglass pieces, McMannis testified that he looked at the damage to the bike to see what it could tell him about the crash. And because the coroner found laminated glass in Andrew's clothes, that discovery pointed to damage to the van's windshield.

Because the two pieces of the passenger side ground effect at the scene gave the FCSO key evidence to build an investigation, Mark had to thoroughly explore what the SO knew about that piece of equipment, sometimes referred to in the deposition as the "running board."

To identify the make and model of the vehicle, a deputy took a photograph of the ground effect pieces to show to market stores and dealerships. At one after-market store, a guy identified the part as manufactured by the Glaval Corporation, installed on Astros. A large dealership confirmed that Glaval Corporation manufactured that part and installed them on Glaval's converted Astro vans.

McMannis said that despite targeting dealerships and after-market stores, he "*could not find that piece*"—that he did not see that part on any van, Thursday, August 6, 1998. He did no investigating the prior week on Sunday, Monday, Tuesday, or Wednesday because he was out of the office. This absolute assertion in 2000 that he could not find an actual ground effect on Thursday stood out in direct contradiction of a later, 2003 deposition, wherein he will testify that he saw one the day before! You'll see why that's important in the 2003 deposition.

Not until the November 2003 deposition did we learn for the first time that on Monday, the day after Andrew was discovered but two days after he was killed, no one from the FCSO was working our case. On the Monday, Tuesday, and Wednesday of that week, McMannis was in London, Ohio for training. Not until Thursday, August 6, 1998, when he returned to his office did he determine the make and model of the vehicle involved. *Five crucial days were lost* before the FCSO canvassed dealerships and after-market stores about the fiberglass pieces only to come up cold in seeing one as per his deposition in 2000.

McMannis testified in 2000, almost two years after the crash, that he and others clearly did not know what make of vehicle lost those pieces until he canvassed stores and dealerships on Thursday. We learned three years later that from Sunday, when Andrew was found, to Thursday when McMannis returned after training, that the FCSO conducted no investigation.

During the next several weeks after the crash, McMannis did make a few phone calls. After he learned that the pieces were manufactured by Glaval, he faxed Glaval's customer service manager, Brad Sherwin, a picture of the broken ground effect. Sherwin confirmed that this was Glaval's part, installed exclusively on their converted Chevy Astro vans. After the 1994 models, Glaval scrapped the part. Sherwin added that Glaval used gel-coating as a paint finish after 1990. The white pieces of the ground effect at the scene were gel-coated. Sherwin reported to McMannis that their ground effect, because of the configurations, would fit only Chevrolets.

Furthermore, because Glaval was a custom-conversion van company, the fiberglass part was *custom-installed*—a detail that Mark grasped when he asked McMannis, "Assuming that the running board has been removed, we would be looking for a van that these running boards fit and as I look at the two pieces, there's at least two holes that would have to line up to include that van as a possible suspect for the accident, correct?" To make the case even stronger, Glaval revealed that ground effect parts when installed were *randomly drilled* so the holes on the van that killed Andrew had to absolutely line up. Andy and

I hadn't fully realized how insightful Mark's question was—as the ground effect was custom-installed to each van, individually.

The guilty van, if repaired, would have a replacement ground effect, thereby introducing another set of holes on the rocker panel, helping the FCSO to identify a suspicious van in a group of area vans. The screw holes of the part and the corresponding holes on the van would become the crucial determiner to tell which van killed Andrew.

To help the Sheriff's Office even further, several weeks after the crash, Glaval sent to the FCSO a list of their 1990-1994 Chevy vans with the fiberglass part sold to all Ohio dealerships. Common sense and basic practices would ordinarily dictate the traffic department's use of the list. The guilty van was practically put in McMannis' hands.

Mark questioned McMannis as to how he used the list as a tool in his investigation. McMannis responded, "We didn't go to the list with each one to see if it was on there." This was the closest statement McMannis made to admitting that he did not use the Glaval list to narrow down the van possibilities. Later testimony proved that he ignored the list, a tool that could have put this investigation to rest in a matter of days.

He claimed that "regardless" of the kind of van a tipster suspected—a Toyota, Ford, Chrysler, etc., he checked all of them. That made no sense. The Glaval ground effect did not fit other vans.

The one van on the list McMannis did see was to become a suspect van— that van was owned by a man in Reynoldsburg and the one McMannis photographed and subsequently used as a model in Crime Stoppers publicity. A sweep of registrations on the Glaval list would have put the criminal van (originally sold out of Dayton) in Reynoldsburg, a Columbus suburb, in August 1998. It would have become a van that needed checking.

The part of this deposition dealing with LEADS (Law Enforcement Automated Data System) slowed the pace of the questioning down to a routine and uninteresting crawl. I could not have known then how crucial this information would be when we began to prepare for our civil trial in 2004. It provided a piece of the puzzle, pointing to the guilty van. Mark asked McMannis about the kind of vehicle information LEADS could provide him. McMannis answered, "We get make, plate and VIN and owner. As to exactly everything LEADS will do, I don't know." McMannis admitted that under oath! The LEADS question will rear its ugly head again in McMannis' 2003 deposition. It is then that McMannis' LEADS testimony becomes critical.

Of course, LEADS or the Bureau of Motor Vehicles could not designate which Chevy vans were Glaval converted. Glaval's own list gave us that.

Mark asked him, "In terms of figuring out who owned a van on the date of the accident," what could he access? McMannis answered, "That would be a question for the bureau [Bureau of Motor Vehicles] or title department. I don't know about that." The question as to who owned a Glaval van on August 1, 1998, in the Columbus area would be a question for the Bureau of Motor Vehicles (an office that doesn't investigate crimes), and not McMannis, because he didn't know about that. The fact that Mark nor we didn't jump across the table proves that we knew little about police work.

McMannis admitted under oath that he was mystified as to the kinds of resources available to him as an employee of the Sheriff's traffic office to update vehicle ownerships!

Most of the time, the victim's family does not get involved in the investigation, but we wanted to help. And did. If it were not for the Glaval list and our inability to contact McMannis at the SO, we would have stayed home that terrible fall season—me, walking the cemetery, grieving and Andy, raking leaves or working on the garage with his friend, Bill. If it had not been for that list and our talking to van owners (we recorded each visit), we could not have had concrete evidence that McMannis was not working the Glaval van list.

According to the list of vans that McMannis claimed he checked, he should have been able to discuss why any number of them were specifically eliminated. His testimony contained no such information.

Any van deemed suspicious, per Don and Jack, should have the ground effect removed by simply using a screwdriver. If no additional holes were bored into the rocker panel, the probability that the van was involved earned a zero.

When McMannis was asked about checking vans on the Glaval list, obviously a sensitive issue, his answer produced an incoherent, jumbled, illogical response—a tipoff as to his emotional state and his attempt to cover-up his willful neglect. He said this about checking the van list: *"From this we made a sheet that where we went out and we highlighted them as we saw them, or Delaware County may have went (sic) and looked at or another county or another agency or someone else may have went (sic) and viewed the vehicle."*

What? Maybe Delaware County? Maybe not. Or another county? Another agency? Fill in the blank—(?) Police Department. And someone else? The man in the moon? And that above response pretty much describes this investigation.

18

IF YOU EVER ATTENDED THE taking of a deposition, you would notice that the attorney asking the questions will move from one subject to another and then back to a previous subject. Sometimes the flow of the questioning demands that the attorney do that. Sometimes an idea will be presented in a witness's answer and rather than ask the question later at the risk of forgetting it, the attorney asks it then. And other reasons, sometimes strategic, cause the attorney to revisit a previous topic.

For the record, Mark had to explore also the physical damage to the bicycle and any other detail he thought was vital about the impact. Even though Mark had pictures of the point of impact, he had to hear confirmation from McMannis that Andrew was as far to the right as was possible in the westbound lane. FCSO photos showed his thin tire mark to the right of the white. Stunningly, the van's tires were off the road when it hit Andrew squarely from behind.

Mark: Anything else about the bike that helped you to try and decide how this accident happened?

McMannis: Yes. There appears to be some white, hopefully, vehicle paint on the frame, the forward vertical tube.

[The crash took place twenty months ago. The paint on the bike had not been noticed or tested before this deposition?]

Mark: You have indicated to me before we began that you would be willing to have—is it B.C.I. [Bureau of Criminal Investigation] …take a look and analyze it?

McMannis: Yes.

Mark: Great.

[McMannis stated under oath that he would be willing to ask BCI to take a paint sample and test it. *Only he never asked BCI. Never.* More than a year and a half had lapsed since the crash and Andrew's clothes were never examined for vehicle paint — in a hit-and-run fatality. And just before Mark finished the deposition, he extracted an empty promise from McMannis who repeated that yes, he would see that the paint was tested.]

Since police place a great deal of confidence in witness information. After scouring the crime scene, an investigator's next step would be to talk to people living on that stretch of Central College Road. But the deputies went to only one house, the Thompsons—the site of a large biker party that weekend. They got nothing. Without a doubt, the death of our son is tied to that party.

McMannis said that he talked to Mrs. Thompson after the crash. She revealed no names of party guests. McMannis testified, "She said...people come from out of state for the party and camp all weekend...friends of friends, friends of relatives. We never got an actual list..." When Mark then asked McMannis for a report of that conversation, McMannis didn't have one.

Since the 1999 party, we had the names of guests through our surveillance and Steve's attendance. Interestingly, most addresses were local—right there in New Albany's back yard. Surely, Mrs. Thompson knew the names of her friends and relatives. But McMannis said he didn't ask.

By August 2000 and 2001, we discovered that some of the same people surfaced at all three parties. Did Mrs. Thompson entertain the notion that somehow she or her family would be held responsible if a friend or relative had killed Andrew?

As expected, McMannis did recognize the possibility of a connection between the Thompson party and Andrew's death. If Andrew had only passed the party site, no more than a half mile from where he died, I believe that he would be alive today. Most hit-and-run drivers are impaired. They run because they're drunk, high or impaired in some way.

Towards the end of McMannis' deposition, someone's phone rang. Mark used that as a signal to break so that we could confer with him. He announced, "Before we wrap up your testimony, I'd like to talk to these folks in the next room." McMannis nodded.

Andy and I, along with Don Sonney, adjourned to a small room across the hall. Closing the door, Mark asked, "Do you have any questions, concerns?"

Don spoke up, "Before the deposition started, I briefly looked at the pile of exhibits on the table. In the pile of Crime Stopper tips, I noticed several with Barry Snidka's name on them. I'd like to see those. I'll follow you guys home."

It would be months before our second year without Andrew—the case might have been considered cold by the authorities, but it was anything but that for us. Not by a long shot. For us, finding Andrew's killer had by no means hit a dead end.

19

WE LEFT THE PROSECUTOR'S OFFICE and like two toddlers hanging on to a mom's coat, Andy and I flanked Mark on both sides. Walking to the parking garage, we searched his face for clues. At times, this scrutiny had to be unnerving.

At last we had something tangible—McMannis' files. Certainly, after the twenty months with the FCSO these many pages must contain some information to help us. The deposition turned out not to be as stressful as I had imagined. Ignorance *is* bliss.

Mark commented that the deposition had gone as expected. We agreed. The soft spring air and bright sun helped to lighten our moods. At last we were making in-roads. Mercifully, we humans don't always know what's around the corner.

Before we parted company, Mark stopped at the garage entrance. "You should take the fiberglass pieces to Glaval and have their people examine them. I have some questions."

"How do we go about getting those pieces?" Andy asked.

"Don's had experience with handling evidence. He can talk to the Sheriff's Office about custody."

"Will the FCSO give those pieces to Don?" I questioned.

"If Don is the only one who handles them. Until Glaval sees those pieces, I'm not convinced that we have all the information. I'll call Glaval's attorney and make arrangements and then email you my questions so you can take those with you."

Navigating traffic toward Westerville, Andy offered his impression of the deposition. "When they were looking at the bike before the deposition, did you hear Holland explain to McMannis what the bike's damage told him?"

"Yeah, I noticed that Jack did most of the talking. I heard him point out to McMannis the white paint on one of the bars. And did you hear Mark get McMannis to say he would have the paint tested?" I asked.

"Yeah, but why in God's name wasn't that done? Sounded like this guy had plenty of training. Could be paint from the van." Andy said, shaking his head.

"Do you think?"

"Did you hear him say that he thought the biker party probably had some connection to Andrew's crash, but he doesn't investigate the party either?"

We had no answers, just disgust. We turned into the drive and saw Don in his car waiting for us. What had Don noticed when he leafed through the Sheriff's files?

We dropped the files on the dining room table. Deceptively, it looked as though McMannis had given us a lot of information. Unfortunately, he made multiple copies of items like LEADS printouts and "Called While You Were Out" messages. Only two Sheriff reports were in the entire file. One was the crash report on Sunday, August 2, when Andrew was discovered, and the other was a partially typed and hand-written report about Barry Snidka—the *only* report, incomplete, that McMannis ever wrote for our case.

The Snidka report involved a call McMannis received from Detective Tom Randle of Crime Stoppers on August 5, 1999, a year after the crash, and then what McMannis did on August 6, 1999, as a follow-up to that call. A one-page typed report, including some handwritten notes, mentioned a trip to Galena and Sunbury and then nothing.

"Would you expect to see some indication that this is a good tip or not?"

"Yeah, I wonder what McMannis did with this tip? This report tells us nothing."

"This tip came in last summer," I remarked. "It's already a year old."

"You have to understand that most tips are suspicions. And until they have good information, you aren't going to hear about it."

"Yeah, let's rely on the Sheriff to get good information."

"That's my job. We should look into this," Don said, wrapping up the meeting.

20

ON A FEW OCCASIONS, ANDY and I drove past Snidka's father's house. While Andy drove and then paused, I took photos of the van parked in the drive. It did resemble a Glaval van, except for running boards and the conversion logo, American Road. The houses on his short street were a mix of homes in disrepair and others well-cared for. The Snidka house needed care. The windows of the split level appeared to be covered with blankets. The drive had three or four battered vehicles parked one behind the other. A few of them, like the van, rarely moved from their spots—probably not drivable. Odd pieces of metal, like down spouting, lay piled up in front of the garage

That evening as I prepared to go to bed, I couldn't shake the image of Andrew's mangled bicycle. We had not seen it before the deposition. As events of that day played over and over, I couldn't turn my mind off. Andy, too, having trouble resting, awakened in the middle of the night, and swallowed some aspirins to dull a headache. Rising early, I made the coffee. No use in trying to rest. In the two years since Andrew's death, my face had aged ten years.

What echoed in my mind—like someone standing on a mountain top yelling into the canyon below—was: Glaval van, Glaval van, Glaval van. We had that one absolute fact. A Glaval van. If Barry Snidka killed Andrew, he was driving a Glaval converted van.

21

NO MATTER HOW TIRED MARK was at the end of the day, he met with us and gave us his best. After taking Deputy McMannis' deposition, he graciously committed his time to meeting with Don Sonney and us on a regular basis in his firm's large, comfortable conference room.

Andy and I took our seats at one end of the table with Don directly across from us. When Mark entered the room, the squall inside my stomach subsided. His manner said, "Everything will be okay—we're going to do this." We believed he had the answers and if he didn't, he knew how to get them. Tucked under his arm were our files and after greeting us, he took his place at the head of the table.

We let Don have the floor. He would cut through the detail. "We looked at the Crime Stoppers' tip that Tom Randle gave to McMannis. Rumors were circulating in Sunbury and Galena [towns near New Albany], naming Snidka. The tip says that three brothers who know Snidka are talking. I'd like to see what that's all about."

Andy and I nodded in agreement. So far these were just rumors.

"We have one other item," Mark said. "We ought to talk about the ground effect. Right now that's prime evidence. Glaval needs to see the actual pieces. Also, we should tie up some other loose ends. We still don't have any information on paint tests and the coroner found a piece of glass on Andrew believed to be windshield glass."

Before we left Mark's office, he and Don compared calendars. When would Don be available to go to Elkhart, Indiana, Glaval's headquarters with the ground effect pieces?

"Just as soon as I can get chain of custody from the sheriff's office. I'll give you a call," Don said, nodding to Mark.

With a hint of urgency in his voice, he repeated the necessity of knowing all we could about the part those pieces were torn from. As insightful as Mark was, he could not have predicted how crucial our doing that was.

I spent hours on Sunday drafting a letter to the president of the Glaval Corp., Richard Strefling, seeking his "permission" to allow Andy, Don, and me to talk to experts at his company about ground effects.

At Mark's end, he was to contact the attorney for Glaval, Michael Cosentino. We had to explore every detail possible about the ground effect part, broken into two pieces. McMannis testified in his deposition that the pieces found at the crash came exclusively from Glaval. His calls confirmed that Glaval sold that part to no other conversion company.

Would some bit of information from Glaval derail all the assumptions we made about that part? Or would some bit of information put us closer to finding the killer of our son? We had no idea which way it would go, or that we would even learn anything new.

Mark asked me to call the then customer service manager, Vickie Stout, later a president of one of Glaval's subsidiaries, to confirm the details of our visit. At the time, when Andy and I were so fragile, Vickie's assistance and compassion gave us resolve.

Vickie arranged a meeting in June with Dewayne Creighton, installation supervisor, Mike Givler, Glaval's legal counsel, and her. Creighton was the avowed expert on the part, and Vickie understood the paperwork dealing with the ground effect.

The next step was Don's responsibility. He had to convince the deputies in the Sheriff's traffic department to give him chain of custody to the ground effect pieces. Having been a trusted member of law enforcement, Don appeared at the Sheriff's Office late in the afternoon on June 6, 2000, and without fanfare, one of the deputies handed him a cardboard box, wrapped securely with tape, containing the pieces from the crash scene.

Early the next morning Don met us at the house and the three of us drove to Elkhart, Indiana, a trip taking a little more than three hours. Promptly at nine o'clock we were in front of the main building where Vickie Stout, head of customer service, asked us to meet her. Glaval's plant and office buildings, surrounded by chain link fences and strips of green grass, seemed to go on for miles.

In my hands, I clutched a folder with a list of questions that Mark had emailed to us several days earlier. The answer to these questions held valuable information. Vickie, welcoming, led us to a conference room where Givler, and Creighton were waiting.

After introductions, Andy reviewed our situation, explaining that during Andrew's crash, the bicycle's handlebars caught the passenger side ground effect, tearing off two pieces. While he talked, Don cut the tape and opened the box with the ground effect pieces and laid them on the table.

"We're not sure what the Sheriff knows about this part, if anything. We're not on the best terms with them. To get a better idea of what we have here, Mark Adams, our attorney, has prepared several questions for us to ask."

Creighton picked up the pieces and fitting the two pieces together said, "This is ours. These pieces came off a part from one of our vans."

"Is there any doubt?" Don asked.

"None. It's a patented part and put only on our vans."

"Could it be installed on other vans?"

"Anything's possible, but I've never seen it," Creighton offered.

Looking at Mark's notes, I asked, "Dewayne, what can you tell us about these parts?

"The part is made of fiberglass. These pieces look to me like they came from a part made in the early nineties. I would expect more yellowing from an earlier part. And earlier parts were painted – later ones gel-coated. This is gel-coated. Actually, we stopped installing these after 1994."

"Can you paint over gel-coating to cover up scratches?"

"Sure. Just like any other external part."

"Say that I need that part for a 1994 van. Can I still get one from Glaval?"

"Sure. A repair shop would call here and order one."

"OK, say I had a Glaval van but didn't want to take it to a repair shop. Could I have one delivered to my home?"

"No, parts are sent to repair shops or dealerships. Retail customers are very rare," Vickie interjected.

"Could I possibly get one at a salvage yard?" Don asked.

"Yeah, just like any other part. Screws secure the ground effect. All you should do is remove the screws.

Checking Mark's notes, I asked Dewayne about the installation and screw holes.

"The installation of the ground effect part is tailored to each van. Screw holes could be matched up as one of a kind as all vans are different. No two are exactly alike."

Puzzled Don asked Dewayne, "Are you saying that there is no set pattern to this installation?"

"Exactly. If you had a van that you strongly suspected, you could match the holes in these pieces to the van's holes. Even if the van owner put on a replacement part, new or used, those holes would be different, but the original holes would still be there."

"How does that happen that the holes on each van are drilled in a different place?"

Dewayne explained, "When the part is installed, workers drill holes randomly in the part and in the van. It's wherever they decide is best for that van. Some installers are sitting, most laying on the floor, some kneeling."

"OK, now I get it. Would a mechanic use the same holes—the original holes for a replacement part?"

"That would be next to impossible to match those original holes. Just drill new holes."

"So even if the driver who killed Andrew replaced that part, the van will have some extra holes that match up to the holes from the pieces at the crash."

"Yes. If there is only one set of holes that match the ground effect on the van, that ground effect was not replaced. That's not your van."

"Could you tell by looking at the van that the part was replaced?"

"No, only if the driver's side didn't look like the passenger's side. The colors might be off. The only way you can tell is to remove the ground effect and check for additional holes."

Here, Creighton stopped to describe what equipment Glaval installed on a basic van to make it a comfortable vehicle.

Wrapping up the meeting, Don asked Vickie how Glaval tracks orders for parts.

"When a shop orders that part, the person gives me a VIN. I'll write up an invoice, taking down the name of the person ordering, the body shop and the body shop's address. The only way I can check an order on the computer is through a VIN, otherwise, we have to go through the invoices."

It was almost lunch time. Mark's questions had been answered. We thanked Vickie, Mike, and Dewayne. The meeting revealed some of the most crucial information we needed to gather. We will never forget the kindness and compassion of the people at the Glaval Corporation.

Not once did my voice crack or my eyes well up while we were at Glaval. I found that when I passed out fliers or looked at vans, I could talk without becoming emotional. But the tension would build as the day wore on—an overwhelming feeling of futility and longing.

We postponed lunch to stop at Tony Packo's, outside of Toledo. We were seated in a room off the dining room. Our server took our orders of German potato salad and cabbage rolls. From our table I could see the activity in other parts of the restaurant. I caught a glimpse of a young man, waiting on tables. I could just see his back. I noticed his perfect posture—like Andrew's. His brown hair—cut like Andrew's. His build—like Andrew's and his shirt, tucked in, the way Andrew tucked his—sort of pulled out. I had had similar experiences before but never with this much similarity to Andrew. Usually, the young man would turn around and his face would be very different. I watched this young man move from table to table and then to the cash register. I saw his profile. I went into a kind of shock. The resemblance was uncanny. Tears flooded my eyes. Thinking that I had an attack of grief, Andy asked if I wanted to leave.

I nodded, "Yes" and motioned for him to look in the direction of the main dining room. He saw the server and as we left said, "That sure looked like Andrew, didn't it?"

22

ROLLISON KNEW THAT WE WERE checking every nook and cranny to verify his tip about Barry Snidka. In addition to his tip, Don was investigating the Crime Stoppers' tip about Snidka. Despite the inaccurate details about Snidka and the problem of tying him to a Glaval van, we had to check these tips before we handed out any reward money. Most importantly, we had to confirm Snidka's access to a Glaval van.

Don, our PI, showed up one evening at Rollison's house and recorded his statement. During the six months that Rollison and I talked on the phone, he remained adamant about the truth of his tip, and we found no changes in his original story.

Right after Rollison received the subpoena from Mark Adams to have his deposition taken, Joey called me, said he was in the area and wanted to come by and meet with me. I wasn't sure this was a good idea. More than once, he commented that he came from a rough family. But on the phone this young man presented himself as sincere and polite despite his background. I was as curious about him as he was about us, so I gave him directions and ten minutes later a truck pulled in the drive.

From the kitchen window, I watched Rollison as he strode up the walkway. I opened the door, greeted him, and extended my hand. He could have been Johnny Depp's twin. By Joey's own admission he came from a rough family and so did Snidka—his relatives were well-known criminals in Columbus.

We sat down at the kitchen table. I had made a pot of lemon herb tea to soothe my jumpy stomach and offered him a cup. Without hesitation, this tough young man accepted a cup of herbal tea. While he drank his tea, I took note of his eyes, his voice, his clothes. I had nothing to be afraid of.

As we talked, he asked about the subpoena he had received in the mail. "Why do you want my deposition?" he inquired.

"It's our attorney's idea. He needs to clarify some of the details."

"But I don't feel right about that. Someone could see me," he said.

I heard his apprehension, but I didn't want him to back out. "Mark's office is not on a main street. You can park in the back and use that entrance. No one will see you. It's where we park."

On the morning of Rollison's scheduled deposition, he didn't show.

23

THAT SUMMER BETSEY'S JOB AT times entailed overseas travel. She had a trip to France on her calendar and after wrapping up her business meetings, she scheduled four days' vacation in Paris. When Scott couldn't join her because of his job, she asked us if we wanted to meet her in Paris. No matter where she was going, we would have gone with her. She could give us the kind of comfort no one else could. We spent long evenings at a Paris café across from our hotel. She preoccupied us with stories she remembered about Andrew and their childhood together.

At the time, some of the stories happened, they weren't funny to me at all, but as the years passed, they became legendary—funny family stories that Andrew and Betsey repeated to illustrate that Andy and I weren't anywhere near perfect parents. "Remember the Christmas when Andrew asked for Data Man?" Betsey asked. The sting of that Christmas story had lost its potency when Andrew laughed and embellished it every time it was told. Data Man was a hand-held electronic toy with buttons and a screen—a kind of a precursor to today's video game toys. She continued, "That was the only thing he wanted, but you couldn't find one."

"That must have been the toy that every boy in Columbus wanted for Christmas. None of the stores could keep it in stock," I said, once again offering excuses.

"You saw one on the shelf at Radio Shack. It was the last one and you grabbed it," she said.

"Yeah, and the thing about it, I was so proud of myself because the clerk had said Radio Shack was completely sold out."

"But you never checked the box," she reminded. "And when Andrew opened his gift on Christmas morning, nothing was in the box. At first he didn't know what to think. Then tears started rolling down his eyes."

"We blamed it all on Santa. Santa must have grabbed a display box. I was not happy that Christmas, but we made it up to him the day after."

"That year I got Big Dogey. Mom, do you still have the kids?" Yes, and today I still do. A very large plastic bag of our children's "kids"—stuffed animals—Big Dogey, Peachy, Roosevelt, Pooh, Little Dogey, and others, stored in the attic. Of all their toys, these were the lasting ones. Maybe because we lived in the country, our children turned to imaginative play with their "kids"—the baseball games, the ship wrecks, and Peachy and Roosevelt's divorce. "Now where did they get that?" I asked my husband one day, totally oblivious.

France allowed us some respite from reality. Back in Columbus, despite jet lag, Andy and I disembarked from the plane with optimism.

24

FOCUSING ON THE CRIME STOPPERS' tip in McMannis' file about Snidka, Don began digging around in Sunbury. Named in that tip were three brothers, friends of Snidka. Sources revealed that McMannis and another deputy met with the three brothers. A Sunbury policeman confirmed that McMannis met with the three brothers in a field behind a nearby bait shop. Curious about the meeting and exactly what took place, Andy and I scoured the police files McMannis had given to Mark at the 2000 deposition for information about that meeting. *Nothing.*

Mark subpoenaed the Sunbury policeman to explore the tip. About the bait shop meeting, the Sunbury officer answered, "I don't know if he [McMannis] kept notes of it because he wasn't writing it down. *He probably did a report.*" No, he didn't write a report of that meeting.

Another interesting detail surfaced in the policeman's deposition about that meeting. He testified, "They [the brothers] gave him [McMannis] a lot of names, a lot of people that was at the party. I think it was the party the night he [Andrew] got killed, there was some kind of party on that road."

Where was the list of these people? McMannis was given names but the Sunbury officer said that McMannis wasn't writing the names down. Even if McMannis was skeptical of the rumors about Snidka, he now had names of people attending the Thompson party. That had to be worth something. The omissions kept adding up. Basic investigative tools like taking notes, and making reports had been summarily ignored.

One day when we were amid investigating Barry Snidka, and after McMannis had left the case, I called his successor, Sgt. Staggs, with some information Don had uncovered. I told Staggs, "Snidka is going around bragging about killing some dude on a bicycle."

Staggs retorted, "It's not a crime to say that you killed someone."

Stunned by his response, my mind went blank. If my neighbor had been murdered and I bragged that I killed him, would I expect the police to be on my doorstep the next second? Not Staggs. Because it's okay to say that. It's not a crime. If you're bragging that you murdered someone, you'd better hope that a certain sergeant in Franklin County is investigating your case.

I cried for two days. Later when I had time to step away from the comment and replay the conversation with Staggs. OMG, I'm in a Keystone Cops movie. This isn't real, right?

I was not giving up. Eventually, the FCSO would have to look at incontrovertible evidence—when we had it. We were in the process of preparing to convince Staggs, the investigator in charge, to look at Snidka's possible involvement. Still missing was a huge piece of the puzzle—the Glaval van.

The first weekend in August 2000 was approaching and our thoughts turned to the biker party hosted by the Thompsons on Harlem Road. By this time, we knew considerably more about hit-and-run fatalities. A detail that stuck out for us was the confirmed impairment of perpetrators who left the scene. The mother who founded Mothers Against Drunk Driving did so because her daughter was killed by a drunk driver who ran and hid.

Luckily for us, the party host was a creature of habit and just like clockwork, we observed party preparations under way on Friday evening. The Thompsons' ranch sat off the road on several acres of land. This was an outside affair with tables and chairs cluttering the yard, a large metal tub for barbecuing and various other containers for food and drink. A string of Christmas lights draped the open entrance to the garage.

We knew that the partygoers would park their motorcycles, trucks, cars, and vans in the yard and along the road. Since we had had the party under surveillance the year prior, we knew what to expect: the setting up would begin on Friday night with enough people showing up to help and begin partying. Most of the guests would arrive Saturday evening and some would stay overnight in tents.

Because the house sits on a busy country road, we could drive past and observe the activity. Cars passing the house slowed down and eyeballed the yard. But because we had an ulterior motive to gawk at the party scene—we wanted license plates—we were visibly nervous. With my pad and paper, I wrote down plate numbers as we crawled past vehicles. In a moving car that was an extremely difficult thing to do. Just as I wrote one number down, I'd come upon the next plate

I used every data base available to the public to get information. I was more certain than ever that hidden in the shadows under the party lights lay some answers.

Before we knew anything about McMannis' successor, Ross Staggs, I convinced myself of the possibility that a new guy might get results. We had evidence, we knew the make and model of the killer vehicle, we had an important list of vans, we had the license plates of more than thirty people who attended the biker party and we had the interest of the public.

A successor usually means a fresh way of looking at a cold case. We knew practically nothing about police culture—such as that fierce loyalty to fellow officers whose job performance shouldn't be questioned even if the case screams incompetence.

We never thought that police work was easy. On the contrary, we learned that the process is more like trial and error in criminal investigations. An investigator, trying to get answers, will make mistakes, or hit a dead end and backtrack. Start over. Question assumptions: Andrew, almost off the road to the right of the white line, could have been targeted. Vehicles can be murder weapons. A detective should never be someone who merely passes a test, but a person who possesses curiosity, an interest in human behavior, common sense, and a perseverance to gather pertinent information to solve the puzzle. Someone who despises injustice. Someone with a deep reverence for life. Someone like Deputy Wooten—a person we had yet to meet.

Mark Adams, our attorney, contacted Staggs about testing the paint on Andrew's bicycle. McMannis testified in his deposition that he would have the paint analyzed. *He didn't and neither did Staggs.* Two years had lapsed from the time of the crash and still the paint on the bike had not been tested. Why didn't we scream bloody murder that this very, very basic test had not been done days after the crash?

Part of our patience with Staggs stemmed from Mark's rapport with him. Still, I believed we were seen like the flies you couldn't swat.

All along we had communicated with Staggs, but he said little in response to information we were passing on to him. This new investigator was an unknown. At some point, each of us had spoken to him on the phone, but as late as six months after he inherited our case, we still had not met him.

Mark advised that he would write Staggs a letter requesting a meeting with him, but he cautioned that since a letter could go unanswered, Andy or I should follow-up with a call to Staggs. Eventually, Staggs did return our call. I answered the phone. After an exchange of civilities, he said, "I didn't appreciate some of the comments your attorney made in his letter. I was offended by his comment about the lack of cooperation by the Sheriff's Office."

I wanted to respond, "You're offended? Our son is dead and no one there has yet tested the bicycle paint or found what Glaval vans were registered in Columbus? You won't work the case and yet you won't give it to the Highway Patrol. You could have easily been rid of us. The State Highway Patrol advised us they would take our case. We didn't publicly complain. We took constructive steps. The FCSO is guilty of dereliction of duty and *you* are offended."

Did I say that? No, I tried to smooth it over. I prayed that we could motivate him. I wanted to meet with him and give him what we had. We wanted Snidka questioned. That's all. Rule him in or out.

When I replayed my conversation with Staggs to Don, he said, "Don't tell me. I'll bet Staggs said, 'We have been doing everything' blah, blah, blah 'working very hard on this case' blah, blah, blah, blah 'running down every lead' blah, blah, blah.'"

In this conversation with Staggs I mentioned that Snidka's father had a van. Staggs was surprised. I guess he didn't read the file.

Before I ended my conversation with Staggs, we set up a meeting at the FCSO traffic office for the following week. Don and Mark both would attend. In preparation for the meeting, I made copies of documents to lend credibility to the information we'd gathered about Snidka.

The traffic office reminded me of an old school, built in the early fifties—the tiled brick beige walls, the linoleum floors, utilitarian, a place for a desk, filing cabinet, telephone and not much more. When Mark, Don, Andy, and I approached the receptionist, she said that we would be meeting with Staggs and Chief Deputy Gil Jones, in Jones' office.

Tall and impeccably dressed, Jones came into the hall and directed us to his small office where several chairs for visitors were pushed against the wall. From the moment we met him, Chief Jones treated us kindly.

Staggs entered, as did Major Tom Bateson. Staggs, then, had a kind of chubby, baby face, probably in his early or middle thirties and Major Bateson was a man in his fifties. Earlier, I discovered that I had been Tom's eldest son's teacher at Gahanna. Chris, a good student, was one of those neat kids I remembered and liked.

After I had distributed my handouts, I gave a brief overview of our investigation and our goal—bring Snidka in for questioning.

Sitting at the opposite end of Chief Jones' small office, Staggs listened, arms crossed against his chest. We had encroached upon his investigative realm. At one point, he repeated what he had told me on the phone, "Dave McMannis is a fine investigator. He worked very hard to solve this case." Staggs must have been reading between the lines because, in truth, we were baffled by McMannis' role. But we made no overt criticism of the FCSO. Mark had cautioned us not to be accusatory.

Because this meeting took place in October 2000, two years and almost two months after Andrew was killed, Staggs felt compelled to say in a defensive, harsh way, "This was *just* a misdemeanor. The statute of limitations is up." Not if it was a deliberate hit—that's murder, a voice inside my head said.

Even today when I mentally recreate that scene and hear that disgusting declaration "*just a misdemeanor*"– my son's death was "*just a misdemeanor*"— my face contorts with grief. We knew that hit-and-run accidents under the law were misdemeanors. A death by a multi-ton weapon was a misdemeanor. So does this mean that because it was "*just* a misdemeanor," our son's homicide didn't deserve investigating? That was the message I was getting.

I took a deep breath and began explaining a one-page summary of the facts about Snidka: the tips, he drove with a suspended license, he lived near the crime scene and had been arrested on numerous occasions. We did make it clear that we were not able to connect Snidka to a Glaval converted van.

During the meeting, I could see Staggs' temperature rise. Thinking that we were somehow berating McMannis' investigation, he repeated his support of McMannis. Before the meeting, we had promised Mark we would keep ourselves under control and stick to the facts. Chief Deputy Jones managed to say, "Looks like we dropped the ball on this one." Just words.

Every time Jones or Bateson offered some sort of credibility to what we said, Staggs, using a hostile tone, would bring the discussion back to McMannis and how much he worked our case.

All through this, I had one nagging reservation—we couldn't put Snidka in a Glaval van. But maybe the police could. Yeah, maybe. An absolute outside chance because we were more thorough than they could ever be. We would not want Snidka charged without the van and sufficient evidence. But we did want him questioned.

In our case, we viewed each tip with skepticism. Experience taught us that. As we tracked down tips and did some basic checking, we found most to be groundless. Nevertheless, we are grateful that people passed on their suspicions. We kept each person named in the tip confidential. And glad we did, as most tips quickly fizzled after a brief checking.

Mark Ferenchik with the *Columbus Dispatch* wrote a story on the second anniversary of Andrew's death. In August 2000, we were no closer to answers than we had been two weeks or two months after Andrew died. One concern was our relationship with the FCSO's traffic department. We confided in

Ferenchik that despite good information and the evidence found at the scene, the investigators hadn't followed through on basic duties.

Ferenchik came to the house several times and spent hours listening to our story. This was our first, serious experience with someone from the press. Despite our long ramblings—detail connected with Andrew's death, Mark never expressed any kind of impatience. Solemn and alert, he asked probing questions. Absolutely, he was on board about our concerns with the Sheriff. We kept crying "wolf," but then would tell him to hold off writing anything.

Holding off was my idea, not Andy's. Andy wanted to lay it all out there. If we came out against the FCSO, I feared we would put an end to any cooperation from them to get justice.

An email from Ferenchik in October 2000 reads, "I will call you to set a time and day, do you think you feel free to criticize the sheriff's department?"

Today, I'm ashamed. Did I not have the backbone to stand up for our family's right to be afforded a basic investigation into the homicide of our son? Apparently not. I vacillated on Mark Ferenchik's offer to give us a voice.

What I didn't recognize was the power of the press in a democracy.

How stupid.

25

STAGGS HAD BEEN IN CHARGE of that meeting in October. Maybe Major Bateson and certainly Chief Jones never needed to react to Staggs' angry and insensitive comments. When we left the meeting, Chief Jones assured us that the investigation would continue and thanked us for our hard work.

When I emailed Mark Ferenchik of the *Dispatch* with the message, "I'm not going to hold my breath," I had serious doubts about any progress. But several weeks later—we were now into November—Don called. "I have some really good news. I just now talked to another deputy assigned to your case. I have to tell you he sounded like a breath of fresh air. He wants to meet with us."

Don's positive message was unexpected. The new guy was more of a gift than his supervisor guessed or wanted him to be. Eventually, he'd be snatched away.

"Who is this guy? What do you know about him?" I asked.

"I don't think he's a detective. He identified himself as Deputy Ken Wooten. From what I understand, he was handed your file with 'this is yours.' I think he had some knowledge of the case from talk in the office."

"I wonder why this Wooten guy got our case?"

"He's been on light duty for several weeks. I'll bet Staggs gave it to him."

"What's light duty?"

"He's been taken off the street and put behind a desk. I think he drove a cruiser. He said he injured a knee."

"So you think he might be interested in helping us?"

"Yeah. I think we got a good one. He wants you to call him."

I took down the number Don dictated and dialed Ken Wooten's cell. For two months, Andy and I were on a high. Deputy Wooten had all the qualities we thought a police officer should have. If any young man in the FCSO lived up to an ideal, it was Wooten.

When Ken answered his phone on that November morning, I heard a voice that sounded almost identical to John Walsh on *America's Most Wanted*. He had been assigned our case and wanted to meet with us. I asked, "What about today? How about noon?"

After breakfast that cold morning in the warmth of the kitchen, I chopped onions, celery, carrots, and potatoes to simmer on the stove for several hours in beef stock. I cook because it's comforting—an emotional outlet. I thought that if Wooten arrived about noon, we could offer him lunch.

Almost to the minute, a red sports car pulled up in front of the house. If you can tell anything about a person by his face, we liked and trusted him from that first minute he walked into the door. Light brown short hair, handsome and young—early thirties, I thought, although he looked younger—his greeting immediately put us at ease. I had the table set and offered him lunch. He didn't hesitate. The FCSO could not have sent a better emissary. We were hooked. In our dealings with him in the next several months, not once did he say he was going to do something and not do it. And not once did he fail to return our calls.

One fact that surprised us about Deputy Wooten surfaced when we discussed his investigative experience. He had none. He drove a cruiser and chased thieves on foot—that kind of duty. But his injuries prevented him from his usual duties; hence, light duty. Then one day Sgt. Staggs handed him our file. According to Wooten, he took the file home that night and read all the material.

As we ate our soup, he asked questions about Andrew. He was gathering information—he wasn't being nice. He was the first investigator to do that. And we could see the importance of his knowing who Andrew was. After we had filled him in on a brief chronology of what we knew had happened the day Andrew was killed, he asked for copies of all the depositions taken thus far. That was a stunning request. He was going to read the depositions? Yes. He said that he needed to get a complete picture of our case.

As soon as he left, Andy and I looked at each other. Were we dreaming?

Within the week, Wooten called to report that he had read the depositions, but he was especially interested in the Joey Rollison tip. "I'm not sure how Rollison fits into all this," he said.

"He knows Snidka through his cousin."

"Yeah, that's what I saw but I'd like to confirm some information with Don. Do you think that Don might be able to get him to come to the station so we can talk to him in person?"

"I know he'll try. What do you think of the Snidka tip?"

"I don't know. We can find that out if we can question Rollison at the station. You did say that his cousin dated Snidka?"

"Yes. Rollison said his cousin and Snidka had stopped by his house one day, and while the cousin was in the kitchen, Snidka confessed to him. Oh, one little thing—he did say they were smoking pot."

Wooten noticed the caveat. "Do you think it's the pot talking?"

"The fear I have is that Joey is getting his information from Charlotte, his cousin. She suspects Snidka, but has no proof. All of them know about the reward money. That could be the motivation."

"Did she ever say that Snidka confessed to her?" Wooten asked.

"She has been asked a few times, and she has always answered, "No." She'll go just so far in saying things. It could be the reward."

"She's suspicious because he tore a reward poster off a pole."

"Exactly. His father's van is a Chevy Astro but it isn't Glaval converted. We can't put him in a Glaval van."

"And Charlotte never said that Snidka confessed to Joey. She had to know that, but never said that. Do you think that anyone from the Thompson party knows anything?" Wooten asked.

"That's worth considering. We gave the Sheriff's office a list of plates and names of some people at the party. But I'm sure they never called those people. Did you happen to see a list of plates and names?"

"Yeah, I saw that. I'm going to start calling these people. And you can talk to Don about getting Joey's statement. I'll start tracking down his cousin See what she has to say."

I hung up the phone, in shock. Some basic stuff—he wanted to talk to people. And we were grateful.

It was November, the holidays were approaching and I knew from experience, the investigation would come to a standstill. But not this November. We met several times with Wooten, and he was taking our calls.

Getting Rollison's tip on tape at the Sheriff's Office merited top priority. Since Rollison had failed to show for a deposition in August, we had doubts that he would show up at the Sheriff's Office. Despite that, Wooten contacted Zach Scott in the Detective Bureau—someone he respected—to conduct the interview. Scott consented to question Rollison to test the tip's credibility. It was Don's job to get Rollison to agree.

On a cold winter evening, Don sat in his Buick outside Rollison's home on the west side, waiting for Rollison's truck to pull up. When it did, Don followed Rollison into the house. Don had to pull every trick out of his investigator's hat to persuade him to talk to Wooten at the station. No statement; no reward. Like someone needing to see the dentist—the sooner the better. Rollison agreed to show up at the Mound Street station after work the next day. In the morning, Don called Wooten and the arrangements were made.

Unfortunately, Wooten was told that his detective buddy would not be doing the interview; it would be Staggs. Wooten didn't offer an explanation to Don why Staggs would now interview Rollison. We took for granted that a sergeant in the traffic division could handle such an interview.

Later, we learned from Staggs himself that he was "not trained in interviewing" and didn't interview. That meant he made an exception in this case. Why? Detective Scott had already consented.

Rollison's questioning was out of Wooten's hands. He did everything he could to see that Rollison showed up at the FCSO to give a statement. So here is the scenario: Rollison shows up. Wooten greets him and takes him to a room where Staggs will question him. Staggs comes in. Sets up the tape recorder. Questions Rollison. Rollison leaves. *No tape in the recorder.*

Andy said, "Are we in a cartoon or what?"

Wooten didn't go into detail about the Rollison meeting. Not long after Rollison's appearance at the FCSO, he ran off to some distant state with another woman. He disappeared.

But that didn't stop Wooten. He began to track down Rollison's cousin, Charlotte, the former girlfriend. Rollison reported that she was living in a motel room with her pimp. He had no idea where, but he did give Wooten the pimp's name and the last cell phone number he had for his cousin.

Wooten's perseverance in finding the ex-girlfriend who moved in and out of motels paid off. Many times he did his searching while off duty—long past his shift. Charlotte was not hiding. This was the way she lived.

At one apartment building he kept watch for two days where the mother of the pimp said he and Charlotte were living. When Charlotte and her "boyfriend" left the apartment, Wooten called her. He reminded her that her information, if it checked out, could get her some reward money and suggested that they meet at an area Taco Bell. When Charlotte's boyfriend heard "reward," they agreed to meet.

By the time Wooten arrived, Charlotte and her six-foot-four, two hundred-fifty-pound boyfriend were seated in a booth, waiting for him. Although muscular and of average height, Wooten congratulated himself on suggesting a public place.

Throughout the conversation, the boyfriend/pimp glared at Wooten as if to warn him not to pull any funny stuff—like arresting Charlotte. Coupled with the glaring boyfriend and Charlotte's nervousness, the meeting didn't give Wooten any new information.

Charlotte repeated the same answers to questions we had asked her previously. Yes, she thought Snidka did it. No, she wasn't with him. Theirs was an on-again-off-again relationship. No, he never confessed to her.

Then Wooten asked the obvious, "Why do you think he killed the guy on the bicycle?"

"Because he tore the reward sign off the telephone pole and his daddy had a van that looked like the one on the pole." Almost the exact same reason she told me and later related to Don. Then, after a few more minutes, the boyfriend got up, signaling that the conversation was over.

When we had a chance to think about her suspicions, I didn't believe that tearing down a poster would hold up in court.

Now, back in the office, Wooten resumed calling the people whose license plates we had identified as having been at the Thompson party. Scrolling down the Thompson party list, Wooten left messages on answering machines, asking for a return call to the Sheriff's Office. I can only speculate, but if Wooten gave any indication as to why he was calling, that would account for the lack of return calls. That and the guests' probable relationship with police.

In one of Wooten's calls, he did manage to reach a woman who had just arrived home from work. We read an account of his conversation with her in one of his reports. Two and a half years after our son was killed, Wooten talked to an invitee who attended the Thompson party in 1998 and wrote a report.

The woman said that she was an acquaintance of the elder Thompsons. She spoke openly about not being a close friend and knowing only a few people at the party. Later, when our new private investigator, Linda Granville, appeared on the woman's doorstep one evening, she talked willingly with Linda about her experience at the party. She did know that it was an annual party and gave Linda several names of other people she knew who attended. The party lasted on into the night, but she stayed only a few hours.

Did any of the other party guests eventually call the Sheriff's Office with information? We don't know. Suddenly, after Christmas, Wooten was yanked off the case. A deputy who made inroads was suddenly ripped away from us.

Don, like us, felt comfortable in communicating with Wooten when we had a thought. Even though he no longer was assigned our case, he always returned a call or answered an email. Deputy Wooten was the textbook cop—the policeman in our elementary textbooks, depicted as our helper and friend, as well as the unrelenting, street-smart deputy who took his job seriously to protect us. After the holidays, he was sent out to the Cop Shop at the Westland shopping center. Deputy Wooten could offer no explanation. When we expressed our great appreciation for his work, he brushed it off saying, *"I was just doing my job."*

2001

26

BY THE TIME THE NEW Year ushered in 2001, a Cleveland law firm that used Don's services in dealing with environmental issues needed an investigator. Don's expertise focused on environmental concerns. Consequently, he would eventually live in Detroit during the week and come home on the weekends, if then. We didn't relish the idea of hiring another PI. Andy and I relied on him for more than investigating.

Before he departed in April for Detroit, we sat down with him one afternoon to discuss what needed to be done before he left. For the last six months, he and his young partner, Ted, had spent hours tracking down Snidka's friends. A typical situation involved one of Snidka's friends who lived with his mother. One evening, after a few unsuccessful attempts to get someone to answer the door, a middle-aged woman finally opened the door a crack. The woman had obviously been drinking since her speech was noticeably slurred. Spewing expletives, she refused to respond to Don's request to tell him where her son was living. She chased him off the porch.

We had to pin something significant on Snidka, or we had to move on. We had spent most of our savings with no results. After Ken Wooten left our case, communication from the Sheriff's Office ceased. Add to that, Don's leaving. Thus, before Don left for Detroit, we had to consider what Don had to finish. Confirming the information about Snidka was like wandering blindfolded through a dark labyrinth of rumors.

Some of the Thompson party guests were friends of the host's son and daughter in their mid-twenties. These were the people likely to know Snidka, and surely one of them would talk. Having names on the list from the party and friends of Snidka, not at the party, we directed Don to talk to them. Two on the list were incarcerated at the Southeastern Correctional Facility in Lancaster.

On a particularly warm, spring Saturday, Don and I drove the country roads, looking for the addresses of partiers and acquaintances of Snidka. At one house a young woman, whose name and license plate we had, was out watering her garden. She seemed to answer our questions honestly, but we had no way of knowing that. Denying that she knew Snidka or that she recognized a photo of him, she could tell us nothing about him. Each of the younger partygoers had a different story, but none of them claimed to know Snidka. Some of them admitted going to the Thompson party; some of them denied it. In the end, we came up empty-handed.

On the list of items was a thorough check of Snidka's father's Astro van by going back and talking to the original owner. We discussed this with Don several times, but since we didn't see it as a high priority item, it remained on the list for several months. Not talking to the original owner of the Snidka van when we first put it on the list in late 2000 turned out to be a huge blessing.

If Don had talked to the first owner of the Snidka van in April 2001, events would not have played out as fortuitously as they ultimately did. In retrospect, what happened was nothing short of astounding. Certain events had to align in synchronicity for us to get the break we so badly needed. Had Don talked to the original owner of the Snidka van before he took the Detroit job, this story would have been a different one.

To explain: in an email to Don, I thought that he should talk to the person who owned the van before the Snidkas bought it. A history revealed that the van's original owner lived in Indiana. American Road in Indiana had converted the van, sold it to an Indiana dealership where the original owner, Gary Bailey*, bought it. The van ended up in Central Ohio because Bailey transferred jobs here. Eventually, the Baileys traded in their van to Quality Chevrolet, who sold it to Snidka's mother. Because the Baileys lived in Columbus, I could ascertain the kind of ground effects installed on the van when they had it and the ground effect's color. The bottom part of the Snidka van was a purplish red. I was curious as to whether the Bailey van had white or red ground effects. And anything else they could tell us about the ground effects.

In talking to van dealers, without exception, we learned that if a van was converted by Mark V, for example, parts for a Mark V van would be ordered from Mark V and not another conversion company. The same for American Road and for Glaval and all the other converted vans. Conversion companies customize their products to fit their vans, regardless of its make. Don knew that the chances of the Baileys using anything other than American Road custom parts would be zero. He was right. Only I wasn't convinced.

Unknown to me during the early months of 2001, the important break would be in the timing of our call to check out the history of the Snidka van. Luckily for us, my call to Quality Chevrolet wouldn't be made for several months yet.

27

BY MAY 2001, DON HAD settled in Detroit. Again, we were without a private investigator. All along Mark Adams had been our sounding board—the go-to person for advice. As was his habit, he passed on to us solicitations he received from private investigators looking for new clients. One such solicitation came from the Information Search Group.

The Information Search Group had two principals, Linda Granville and Jeff Adams, Ohio State University graduates with degrees in criminology. Each had plenty of experience working with local private investigating firms and attorneys. Within several days, I had an appointment with Linda to discuss the details of our case.

In no time, Linda zeroed in on noteworthy information and understood the major issues. For the next year and a half, Linda, primarily, worked with us. We soon realized that she was a standout in the private investigation field. She followed through on every task she set out to do. Her reports were thorough. She documented what she did. And she kept scrupulous records of her work time for us. I was to discover that as a junior in high school, she was in one of my classes. This was one former student I would love to take some credit for influencing. But in all honesty, I couldn't.

Linda moved comfortably into Don's place. She agreed to continue to interview the people from the Thompson party. Linda conducted one of the best interviews I was privileged to hear. More than once, Don confided that women investigators have an advantage. People are not usually intimidated and will talk openly; whereas, people are much more guarded in what they say to men. Linda's calm demeanor in some subtle way induced people to answer her questions. A few denied attending the party even though we had strong evidence that they did, but because others were willing to talk to her, she ably added to our information about the party.

One witness told Linda that several different groups of people attended the party: people who worked with the host and his wife; bikers (members of the host's motorcycle club), and the younger friends of the host's son and daughter. The groups tended to socialize within themselves. One person said that the party was called "Dawg and Ears"—serving hot dogs and corn on the cob?

Another person gave Linda a list of people she knew who attended. That bit of information, coupled with our surveillance of the party vehicles for three years, proved that many of the same people attended every year. Mrs. Thompson suggested that the guest list changed each year. Or at least this is what Deputy McMannis said. No, not to any noticeable degree.

Linda learned the names of other guests and from them got several more names. During this entire interviewing process, only one deputy's name was mentioned—Deputy Ken Wooten—as having contacted them. Where was Deputy McMannis in 1998?

We had not been entirely persuaded that the tips had come from rumors. Did a Glaval van lurk somewhere in Snidka's history? That was a principal hang up. We couldn't find one. I made vehicle charts and lists of friends and relatives on poster board. We did find two Astro vans. Linda contacted Vickie Stout of the Glaval Corporation to ascertain if Glaval had converted them or if any parts had ever been ordered from Glaval. Gracious and accommodating, Vickie checked her database. Linda's list also included the Snidka van. Vickie's answer: None of the vans were Glaval converted, nor did they have any record of any parts ordered for them.

Okay, I reasoned, we know that Snidka's father had an Astro van. What if the original owner of the American Road did the unusual, like install Glaval ground effects? This would have been done before the crash. Then, as Linda pointed out, Glaval would likely have a record of that and they didn't. I wanted to go straight to the original owners—the Baileys—and talk to them.

We were nearing the end of June. In nearly one month the calendar marked the third anniversary of Andrew's death. Sitting in the kitchen, with the Snidka file spread out, I looked at the to-do list we had prepared for Don. "No. 8: Find out where the Baileys are living and get a full history of the Snidka van before Baileys sold to Quality Chevrolet, esp. information about the ground effects." Suddenly, an idea came to me—go yourself and see the Baileys.

This was unusual because I had stopped listening to an inner voice, compelling me to take some action. I discovered that as soon as I had identified myself as Andrew's mother, people no longer wanted to talk. But on that afternoon, my inner voice prompted me to visit the Baileys, original owners of the Snidka van. This item had been on Don's to do list since November of last year. I really couldn't explain my sudden, spontaneous interest.

Two Gary Baileys lived in Columbus. I chose one of the addresses, plugged it into MapQuest, got the directions and was out of the drive in a matter of minutes.

The Bailey house, a neat-as-a-pin split level, sat on a manicured lawn along with similar homes. The sun highlighted the flowers in the yard and lining the walk.

When I rang the doorbell, a blonde woman about my age answered. I had my speech ready.

"Is this the Gary Bailey home?"

"Yes," the woman answered, slightly puzzled.

"This may sound a little strange, but did you and your husband own an Astro van and sell it to Quality Chevrolet in 1996? I want to be sure I have the right house."

Later I learned that Mrs. Bailey assumed that I was interested in buying the van and wanted to know its history. "Yes, we sold a van to Quality Chevrolet, but my husband would know more about that than I do. He's at work right now but will be home around four. Can you come back then?"

"Yes, is four-thirty okay?" I thanked her and left. That wasn't so bad. What if I find out that the Baileys had had an accident and somehow changed the ground effects?

Around four-thirty I returned to the Baileys' door and this time Mr. Bailey answered and invited me in. After I explained the reason for my visit, our conversation revealed that American Road ground effects were very different in design from Glaval's design. American Road's part came up over and around the wheel wells. Also, he believed that the ground effect matched the striping, not the van. He said that he thought the part was red because the striping was red. But that he would check with his son and call me back.

When I prepared to leave, Mr. Bailey promised to call me as soon as he talked to his son. The next day Mr. Bailey left a message: "The ground effect was red. I'm sending you a photo of it". Part of it was covered in snow, but I could see the red. We remember with gratitude how helpful the Baileys were.

We were getting closer to eliminating the Snidka van. Yet, I had one more card to play. One more lead to check before I surrendered the tip. And that one card turned out to be an ace—only it didn't have anything to do with the Snidka van.

I waited until after the fourth of July weekend to call Rob Gaminelli*, the service manager at Metro Chevrolet (Quality had sold out to Metro). During the last three years, Andy and I, periodically, stopped by the service department to see Rob. Several months after the crash, he gave us a list of conversion companies with telephone numbers, and answered questions about vans and parts. Whenever we appeared at the service desk, he greeted us with open friendliness. Like others, Rob joined that list of compassionate persons who cared about helping us. I dialed his number in July 2001.

When he answered, I got right to my question. "Rob, we've been looking at a van traded to Metro [once Quality] and later sold in 1996 to people by the name of Snidka. Could you tell us if their van was ever brought in for repairs or for parts and what kind of work was done? We might be interested in buying it," I said, as Don had suggested that we should try buying it.

"Sure, do you have a VIN? I'll put it in our database. Call me tomorrow if you don't hear from me."

Hanging up, I had this premonition we would receive some valuable information. We did. Only it wasn't what I had expected. Today, I call it a miracle.

Expecting a call from Gaminelli the next day, we waited around all morning. When Andy couldn't take waiting any longer, he picked up the phone and dialed Rob's number. Rob answered.

"Rob, you're busy, but did you check out the repair history of that VIN Elaine gave you yesterday?"

"I checked it and we have no record of it being in the shop."

"Okay, I guess that settles that."

"But I have something I'd like you to see. Can you come here now?"

"Sure," Andy said, slightly confused. "What's this about?"

"I'd like you to have a look at this van—a van brought in about a week ago for some repairs. What side of the van hit your son?"

"The passenger side."

"And as I remember, you were looking for a Glaval van, right?"

"Yes, why?"

"Right now, we have a Glaval van in the shop. The passenger side was damaged, and we can tell it's been repaired. And no question the running board has been replaced. I think you should have a look at this van."

"We'll come now. Does the van have anything to do with the VIN we gave you?"

"No. This is different."

That hunch I had to consider the Snidka van repair history turned into one of those groundless intuitive feelings. Or was it? We had no idea what was in store for us, but experience told us to check out this van.

Rob met us at the service desk. Curious to see what this was about, we followed him to the shop area. The van looked nothing like any of the Glaval vans we had seen, except that it had the right kind of ground effects. Most Glaval vans had striping on the bottom part of the van, but this one didn't. And the color was a stark white—devoid of any custom detailing. It resembled a utility vehicle.

Several mechanics stood nearby. After introductions, one explained, "The van was brought in a week ago for a transmission repair. We used the VIN plate on the dash to order the transmission. The VIN says that the van is a 1990, so we order a 1990 transmission, only when it comes in, the transmission doesn't fit. One of the other mechanics looks at the transmission, then looks at the van and says, 'This is a 1993.' The VIN plate on the dash is a fake. It's been glued on."

"When the mechanic looked at the transmission, did he see another VIN?" Andy asked.

No. There should have been a VIN stamped on the engine and some other places, like inside the glove compartment. But they were all sanded out. He could tell by looking at the van what year it was. This is a chop shop van."

"What do you mean by that?" I asked.

"Probably stolen."

Andy looked at Rob, "You said the passenger side was damaged?"

"The passenger side running board has been replaced. And this post, the piece of metal that separates the passenger window and windshield, has been damaged and then repaired. If you look closely, you can see the filler."

For us to get excited, first, the ground effect on the passenger side had to show evidence of being replaced. One way to check that would be to remove the ground effect to see if additional holes were drilled in the rocker panel. If the rocker panel had additional holes, the next step would involve the pieces found at the crash. Do the holes in those pieces match up to holes in the van's rocker panel? Rob and the mechanics reported that the passenger side ground effect had been replaced. We wanted, however, an expert to confirm that.

We called Jack Holland, retired crash reconstructionist for the Ohio State Patrol. Advising us that he had about an hour between seven and eight o'clock to spare, he agreed to meet us at Metro that evening.

Standing in front of Metro's service entrance, we watched Jack Holland's car pull in and park. As we walked with him to the side entrance of the service area, we repeated in greater detail how we had come to Metro Chevrolet. Jack, although friendly and affable, was a person of few words. The years he spent as a top crash reconstructionist for the Ohio State Highway Patrol had honed the skill of separating the wheat from the chaff. All he wanted to know was what he needed to know. Before this, he had examined another van for us. He had mechanics remove the passenger ground effect and upon his inspection, he had eliminated that van because no other holes were drilled in the rocker panel.

The service office had closed at six o'clock but a large side door—much like a gigantic garage door—was left open for us. None of the mechanics whom we had seen earlier were around, but pounding sounds and music emanated from the body shop area nearby.

Jack carried a tool bag, and from it he removed a flashlight and a camera. We watched as he began at the front of the van, examining the hood, the windshield, and the grill; then he moved to the driver's side, squatting down to get a better look at the ground effect. Then he inspected every inch of the driver's side in a kind of sweeping motion with his flashlight. He continued to examine the back and then the passenger side. He seemed to be especially interested in the windshield post and the ground effect. He pointed out that the post had some repair work and that the passenger side ground effect had been screwed in place with flat head screws whereas the driver's side used Phillip screws.

Working quietly, Jack said little. At one point, he picked up his camera and took some photos. Also, from his bag he took out a tool that looked like a nail file along with a white envelope and scraped some paint samples off the van. He handed the envelope to me and told me to mark it. I wrote something like "white van seen at Metro, July 9, 2001; paint sample taken by Jack Holland."

One of the guys from the auto body area spied us and stopping his work joined us. Briefly, we explained our presence and had permission to allow Jack's inspection. He asked Jack what he could do to help.

"I could use a step ladder."

Several minutes later the man returned with a step ladder. Andy extended his hand and introduced us. We learned that the young man, Earl, had trained in body shop work in high school and had ten years' experience. Between Earl's and Jack's expertise, they pinpointed where the van had been repaired. Most of the obvious repair was on the passenger side.

Thin and agile, Earl climbed up and down the ladder, leaned down, forward, and contorted himself to have a look at the van. At one point, he opened the passenger side door and peered into the rubber gasket lining the door—opening the folds of the rubber as he worked his way down. About six inches from the top, he stopped and said, "Well, look what we have here. Would you happen to have a pair of tweezers, Ma'am?" he said to me. "Looks like a hair that's stuck in this gasket."

"I'll bet Jack has something we can use," I said as I didn't have a pair of tweezers.

Overhearing our conversation, Jack offered, "No, I don't have tweezers."

Then, ever so carefully, Earl got hold of the hair as Andy separated the fold. Jack was ready with paper and an envelope. Jack thought that he should wrap the hair in a smaller piece of paper inside the envelope. He did, and the hair was carefully placed in the envelope. Both envelopes, the one with the paint sample and the one with the hair, would be given to the FCSO. This was one young man we would never forget.

At about eight o'clock we walked out of the garage entrance to where Jack had parked. He spoke to us with a seriousness we had not heard before. *"You have probable cause. Contact your lawyer."*

From Jack's tone and his urging to call Mark, we sensed that Jack had serious suspicions about the van and that the van needed scrutinizing—a thorough and minute inspection. Happening upon a suspicious van in this way, unexpectedly, derailed the preconceived notion that the only way we would find the responsible van would be to work the Glaval list until we eliminated all but one van. By 2001, I had to switch from relying on the Bureau of Motor Vehicles for updated van information to an online service, CarFax, that checked a vehicle's history—primarily for buyers. For a special offer of $19.99, I could check as many VINs as I could in twenty-four hours. I used the special offer every time CarFax offered it.

Our greatest fear was that the van was gone—crushed for junk or burned in some isolated alleyway. Could the owner afford to destroy an expensive vehicle, and if a VIN on the Glaval list showed that a van had disappeared, that was a red flag, deserving of inquiry. As it was, the guilty van had been on the Columbus Police Department's list of stolen vehicles in May 1999, just months after the owner got rid of it.

About a year after Andrew's death, a Columbus policeman, Officer Claypool, was killed by a hit-and-run driver during a traffic stop. The Columbus community left no stone unturned to catch the killer. When the vehicle was finally tracked down, it had been taken to Texas and reduced to crushed steel.

Until we had some concrete reason to suspect this van at Metro Chevrolet, I wouldn't allow myself to speculate. One detail that relieved some of that skepticism was Jack Holland's declaration, "You have probable cause. Call your attorney." If Holland didn't think that we had reasonable grounds, his vast professional experience would have prevented him from making such a statement.

Also, as a flashing red light, mechanics told us that the passenger side ground effect had been replaced. Arriving home after nine, we decided we would call Mark in the morning.

When Mark answered, I said, "I think we've got a suspicious van. Jack Holland looked at it yesterday and advised us to call you. He said that we have 'probable cause.'" Then, I relayed to him the events of the previous two days.

Mark's first questions dealt with the ground effect. "How did they know the passenger side was replaced?"

"I don't think they removed it. What tipped them off was that the driver's side showed Phillips screws and the passenger side had flat head screws. At least that's how they explained it to us."

Joining the conversation, Andy told Mark that the VINs had been sanded off. "Jack looked but couldn't find any. Mechanics couldn't either. When the van was brought in, it needed a new transmission. They ordered a transmission based on the VIN plate on the dash, but when they tried to install it, it didn't fit. One of the mechanics said the year on the VIN plate was wrong. The plate was fake and had been glued on the dash."

"What year was the VIN?"

"1990."

"And what year was the van?"

"1993. Apparently, one of the mechanics could tell by looking at it. They went ahead and ordered a 1993 transmission and it'll work, but they haven't installed it yet."

"We have to know what the VIN is."

"The service manager told us that the manufacturer hides a VIN in case a car is stolen. They change the place every year so that crooks won't know. He said to call GM and find out where the hidden VIN is."

"That's something the Sheriff should do."

"That's not going to happen," Andy said sarcastically, using a phrase he had heard before.

"You have to call them. Call the deputy who tried to help you. See what he can do. Then call me back."

"We'll need to tell Rob, the service manager. He should know that we're calling the police."

"Tell him. The police should be involved."

When Andy hung up, he turned to me, "Staggs won't come out. Call Ken Wooten."

A few minutes later, Wooten answered. We repeated the story and that Mark advised us to call the Sheriff's Office. "Could you meet us at Metro Chevrolet?"

"Don't leave just yet," he said. Give me some time to explain the situation and get authority to meet you. You guys know I'm no longer on the case, so I'll have to go through channels."

"Ken, if you don't come out, no one will, or if they do, the van will be long gone. We called you because Jack Holland said we had probable cause. And Mark says that the police need to be involved."

"I'll call you as soon as I get permission to meet you."

With the call to Wooten, we suffered no doubt that he would make it happen and meet us. I called Rob. After I had described to him the events of the evening before and that morning, he agreed that the Sheriff should have a look at the van, but then added, "Hold on a minute while I explain the situation to my supervisor."

When Rob returned to the phone, he was a different person. His supervisor was not happy that a Sheriff's cruiser would be parked in the lot examining a vehicle in the garage area, where other vehicles were being serviced.

We explained to him that the Sheriff had already been advised and that our attorney had recommended it. Sometimes, "our attorney" turns out to be magic words, and sometimes not, but this time they were.

If we knew anything about Wooten, we knew his interest in our case and his desire to see it solved were genuine. Along with that, I observed that he had the curiosity gene. We had no doubt that he, armed with questions, would meet us at Metro and have a look at the van.

The call came soon after. Wooten explained that Staggs was out of the office, and he had to run down Major Bateson to get permission to meet us at Metro.

Metro Chevrolet sat on the corner of two major roads in Columbus in 2001. The showroom and service building were surrounded by new vehicles on one road, and with used vehicles showcased on the opposite side. The compound, decorated with strings of red and white flags, highlighted rows of vehicles.

About noon on July 10, 2001, Andy and I pulled up to the entrance near the service area designated for customers. A few minutes later, Wooten's patrol car pulled up beside ours. Meeting him as he exited his cruiser, we filled him in on a few details before talking to Rob.

"You've got to take a look at this van and see what you think," Andy said shaking Wooten's hand.

"Ken, Rob isn't too happy to have the police here. He was okay with it, but then his supervisor voiced some strong concerns."

Not one to get flustered, "We'll just have a little talk with him. There's nothing for them to worry about. We're not going to make a scene," Ken assured us.

As we approached the service desk, Rob rose to meet us. After introductions, Wooten promised Rob that the activity around the van would be minimal, and they'd leave as soon as they had a look at the van.

To keep the police's examination of the van out of public view, Rob instructed a mechanic to move the van outside to a side garage door area with little activity. The sun offered the best light possible.

While we walked to the outside lot, Wooten asked Rob about the van's present owner. "Is this guy a regular customer? Do you know him?"

"Yeah, we do. He's had other vehicles in for repair. But nothing like this."

"What do you know about him? Do you know where he lives? Where he works?"

"We have a work order with his address but I don't know him. One of the mechanics who worked on another vehicle for this guy might know. I'll get him."

Minutes later, Rob and one of the dealership's mechanics emerged from the garage door. "This is John, one of our best mechanics. He recalled working on a car for this guy last year."

"What do you know about this guy?" Wooten asked.

"Let's say that he is not one of our finest citizens," John answered.

"The Starinchaks said that someone yesterday made the comment that this van looks like it came from a chop shop. Do you think it's stolen?"

"Yeah, it could be. When the VINs are erased, you know something's fishy."

During the conversation, Rob placed his clipboard on the hood of the van. As Wooten was gathering information about the van's owner, I looked at the clipboard. I noticed a license plate number. This was the invoice for this van. Since Rob's attention was diverted, I took pen and paper out of my bag and wrote down the owner's name and address and license plate. I knew the area and possibly the apartment complex. I'd give this information to Linda Granville to check out.

By the time I joined the guys, I heard John say, "I wouldn't mess with this guy. I think we should go ahead and put in the transmission. He's already paid for it. Then when he leaves the lot, you guys can talk to him," nodding to Wooten.

"I don't know. Can I talk to the Starinchaks before we decide anything?" Wooten said.

"Sure. Metro's owner—the big guy here—wants to know what's gonna happen to the van. I'll go inside and tell him. I'll be back in a few minutes."

We watched Rob and John enter the garage. Andy turned to Wooten, "What do you think we should do?"

"I don't think we should let this van go. There are obvious repairs made on the passenger side and there's no doubt that the ground effect has been replaced. We have enough here to warrant a search."

"And what really got us," said Andy, "was Jack Holland saying that we had 'probable cause.' I don't know if you know Jack, but Jack isn't someone who overstates a case."

"Just the opposite," I added.

"I'm going to call Ross (Staggs) and see if he can come out. I want him to see this van."

We no sooner finished our conversation, when we saw Rob hurrying toward us. "Mr. Levy* wants to talk to you. He has an idea to run by you."

Rob led Andy and me through the back halls from the service area to the showroom to Mr. Levy's office. As we entered, an attractive forty-something man extended his hand, introducing himself as Jack Levy.

"I understand from Rob that we have a problem with a van. I greatly sympathize with you and I'm sorry about your son."

"I hope we haven't caused you any problems," Andy said.

"Actually, you have. From what I understand the owner is not someone we should mess with. What I'd like to do is to finish the job, give him his transmission and allow him to leave. When he comes in to get his van, we can call you and when he leaves the lot, someone can follow him."

"Deputy Wooten from the Sheriff's Office is outside making some calls. He thinks the van warrants a search. And last night our crash reconstructionist looked at the van and said we had 'probable cause.' Wooten thinks it's a mistake not to take it in," I said.

"Okay, look, this is what I can do. We have a state-of-the art tracker, worth more than $500. We'll attach it to the van. The police would be able to tell within a twenty-mile radius where that van is at all times."

Andy and I were uncomfortable interrupting this man's business. We had reasons for being suspicious about this van, but nothing was certain. We left Mr. Levy's office to talk to Wooten about the state-of-the-art tracker.

We found Wooten talking on his cruiser phone to Staggs. "Ross is on his way. He wants to get a look at this van."

For Wooten to do anything official, he had to go through Ross Staggs. This was a necessary step. For us, that was okay if Wooten was involved.

"Wait 'til you hear what just happened. The owner of Metro wants to put in the transmission, allow the guy to leave, but stick a tracker on the van so police can trace him," I explained to Ken.

We could tell by the look on Wooten's face that he wasn't buying the plan.

"No, we can't take the chance. Lots of things could happen. If the van checks out okay, we'll return it and the owner won't be out anything. There are too many things that aren't right."

"Yeah, that fake VIN plate on the dash and the damage on the passenger side," I said.

"What gets me is that there are no VINs." Andy added.

"Mr. Levy did say that they would install a state-of-the-art tracker," I said looking at Wooten to see if that would change his mind.

Wooten shot me a look as if to say, "I said no and I mean no."

As we were talking, Rob approached us, wanting to know what we thought of Mr. Levy's idea of installing a tracker on the van. Clearly, Rob was in a difficult situation.

All along he had tried to help us. This was a young guy—late twenties—who had not hesitated to answer any question we had about Chevy vans. If it concerned paint, he pulled out his paint books; if it concerned conversion companies, he pulled out that book. More than once, he made copies of pages for us to have. When he had advised us that he had a suspicious Glaval van in for a transmission repair and urged us to see it, he had no idea what trouble he was causing himself. He had supported us and it backfired.

Wooten explained that the van might have been involved in a traffic fatality. That alone would prevent the owner from driving it away. Too many things could go wrong, like the van never being recovered, especially if the owner were tipped off that the police were interested in it. No, if possible, the van had to be confiscated. Today.

By the time Staggs showed up, one other deputy had stopped by. Three sheriff cruisers were parked in the side lot at Metro.

As Staggs walked around the van, looking here and there, I followed. I still listened and believed what he said. Confessing that is not easy today, but it can give you an idea of how hard it is to doubt what the police say—even with our knowing he was a close buddy of McMannis and wouldn't want to one up him.

"The windshield hasn't been replaced," Staggs announced.

The guilty van had a damaged windshield as the coroner found shards of laminated glass in Andrew's clothes. Engineers we were to hire later to examine the van must dig around the windshield to find out if it had been replaced. But this guy has x-ray vision!

While scrutinizing the windows, I mentioned the hair Earl pulled out of the rubber gasket the day before. I said, "If the hair is Andrew's, that would be proof that Andrew's head made contact with this van. Right?"

"I doubt that we could test it. We don't have the money to do that."

Yes, I felt disappointment. No, I didn't question the response. Either I was a lot more compliant by nature or the "investigation" had taught me not to expect anything. Overhearing Staggs' response, Andy was livid. Not until later, when I replayed the comment, did I feel a snarling anger.

Standing on the lot outside the service area, we had been out in the sun for most of the afternoon, and I was thirsty. As Andy stood talking to Wooten, the other deputy, and Staggs, I left to get some water at a vending machine.

By the time I returned, a lot had transpired. Wooten had convinced Staggs that the van should be confiscated. The usual procedure would involve a court order to take the van. That couldn't take place until the next day. The van wasn't going anywhere—it was without a transmission.

Surprisingly, Staggs had come up with an idea. Making his way to the service area, he asked Rob for the van owner's name and address. Writing the name and address on a slip of paper, he asked Wooten if he would be willing to go to the man's house and get a release to take the van. Wooten said it was a good idea. Staggs pulled out a pad of forms, filled one out and gave it to Wooten. If Staggs wanted to get something done, he could.

In what seemed like no more than a half hour, Wooten was back with the signed release. He was incredulous. "I knocked on this guy's door, told him that his van could have been involved in an accident before he owned it, and could he sign a release so we can have a look at it. And he did." We were all in shock. It's never that easy.

"The only thing he said," Wooten continued, "was 'Will I get my van back'? He said he bought the van several months ago from his cousin for $2,000."

Staggs had more confidence in his plan than any of us because he had already ordered a flatbed truck to come and take the van. Probable cause.

Before we climbed into our car to head home, Andy and I discussed what we should say to Mr. Levy, the head guy at Metro. At least to express our thanks and report that the van owner was cooperative and would get his van back if it checked out.

If you have ever read Daphne DuMaurier's novel *Rebecca* or seen the movie, one scene stands out as a lesson to us gullible people. Rebecca, the first Mrs. DeWinter, is dead when the novel begins. Rebecca's housekeeper, Mrs. Danvers, stays on after Max DeWinter marries a second woman – nice and gullible. So trusting you want to shake her. Anyway, Mrs. Danvers, loyal to Rebecca's memory, is jealous of the new wife and pulls every underhanded trick she can to make the second wife look stupid. In one scene Mrs. Danvers offers the second wife help in designing and making a costume for a large party Max will host. By this time the second wife is on to Mrs. Danvers' game and is suspicious of her help. It begins with the second wife speaking with disdain to Mrs. Danvers, but Danvers feigns concern and offers to help design a costume. Not having fully learned her lesson, the second wife falls for Danver's feigned interest and suffers still another humiliation.

Did Ross Staggs just pull a Mrs. Danvers? By getting the release from the van's owner and ordering the flatbed, I went from being angry and skeptical of him to being reeled in. Yes, I was like the second wife in *Rebecca*. Given what we were to discover next about the van and the FCSO, I doubt that he ever intended to help us. .

Some hazy doubt lurked in the back of my mind about what the FCSO would do with the van. My paranoia was fueled by the FCSO's brand of investigation. We knew the first action Staggs should take: remove the passenger ground effect, see whether additional holes had been drilled in the van's rocker panel and if they had, determine whether the holes in the pieces of the ground effect lined up. When we returned home from Metro Chevrolet after the Sheriff's flatbed drove off with the suspicious van, I called Betsey.

"Mom, we've been through this a million times. You need to meet with someone in the Sheriff's Office and get a commitment from them what they're going to do if the pieces fit."

"Let's say that the holes match. How do I get a commitment?"

"Ask them directly what they intend to do, and then ask how long it will take them to do whatever it is that needs to be done and repeat the time or the date and tell them that you will call them. Mom, they're working for you."

I can't begin to estimate the number of times I called our daughter for advice on how to motivate the Sheriff's Office to help us. She was used to working with business people who lost a client if they failed to follow through.

"Dad wants to go to the press. He's really fed up." I announced.

"Call Yolanda Harris of WSYX. Or call that reporter dad likes a lot – you know the guy from the *Dispatch*."

"Mark Ferenchik," I said. "If we complain to the media, any chance at mending fences with the police will go down the tubes."

"Mom, face it. It won't matter if you go to the media and complain or if you don't complain. You might as well get the truth out. At least you'll have that."

"Before we start thinking the worst, maybe we should be patient and see what happens from here. If the pieces don't match up to the van, then it's a moot point."

"When do you think you'll hear if they're a match?" she asked.

"I have no idea. That's the first thing they'll do—see if the pieces match up to the van and then they'll call in someone to find the hidden VIN. As soon as we know something, I'll call you."

We were lucky to have our daughter. Some of our friends in The Compassionate Friends organization have lost their only child. Imagine that living hell.

28

UNKNOWN TO ANDY AND ME, with the confiscation of the Metro van, the real investigation was about to begin. The next morning I called Linda Granville to describe the events of the past two days.

Linda knew that on impulse I had contacted the original owners of the Snidka van to ask about the ground effects on that van. Meanwhile, she and Jeff had been tracking down the title histories of vans on Glaval's list. This was the way I believed we would find the van that killed Andrew—by checking out the list of vans, one by one. She expressed her surprise at the turn of events. She was particularly interested in the hidden VIN and discovering who owned the van at the time of the crash.

A day earlier when Rob, the Metro service manager, laid his clipboard down with the work order for the van on top, I saw the present owner's name, a John Brown*. Did he remove the VINs? Did he own the van at the time of the crash, kill Andrew and then remove the VINs so the van could not be traced back to him?

No, that didn't make sense. Why would he take the van to Metro for repair and give them his real name if he wanted to hide his ownership? Or maybe John Brown was an alias. Eagerly, we waited to get a status report from Staggs.

Instead, about one o'clock in the afternoon, Wooten called.

"They found the VIN," he said. "Some guys at the garage know about stolen vehicles and they called in an expert. He knew where to look."

"Do you have the VIN? I'll give it to Linda and have her do a check on it."

"Steve Fickenworth has it. Call him. He'll help you."

"Do you know if the pieces line up?" I asked, expecting that they didn't.

"Steve said they were a good match but that's all."

"So I wonder if a good match means that the holes in the ground effect pieces and the holes in the van line up?"

"Steve said that they were a close match."

"What do they do now?"

"I don't know."

Standing by the phone, Andy could piece together what Wooten told me. The pieces matched or at least Wooten reported that Fickenworth said it was a close match. And Staggs called in an expert to find the hidden VIN. We could have made some strong assumptions but we didn't.

I dialed Deputy Steve Fickenworth's number.

While events were happening to us during the investigation, we took them at face value. Months after the discovery of the Metro van when information about it began to gel, I had one of those moments of understanding the consequences of a detail which seemed insignificant at the time.

The stars in my or Andy's horoscope again had to be aligned. Sergeant Staggs was scheduled to go on vacation and, as a result, our case was put in the hands of Deputy Fickenworth. A lucky break for us.

Ross Staggs was not only McMannis' successor but also his close buddy. If Staggs had remained in the office instead of going on vacation, it's my gut feeling that he would have called his friend with news of the van, because McMannis was the investigator before him. And I believe that after a conversation between the two, it would have been unlikely that BCI ever would have seen the van. I based this on facts—what happened after BCI's exam and the subsequent halt to the investigation of the van. Stopped cold—despite a BCI's scientist's findings that screamed for an investigation.

McMannis' revenge.

When I made the call to Fickenworth to get information, I could not have imagined that events would play out as they did. In the next several weeks Fickenworth was to be our contact person with the Sheriff's Office. He always took our calls.

"Steve, Andy and I are wondering if you guys were able to find the VIN."

"Yeah, we did. We called in an expert and GM told him where to find the manufacturer's hidden VIN. It changes every year. Only the manufacturer knows."

"Were you able to take off the ground effect?"

"We did and found other holes in the van. There have been three ground effects on the van and *one set matched up perfectly.*"

Wait. Wooten told us that Fickenworth said that the match was "close" and "good". Now he used the word "perfectly." The word jumped out at me.

"You're saying that the pieces of ground effect match up to one set of holes *perfectly,*" I repeated, trying to take a breath.

"A near perfect match," he said when he realized he had just said something that he shouldn't have. But I had heard him the first time. I have his word "perfectly" authenticated in a letter I sent to our attorney, Mark Adams, dated July 17, 2001. "So what do you do now with the van?" I continued.

"We've decided to take the van to BCI (Ohio's Bureau of Criminal Investigation) and have them look at it."

"When will you do that?" I asked.

"We were going to do that this morning, but I thought that we'd better get a judge to sign a court order. I'm heading out to get the order signed now and when that's done, then we're legal and can transport the van to London. Probably tomorrow."

"How will it go to London? I mean, will you take it on that flatbed?"

"Yes, and I and another deputy will go with it."

"Could you call us after you take it?" I wanted to be certain that BCI got the van.

"You can call me tomorrow afternoon. I should be back in the office then."

"One other thing. Andy wants to know if you can give us the VIN."

"I have it right here. It's 1GBMX...."

"Is there anything else we should know about this van?"

"Not that I know of. When we get BCI's report, we'll be in contact."

The look on my face when I hung up told Andy that I wasn't exactly happy with the conversation. "At first he said that one set of holes in the van matched up perfectly. He used the word 'perfectly,' then changed it to a 'near perfect' match.

"Maybe, they need to get BCI's examination report before they can make any statements," Andy figured.

"You and I know that that van would not have been put on a flatbed and taken to London if those pieces didn't match up. And with a court order and two deputies as escorts no less," I said, getting my two cents in. Probable cause.

"What do you make of that—that the pieces match up? Perfectly to one set of holes?" Andy asked.

"It's a red flag, that's for sure." What an understatement. Had we forgotten Glaval's installation supervisor Dewayne Creighton's exact words, "If you find a van with holes that match up to those pieces, you've won the lottery."

Understanding what the ground effect was all about was a process—a gathering of information and analyzing it. We had the facts but had not processed them yet. And the three sets of holes meant that the van had had three different ground effects. One set we knew had belonged to the ground effect presently on the van.

"I'm surprised Fickenworth gave me the VIN. I'm calling Linda to see what she can find out about it."

Before I could pick up the phone, Andy got this look on his face. "Hey, get the Glaval list. Let's see if it's on there." In a flash, I had the Glaval list in my hand—always within reach as we constantly worked on it.

Starting with page one—of fifteen pages with approximately forty VINs on each page—Andy scrolled down with his finger while I looked over his shoulder for the last three digits of the 17-character vehicle identification numbers. We got to page 13 where we stopped dead, repeated the number several times—just like when you win the lottery—and were satisfied that we had it.

The original owner was listed as a man who lived in Dayton. But more curious than anything, Andy had written next to the VIN, "checked."

And this was on page 13. That made no sense. We were nowhere near page 13 in checking the Glaval vans. But there it was, this particular van, this van with its VINs all ground off, only this van with holes to match the ground effect pieces found on top of our son's bike, marked "checked."

"We have to backtrack," I said to Andy. "At some point, we must have seen this van. Let's think this through."

"That's my handwriting, but I don't remember writing that," he said.

"You did, so we must have had some involvement with it. Could it have been a van that we spotted at a shopping center, took the VIN off the dash and had Don check it?"

"Maybe," not quite accepting that theory.

"I wonder if somehow I took it from the Glaval list and gave it to the BMV for updating and we went to see it? If we went to see it based on a BMV report, I'll have a record of it in my notebook."

In checking Glaval vans, I used a form to keep track of information: the VIN; the date; the time of day; the van's color, and comments about what happened and our evaluation of the van. I had no record of this van in my notebook. The likelihood that we tracked this van down from the Glaval list and BMV records was zero. There had to be another explanation. Of all the Glaval vans listed on their fifteen-page report, this was the *only* van that had been marked "checked." We were stymied.

After Fickenworth had given us the Metro van's VIN, the first document we grabbed was the Glaval list of vans. That made sense. It was the foundation—the building block—on which the other information rested.

"This sure is strange. I'm going to give Linda a call," I said.

I heard from Linda the next morning. She had researched the Metro van's vehicle history. Besides giving her the authentic VIN, I also gave her the VIN on the plate glued to the dash. The first puzzling bit of information she found was that the alleged present owner (now 2001), John Brown, at the address we gave her, did not have title to the 1993 Chevy van found at Metro. The hidden VIN's title rightfully belonged to Nationwide Insurance.

"But," Linda said, "the bogus VIN comes back to him."

"What does that mean?" I asked thoroughly confused.

"Brown doesn't own the van at Metro—at least not according to the real VIN."

"Why remove the VIN plate and put another in its place?" I asked.

"To hide it because it was involved in a crime. If a vehicle is stolen, to hide it, thieves will remove the real VIN and replace it with a VIN plate from another vehicle. But Brown could have bought it without knowing the title wasn't legitimate. If a vehicle is stolen, the VIN makes it possible to track down."

"Did you find out anything about the VIN glued on the dash?"

"That VIN comes back to Brown. When he bought the van two months ago, the bogus VIN had probably been glued on the dash. The title to the van Brown bought says that the van is blue and a 1990. The original VIN says that it's white and is a 1993. Which is what the van at Metro is."

"How can this happen? How can someone go to the Bureau of Motor Vehicles and get a legitimate title with a bogus VIN? Does anyone check the vehicles?"

"No, no one checks. And car thieves know how to mix up titles. It's not hard. If the running board pieces match up to the van, we need to know who owned that van when Andrew was killed. From July 1996 to September 1998, the van was owned by a guy in Reynoldsburg."

"I thought you said that Nationwide Insurance owned the van," I said.

"They do. From the title, the Reynoldsburg owner, a James O. Sapp, sold it to Spitzer Dodge in September 1998. He owned it when Andrew was killed. Then Spitzer sold it to some guy who's now in prison. Looks like the van was stolen and then Nationwide took title in May of 1999. After that, we have no history. It's James Sapp in Reynoldsburg that we need to look at."

"The Glaval list shows an Edgar Winn* of Dayton buying the van from a dealership in Dayton," I said looking at the list.

"That's right. Winn is the original owner. In 1993 he bought the van in Dayton and then sold it in 1996. That's when Sapp, living now in Reynoldsburg, bought it in Dayton. He was the owner on August 1, 1998. I'm on my way over with a copy of these title reports. We can talk then."

When Linda sat down at the dining room table, she spread copies of the titles out on the table. "I have the guy's address. He lives in Reynoldsburg."

"While we're waiting for the BCI report, see what you can find out about him," Andy said to Linda.

"Linda, what disturbs us is that Andy wrote 'checked' next to this VIN on the Glaval list McMannis gave us. And we don't know why he did that."

"Well, now we know the van is local. We can't do much until we know more about this van. Did they tell you how long BCI will have it?"

"We have no idea. But if the report comes back that the pieces match up, we'll need your help. Right now, I'm puzzled about writing 'checked' next to this particular van. I can't remember how that happened."

"I think we should get Jeff to go to the Reynoldsburg address and have him look around. Once we start getting information on this van, it'll probably come to you."

Linda was right. We just had to keep digging. Linda's information about James Sapp who owned the van in 1998 meant nothing to us. We didn't recognize the name or address. Unexpectedly, the details of BCI's damning report would also lead us to other incredibly important information.

In Staggs' report to his supervisor, Chief Deputy Gil Jones, before Staggs left on vacation the day after the van's confiscation, he stated, *"If the ground effect pieces match up to the van, then Sapp becomes a suspect."* (See copy of Sgt. Staggs' report, 7/27/01)

BCI's report confirmed what Staggs and Fickenworth and every other deputy in the traffic department knew at the time the van was brought in from Metro Chevrolet—the pieces of the ground effect matched up perfectly. Everyone in the FCSO by this time, including Chief Deputy Gil Jones, knew that the ground effect pieces were custom-drilled and the serious implication of the match. So why didn't the FCSO question Sapp? What was the obstruction? Guess.

Also, in referencing Dr. Kwek, BCI's forensic scientist, about DNA testing (the hair pulled from the gasket during Jack Holland's examination at Metro Chevrolet) in the report, Staggs told Gil Jones that Kwek had declined the testing because "of the time element involved." Dr. Kwek testified under oath later that Staggs was the one who vetoed the DNA testing. Additionally, I believe that had Staggs not gone on vacation that week, Steve Fickenworth would not have been granted permission to request the BCI to test the other items, let alone flat-bed the van to BCI.

SGT. R. STAGGS REPORT – July 27, 2001

July 11, 2001 : Ken contacted me regarding a van matching the suspect vehicle. It was at Metro Chevrolet near Morse Rd. and Westerville Rd. I responded and inspected the van. The Glaval Package was present and the ground skirting had been replaced on the passenger side. There was also evidence of sheet metal damage to the roof and fender on the passenger side. I contacted the current owner, George Green, and asked for permission to remove the vehicle from Metro Chevrolet. He gave me permission in writing. While inspecting the van, we realized the VIN had been altered. All original VINs had been removed. Through Dep Tony Breece, the National Insurance Crime Bureau was contacted. They advised where a hidden VIN could be found. We disassembled a portion of the van and located the number. Through a title search, we found out who owned the van at the time of the crash in 1998. James O. Sapp, 6490 Rugosa Ave. in Reynoldsburg was the owner until 10-01-98. Snitzer Dodge gets a new title at this time. Dep. Steve Fickenworth will try to match the evidence piece to the original screw holes. If this is a match. Sapp becomes a suspect. I feel BCI should be called in at that point to process the van for damage evidence. We may also need to send in a paint scraping from the van. I will be out of the office until 7-24-01.

July 25, 2001 : The van was taken to BCI while I was on vacation. Dep. Fickenworth felt the Glaval evidence we had was a good match. Karen Kwek is a BCI investigator. She contacted me to explain her progress. She stated the paint was a microscopic match to paint chips found on Andrew's shirt. This does not prove it came from our van, but shows it came from the same paint shop and same color base. I don't know all the details. She assured me this information would be forthcoming in her report. She told me the DNA lab at BCI had declined to search for evidence for specific reasons. They felt the evidence would be too inconclusive, even if detected, because of the time elements involved. I don't know the details of this either. She told me she had other tests to conduct and would contact me when she had finished. No other progress to report.

Sgt. R. Staggs

7-27-01

Sgt. Staggs Report, 7/27/01

August 1, 2001, on the third anniversary of our son's death, Chief Deputy Gil Jones wrote a letter to Attorney Wolman enclosing a copy of BCI's initial report of the examination of the van (see copy of Jones' letter, 7/31/01). On Mark's advice, we talked to Atty. Wolman, a leading attorney in Columbus on civil rights. Wolman sent the FCSO a Writ of Mandamus—**do your job**.

The lead BCI scientist, Dr. Karen Kwek, reported that her examination matched up the pieces of the ground effect to two holes found in the Metro van, and matched paint chips found in Andrew's clothes to paint she had removed from inside the door of the van. The paint samples' chemical composition and the microscopic layering were a match. Two huge red flags.

Glaringly, Chief Jones's letter about the BCI report omitted that the ground effect pieces found at the crash matched the van from Metro. Read it yourself. The omission was beyond belief. That was the reason for BCI to examine the van. Is Jones tacitly protecting McMannis? He was afraid. Of what? That we might sue? He had plenty of evidence to know that we were interested only in holding the person who took Andrew's life responsible. I lost every ounce of respect I had for the man.

As stated in Jones's letter, McMannis told Jones that he (McMannis) had seen this van (the Sapp van) "within one or two weeks" after the crash. How does that affect BCI's scientific conclusions and the facts about the van? It doesn't. Was Jones suggesting that despite BCI's findings and Glaval's custom-drilling methods, McMannis' declaration that he saw the van "within one or two weeks of the crash" trumped the conclusions of BCI's scientist? First, "within one or two weeks" is a ball park time frame. The "within one" week doesn't work because McMannis was in training and didn't know until six days after Andrew was hit, the make and model of the vehicle. At the media conference on the seventh day, Friday, he had no photos of the Sapp van. It was at the end of the second week, that he spotted the Sapp van. And from a deputy that Jones knew kept no records to prove when he performed any official task?

If Jones wanted to get the message across to us that because Deputy McMannis claimed he saw this van within a week or two of the crash, that this couldn't be the van, he grossly underestimated us. Did he seriously think about BCI's report as well as the facts about the van and what that meant? Or did he ignore the report and keep the peace in the department by supporting McMannis, a deputy with friends in the FCSO? If McMannis had seen the Metro van and eliminated it, he did so because the van had already been repaired. The owner, Sapp, had plenty of time.

The red flags as indicated by BCI's examination of the van should have been our Writ of Mandamus, a court's demand that the Sheriff's Office act on this factual, scientific information. The findings of BCI logically and reasonably pointed out that the Sheriff's Office should investigate the van and its owner.

We had the findings of BCI and the statement of a deputy to his supervisor as to an approximate time that he supposedly saw the van and yet, the Sheriff's Office gave no hint that the BCI's final report demanded that they talk to James O. Sapp, owner of the van, at the time Andrew was killed.

JIM KARNES   **FRANKLIN COUNTY SHERIFF**

FRANKLIN COUNTY HALL OF JUSTICE
369 South High Street   Columbus, Ohio 43215   (614) 462-3360

Date: July 31, 2001

To: Mr. Benson Wolman

From: Chief Deputy Gil Jones

Subject: Update of Starinchak Investigation

This update is being provided to inform you what has been transpiring with the investigation, since we last communicated. Please find attached a progress summary from Deputy Steve Fickenworth detailing the progression of processing the evidence submitted to B.C.I. Also, Sergeant Ross Staggs' progress summary dated July 25, 2001 is attached. Deputy Fickenworth has spoken with Mr. and Mrs. Starinchak to bring them up to speed. At this point in time, the verbal communications between B.C.I. staff and Sergeant Staggs and Deputy Fickenworth would indicate paint samples from the van and comparison to samples from Andrew's shirt match. The problem with this information is it does not exclude the potential of other vans being the source, or conclusively identify this van as a unique source.

Not true. He knows the pieces at the scene match up to this van, but will refuse to say it.

The written reports have not been received from B.C.I. for more in depth review as yet. If the exact identification of the paint sample is possible it might be possible to narrow down to a finite number of vans with that paint and possibly narrow down those to a smaller local geographic area. These are still unknown factors yet to be checked, if possible. *If possible! He doesn't know about the GLAVAL LIST?*

During the review of registration and vin numbers related to the van, it was discovered the van submitted for testing is actually a vehicle previously located and eliminated by Deputy David McMannis, showing no corresponding damage, within a week or two after the accident. The van was sent however to gain any possible information and confirm or eliminate its involvement. *the time frame*

Any further information obtained will be relayed to you as expeditiously as possible. As always, if you have further questions or concerns please contact me at (614) 462-3300.

Respectfully,

Chief Deputy Gil Jones
Chief Deputy Gil Jones
Patrol Division

TDB/sd

Jim Karnes, Sheriff, letter 7/31/01

When Attorney Wolman received a summary of the final BCI report, he called us and in turn, we took the report to Mark Adams for his opinion. We barely blinked without asking Mark's permission first.

The report, dated July 26, 2001, was addressed to Sergeant Ross Staggs and signed by Dr. Karen Kwek, BCI's scientist who conducted the examination.

Dr. Kwek observed areas of damage on the van and visible overspray of white paint on the tip edge of the windshield. An examination of paint chips removed from along the leading edge of sliding door and rear right side "revealed that the vehicle has been repaired and repainted several times."

Looking to Andrew's clothes, in the debris from this item, she observed the presence of several glass fragments and white paint chips. These chips from the clothes show the layers: clear coat, white and gray primer. "This three-layer paint is indistinguishable in layer sequence, color and microscopic appearance and similar in chemical composition to the original three-layer paint removed from the rear right side of Item #1 (1993 van)."

Referencing the two pieces of fiberglass—" bearing two holes (which) fit along the rear of the front wheel well of Item #1 (van)—the two holes align with holes present in and around wheel-well. The second piece of fiberglass in Item #3 fits behind the first piece…and the hole present aligns up with one of the two holes in that region of the right rocker panel."

Our trip to Glaval a year earlier revealed the most crucial information that we gathered. *Glaval's ground effects were custom drilled, custom installed—each van was different. Like DNA.* Dr. Kwek's report definitively stated that the holes in the fiberglass pieces aligned with the holes in the van. And that paint scraped from the van matched the paint chips found in Andrew's clothes.

Much was happening at the end of July 2001. One of the most astounding revelations was yet to come. The suspicious van from Metro had been transported to BCI for examination. Dr. Kwek's report was damning. The van turned from suspicious to a van at fault. The authentic VIN of that van was, indeed, on the Glaval list, but Andy had marked it "checked"—the only one he marked in the entire 700 plus vans. We were perplexed. Why had Andy marked only that van? The van with the damning BCI report?

The day after receiving a copy of Chief Deputy Jones' letter to Attorney Wolman, we called Wooten to ask him what he thought of the BCI report. After he had seen the report, he talked to McMannis about the van. He told us to sit down. That we would not believe what he was about to tell us.

"You know the van in your posters? That van is the same van sent to BCI."

I repeated what Wooten had just said to Andy. "The van Staggs took from Metro Chevrolet?" I asked to be sure we were talking about the same vehicle.

"Yes. The van we saw at Metro Chevrolet and sent to BCI. Dave (McMannis) said that it's the same van in your posters. He saw the van two weeks after the accident."

"Dave McMannis said that?" I asked, my mouth agape.

"Yes. He said that he was teaching his daughter how to drive and saw the van. He asked the owner if he could take some pictures of it. In fact, he used it in the September Crime Stoppers television interview."

"The van we found at Metro was the same van in our posters and in Crime Stoppers?" I restated, thoroughly stunned.

"Right. You know Dave lives in Reynoldsburg not too far from where that van was."

Reward Poster

"God, I don't believe this. People asked us all the time if the van in the poster is the van we're looking for and we would say, 'No, no, it's a photo the police gave us.' We stood next to that van during the Crime Stopper's television interview at some person's house. Could have been Reynoldsburg. Something's not right here."

"What do you mean?" he questioned.

"The van from Metro didn't look anything like the van we stood next to for Crime Stoppers except it had Glaval ground effects."

"Well, it's the same van."

"Then, someone changed it. The stripes are gone and it looks like a plain white work van. And it has decals on the back lights. And decals on the back window."

"When was the Crime Stopper's interview?" Wooten asked.

"I'm not sure. Betsey was flying home on the weekends. It was weeks after the crash and still warm. McMannis gave us an address. Some house. That's all I remember."

"See if you can find out when you did that interview," he suggested.

"We might have taped it. It never occurred to us to be suspicious."

"By that time, the van had been repaired. Dave said that he saw it about two weeks after the accident."

"Attorney Wolman's letter said that McMannis told Gil Jones he saw it within a week or two after the crash. I'm trying to remember when he brought the photo here. I'll have to look to see when we made those flyers."

"How would you know?" he asked.

"My niece printed them up for us, and I was emailing her with the wording on the flyers. We gave her the photos to use. I'll see when I did that. McMannis never mentioned anything about teaching his daughter to drive."

"Yeah, they were driving around his neighborhood when he saw the van in a drive."

"That's not what I remember. When he gave us the photos, he said he spotted a van and stopped the driver." Factually, the van wasn't in McMannis' neighborhood. It was on the other side of Reynoldsburg, McMannis' town.

After I hung up, Andy and I sat dazed. The suspicious van at Metro is the same van in the photo that we used in flyers and posters. And it's the same van that McMannis, Andy, Betsey and I stood next to at the Crime Stoppers interview outside some house more than a month after the crash. An auto expert found the hidden VIN. *This was the same van.* We had to think this through. When did McMannis give us those pictures of the van and when did the Crime Stoppers interview air?

Arranged in neat stacks on the floor, black plastic VHS cassettes in their containers surrounded Andy. "I can't find the Crime Stopper's tape. I'll call the TV station and see if I can get a copy."

Later that afternoon I decided to run to the library and check out the *Dispatch* archives. The *Dispatch* and the television station WSYX worked together to publicize the Crime Stoppers crime of the week. At that time, I could only access the *Dispatch* archives by going to the library. Once there, I typed in "August 1998" and "Crime Stoppers." Nothing came up. Then I typed in "September" and "Crime Stoppers" and there it was—the article about Andrew's crash, dated September 8, 1998. Now I had a date. The Crime Stoppers' interview took place five weeks after Andrew's death.

Then, out of curiosity, I headed for the city directories. Leafing through the 1998 directory to find the name of the van owner at the time of the crash, I saw an address in Reynoldsburg. Next, I looked to see where he lived in 1999 and that listing was different—on Oldbury Court in Reynoldsburg. Crosschecking addresses, I noticed the Oldbury Court listed a woman's name as the resident.

The 2000 and 2001 directories listed the van owner as back at his 1998 address. We decided to take a ride to Reynoldsburg to look at the addresses. Seeing the area might jog our memories. Although three years had lapsed and we had no record of the address McMannis gave us to meet him for the Crime Stoppers' filming, we remembered what the street looked like, anticipating that it would be the 1998 address.

Checking the Reynoldsburg map, we followed the same route we took in 1998. Driving slowly, Andy tried to see mailbox numbers on the left while I looked at house numbers on the right. In the second block, I pointed and said, "That's the number. That brown house there."

The house, a small ranch, sat on a non-descript lot. Nearby houses were similar. The street was neat and tidy—a typical Reynoldsburg neighborhood.

"Does this area ring a bell?" I asked Andy. "I don't think we have ever been on this street before."

"Right. I've never been here."

"This doesn't make sense. We weren't here for Crime Stoppers."

"Remember, the street was like a cul-de-sac," he said.

"You're right. I have another address here, but the directory said he lived there in 1999."

"See if you can find it on the map and let's just have a look. Is it in Reynoldsburg?"

"Yeah. In fact, it's not too far from here," I said, looking at the map.

As soon as we saw Oldbury, we knew immediately that this was where we had been for the Crime Stoppers filming. The directory had listed a woman's name under that address. The woman could have been anyone, a relative or the person who owned the house. We were to discover that it was the van owner's girlfriend's house—soon-to-be wife number five, after August 1, 1998.

Although we were unaware at the time, the pieces had started to come together. The van in the Crime Stoppers' interview was the same van owned by the Reynoldsburg man on the date of Andrew's death, August 1, 1998. But why had Andy marked it "checked" on Glaval's original list? And, more importantly, why was this the *only* van on the entire list that he had written "checked"? The very van that BCI had examined. The very van that the ground effect pieces matched with holes in the van. The very van from which paint chips found in Andrew's clothes matched.

The answer to at least one of those questions came days later after we thought more about the period in which Andy would have marked the original Glaval list. The notation occurred after we had begun looking at vans on the list toward the end of September 1998, six or seven weeks after the crash. At that time, I was the one working the list. I had made no marks on the original list—I made copies for my use.

We both vividly remembered that afternoon in October 1998, when McMannis made a visit to our house, alone and unannounced, and the only time he ever accepted an invitation to come in. On that day, he made the statement that he had checked some vans. Vans from the Glaval list? None of those people ever indicated he had been there. Van tips from Crime Stoppers to the sheriff? We can't tell you because documentation is non-existent. But on that day McMannis, running his finger down the Glaval list, stopped at the Reynoldsburg VIN and instructed Andy to mark it "checked." McMannis offered no explanation that this was the van in the photo and utilized in Crime Stoppers. Andy merely did as he was directed. The only VIN marked "checked" at the direction of Deputy McMannis.

In the throes of a terrible grief, we did as instructed without question.

As the information about the Metro van kept piling up, I became fixated on the owner. Was he the driver? Did he have children who drove the van? Other family members? Friends?

Now, Linda, our PI, was busy researching the vehicle titles and owners of both vans—the Reynoldsburg van found at Metro and the van whose VIN plate was fraudulently glued on the 1993 Metro van's dashboard. Her job was to figure out how those two vans intersected. It was apparent that the 1993 VIN had been removed to hide it.

Also, as Linda pointed out, we had to know exactly when McMannis took the Metro/Reynoldsburg van photos—the same photos he gave us to use in our flyers.

"If he gave you those photos within weeks after the crash, we should know precisely when," she cautioned.

Andy and I nodded. "We can say for certain that he didn't give us the photos the first week. We never met him until the second week," I responded.

"The police have their own photo labs. They record when the film is brought in and when the pictures were taken. I'll get over there this afternoon."

"We're getting ready to take a ride to Dayton to see what we can find out about the owner. Apparently, he lived in Dayton before coming here. He bought the van from Frank Z in 1996."

"Check out the Montgomery County Municipal Court. And if you have time, see if he had any cases in Common Pleas."

Andy thought that going to Dayton was a waste. "What do you expect to find out?" he asked. The FCSO, despite BCI's report, wasn't investigating this van, or the owner. To answer his question, I didn't know. From experience, I know that you go to a place where you might learn something.

With the death of a child, you might as well have your heart cut out. You live. Your child dies. The real life of you dies with your child. Someone took my child's life. Someone took my life. Who could leave a human being to die by the side of the road? Who among us has so little reverence for life that they could injure or kill, and then run and hide? I had to know about this person—this owner of the van that killed Andrew.

To paint a picture of the owner, Montgomery County's Court of Domestic Relations gave me the first stroke of the brush. This was a man who had married and divorced four wives. The marriages averaged about five years, with the second one lasting less than two. Records stated he was a divorced man when he moved to Columbus in 1996, having divorced wife number four in the early nineties.

"OK, you know he's been divorced four times. And that means…" his voice trailing off.

"Maybe he has a bunch of kids and they're old enough to drive. But he has no biological kids by any of these women."

"Maybe he has stepchildren living with him."

"No, it doesn't look like that. His fourth wife had kids, but he had been divorced from her five or six years before he came here. These are her children, not his. Nothing here about custody. She's still in Dayton."

"When you were copying records at the courthouse, I saw someone who looked like Don Corbin. You haven't heard from him, have you?"

"No. But I wanted to tell you that several days ago, I came across some notes I took during our meeting with him in Johnstown—right after he was named Chief of Police. Do you remember what he said at our meeting?"

"Yeah, he talked about Chris getting married and having a child. His son moves on and ours is dead." The Corbins lived near us when Andrew and Chris were good friends in elementary school.

"It's hard to hear about Andrew's friends getting married and having children, but would you, in all honesty, want anyone else to lose a son because we lost ours?" No child should die before a parent. "It's what Corbin said about the type of person who killed Andrew. The profile he drew for us," I said looking at my notes from that meeting.

"The only thing I remember was he seemed to think the person would be from Kentucky or West Virginia."

"Yeah, there are six items in this profile, and he did say that. Listen to this. He said the person is in his fifties. He said that the man uses his van to drive around his buddies and might not be married. He works construction and he lives within a six-mile radius of the crash. If it turns out to be this van's owner, then this profile is nothing short of amazing."

"Does this guy work construction?"

"No, but court records indicate he had a blue-collar job with the government. Look at the other things. He's in his fifties and he could be single."

"Yeah, but didn't Corbin say the driver was from Kentucky or West Virginia? This guy's from Dayton." We didn't know it then, but the owner was originally from Kentucky.

"Well, I'm just saying, look what Don Corbin said. Reynoldsburg is less than ten miles from New Albany."

As we were heading out of Dayton toward Columbus, I spotted a Huber Heights sign. "Hey, let's stop there and check traffic records." Huber Heights is a large suburb of Dayton.

A few minutes later we exited the freeway toward Huber Heights. Not knowing where the Clerk of Courts office was, we pulled into a gas station, and asked the cashier for directions.

"You wait here. I'll check it out," I said as Andy parked the car.

Entering the narrow hall, I noticed a sign, "Pay tickets here." The woman behind the counter slid the glass door open, "Can I help you?"

"If someone got a ticket in Huber Heights, is this where I'd come to get a copy?"

"I can give you the case number and the date. What's the name on the ticket?"

"Can you check two names?" I gave her the van owner's name and the woman's name at the Oldbury address.

"We have a ticket for the one person," she said, grabbing a post-it note and writing the woman's name, address, and a 1996 case number and then handing it to me. That post-it note, we were to discover, would put the owner's girlfriend in the same area as an auto body shop that ordered a passenger side ground effect on August 6, 1998.

Because Montgomery County did not have a central clearinghouse for mayors' courts, we would have to go to each of the suburbs to get up-to-date records. We didn't do that. After several trips to Dayton, we knew something about the owner and his girlfriend, now wife. This was the girlfriend's third marriage with a daughter in elementary school.

The van owner's marriages were of interest simply because they might shed some light on the man himself and family. Only the first divorce listed "extreme cruelty" and "gross neglect of duty." The other divorces were dissolutions that required little detail as none of the wives nor did the man have any property to speak of. Records mentioned relatives in Kentucky. Almost without exception to get more information, we'd have to have a law suit in place, involve an attorney and to serve a subpoena. Mark had prepared us for that possibility.

While I scoured court records in Dayton, Linda paid the Sheriff's lab a visit. She watched as technicians checked and rechecked their records. McMannis had submitted no negatives of van photos to the lab in August 1998. Nor at any time in our case.

So how did McMannis get the photos? McMannis had used a Polaroid camera. The photos weren't dated. No official record existed as to when McMannis took those pictures. Ironically, I was to find one of the photos, a Polaroid, inside a church bulletin dated two weeks after Andrew's death.

We remembered McMannis coming to our house to give us the photos. No one from the FCSO interviewed us about the crash that first week, from the time Andrew was discovered on August 2, to the following week, August 10.

Ten days had lapsed since Andrew had been killed. We didn't know the reason for the long delay until McMannis' second deposition taken in November 2003—that he was in London, Ohio, for training until August 6. In charge of vehicular homicides for the FCSO, when asked what the office was doing in his absence, he said, "I don't know. I wasn't there."

Because those pieces found with Andrew on Sunday morning, August 2, were unique, the Sheriff's Office should have had an accurate description of the vehicle ready for the six o'clock news that evening, and they should have swung into gear immediately. Every law enforcement agency understands the importance of getting the word out to the public without delay in a hit-and-run homicide. Instead, on Monday, McMannis moseyed off to London, Ohio, for three days and then six days after Andrew was hit, he returned to the office to have a look at our case. Our first contact with the FCSO about the crash happened at a press conference, seven days after Andrew was hit. No hurry. This was only a young man's life.

On Friday, August 14, when Deputy McMannis handed Andy the photos, he said, "Billie Bob will turn his own mother in, if she did it, for $10,000." In trying to recreate the events of the week after Andrew's funeral, one small detail helped to pinpoint the date that McMannis gave us those photos. He (Andy) had been dealing with garbage cans. After pick-up that morning, he placed the empty cans in the trunk of his car. Heading back down the lane, he spotted a squad car in his rearview mirror. That had to be a Friday. Friday, August 14, 1998, two weeks after the crash. We put out no garbage cans the week of Andrew's funeral. During the whole investigation, McMannis came to the house only twice in August and once in October.

My niece, Susan and her friend, John, stayed with us every weekend for a month after the crash. She and John owned a printing business. When they visited on Saturday, August 15, we gave Susan the photos and upon her return home August 16, she began working to lay out the reward flyers and posters. She and I emailed back and forth, clarifying the language. On Sunday, August 23, with Betsey, Susan, and John's help we drove up and down Central College Road and side streets in the vicinity to put the finalized flyers on mailbox poles. Tipsters could call the Franklin County Sheriff's office or Crime Stoppers. Eventually, those tips, I suspected, were thrown in a box, unread, or robotically marked "C/C."

29

BASED ON DR. KWEK'S EXAMINATION at BCI that the paint and fiberglass pieces matched the Metro van that James O. Sapp owned at the time of the crash, you might think that someone from the FCSO would talk to him, but you would be wrong. Or that the statement Staggs made to his supervisor, Gil Jones, in a written report that *if this is a match* (evidence pieces to van screw holes), *Sapp becomes a suspect,* meant exactly what Staggs wrote, you missed the mark again. No one from the FCSO ever tried to check out the van and its owner.

When McMannis told Chief Jones that he saw the Sapp van "within one to two weeks" after the crash, an ambiguous time frame at best, was that good enough for Jones? Was it good enough for Jones that McMannis kept no official records of any of his comings and goings in our case? And most disturbing, was it good enough for Jones to dismiss BCI's scientific findings when a deputy under his supervision claimed a date that was vague—let alone nothing official?

Astoundingly, in an August 2003 *Dispatch* article about the fifth anniversary of Andrew's death, Staggs is quoted as saying about Sapp, "I didn't feel we had enough evidence to take the time out of his day." This was the absolute antithesis of Deputy Staggs' report, July 11, 2001, immediately after the Sapp van had been confiscated? In that report, he stated, "*If the pieces match up to the Sapp van, Sapp becomes a suspect.*" From July 2001 to August 2003, what changed Sgt. Staggs' mind about the matching ground effect? No further scientific inquiry discovered other facts to dismiss this particular van. *None.* The FCSO had completed no further examination or investigation of this van. What in God's name was going on there?

The traffic office of the Sheriff's Department knew all about Glaval's definitive statement—that the guilty van first had to have the passenger side ground effect replaced and, second, holes on the van had to match up to the holes in the pieces found at the crash. The holes did. The Sheriff's Office knew all about Glaval's custom drilling and installing. Why not keep going to see where this would lead? BCI also determined a paint match. For Staggs to make an outrageous statement to the press that the FCSO didn't have enough to take the time out of the owner's day recklessly dismissed scientific fact. On that statement alone, we should have sued the FCSO.

One day, browsing the book stacks in the library, I pulled out a book, *Unbound,* by a retired Police Chief, Anthony V. Bouza, primarily about police corruption. Bouza's career which began in Minneapolis took him also to the Bronx Police Department in New York. With authority, he writes, *"I found the overwhelming majority of supervisors worse than useless. Several were little more than cover-up artists or apologists for wrongdoers" (136).* The "worse than useless" part we were getting. We had yet to detect or fully realize the "cover-up artists or apologists for wrongdoers." We could not have anticipated what was in store for us.

Reliving that period when the Sheriff's Office did nothing about the BCI's report, I'm repulsed that public officials can ignore evidence in a homicide if they choose to. The fact that the Reynoldsburg van was to languish for a year after its confiscation, outdoors, at the Sheriff's impound lot while the FCSO did absolutely nothing, didn't stop us. Mark Adams filed motion after motion to have the van examined thoroughly by engineering experts—motions that were denied by a Franklin County Common Pleas judge, citing the Sheriff's contention that the case was still open.

To be fair, Deputy Fickenworth worked our case while Staggs was on vacation. He called the Glaval Corp. at the time police confiscated the van and inquired as to whether anyone ordered a ground effect part under the Sapp van's VIN after the date of the crash.

That was a good inquiry. But the fact that Glaval received no order for that VIN after August 1, 1998, should not have surprised Fickenworth. If the van had been involved in a homicide, would you go to a reputable dealer and have them place an order for a piece torn off and left at the scene of a homicide? Or would you find another route to get a replacement piece? So Glaval received no order for a ground effect under that VIN. Any other Glaval VIN would do.

Besides ordering from a dealership, the most obvious way to find a replacement part is the junk yard. That route could be problematic in and around Columbus as Glaval vans were in short supply. The Dayton area, however, has a huge Glaval dealership. That part would not be hard to find in a Dayton area salvage yard.

Another way would be to "borrow" a ground effect from some other van, especially if the damaged van had to be repaired in a hurry. No one in Dayton knew of Andrew's death and a missing ground effect taken from an otherwise perfect van would hardly be noticeable. An auto body shop could order a new part from Glaval under that van's VIN or the van's production number with Glaval. To check out that possibility, Glaval's invoices had to be checked by hand. Checking invoices would have to wait.

Fickenworth's report to Chief Jones confirmed Fickenworth's belief that the Reynoldsburg van was involved in the crash. No doubt, he voiced the obvious—someone needs to talk to Sapp. From the information, we could gather, Fickenworth was moving in the direction of solving our son's homicide. But then unexpectedly his work ended.

All along I didn't have the backbone to publicly confront the FCSO. I kept a tight rein on Andy. We fought every day about how to get the FCSO to investigate the Sapp van. Andy felt that we wouldn't motivate them no matter what we did. "They ignored BCI for Chrissakes." He wanted to storm the FCSO and in plain language and with some cursing spell out our disgust. I strongly feared that the FCSO had the power to do whatever they wanted with the van. I couldn't take the chance on their deciding to turn it over to a salvage yard or to give it back to Mr. Brown, the guy who had brought it to Metro for a transmission repair. I couldn't trust what they would do in retaliation.

James O. Sapp, owner of the van, on August 1, 1998, will deny driving his van on August 1, 1998 and hitting our son. Engineers and scientists concluded his van killed our son.

30

ONE AFTERNOON, LINDA, OUR PI, stopped by the house with all the vehicle documents for the Metro/Sapp 1993 white Astro van and the 1990 blue Astro van. She had spent days at the Bureau of Motor Vehicles, tracking down the vehicle histories and the driver histories of the two vans. Thorough in her research, she handed me a file containing copies of titles, title histories and driver reports.

Brown was the last owner of the 1993 van – posing as a 1990 — in 2001 and that in September, 1998, *and a day after the Crime Stopper's publicized interview, James O. Sapp sold the van to Spitzer Dodge in Reynoldsburg.* Two and a half months later Raymond Farris* bought the Sapp van from Spitzer Dodge.

Why should we care about Raymond Farris? To find out his story, I made a stop at the Franklin County Court House. When I punched his name in one of the computers at the courthouse, several entries popped up. Farris had a serious criminal record. He had been arrested for breaking and entering with intent to burglarize and in another incident attempted to murder his girlfriend.

In March 1999, awaiting arraignment for the breaking and entering charge, he filed a vehicle theft police report stating that after he had parked and exited the van, the suspect "who he had never seen before" jumped in and drove away. The thief was referred to as "her." Was he paid to buy the van and then get rid of it? He does do that.

By May 1999, Farris had his check for the "stolen" van from Nationwide Insurance. Later, Farris or the police found the van. Farris had his check and his van. A police report said that the van had been recovered. God knows he tried to get rid of it, but it kept showing up. It was at this point, that the Farris van (formerly Sapp's 1993 white van) took on a new identity and became a 1990 blue van.

Looking at the owners after Sapp sold the van and their length of ownership, no doubt exists that the van was a hot potato. The van had to go off paper so it couldn't be traced. But who could have predicted that it would turn up again with its new identity when it did?

31

ONE OF THE LAST STATEMENTS McMannis made under oath in his May 2000, deposition involved his agreement to get paint chips and smears found on Andrew's clothes and bike tested by the Ohio Bureau of Criminal Investigation. He didn't. In all the time that he was the lead investigator in our case, he had evidence of vehicle paint left at the scene and never had this evidence analyzed.

The first order of business in an investigation is to look for vehicle paint to ascertain the make, model, and year of an involved vehicle. It's possible that a paint chip can give authorities the unique history of a vehicle, especially if the vehicle has been painted several times before the crash. What traffic investigator would overlook doing something as basic as that?

None of us is above error or the omission of some necessary action in the function of our professional duties. But not having the paint evidence tested is so basic, and so necessary, that it's inconceivable to me why that wasn't done even after McMannis agreed to those tests under oath?

When Dr. Kwek of BCI examined paint chips found on Andrew's clothes and determined a paint match to the 1993 Sapp/Metro van, Mark Adams and our PI, Linda, went to work, gathering information about vehicle paint. Mark called his legal contacts working for General Motors who gave him the names of people in the paint division.

With the match of paint chips in Andrew's clothes to a sample from the inside door of the Reynoldsburg 1993 van, Dr. Kwek of BCI stated that the paint on the clothes and van was a match or similar. Dr. Kwek explained that "similar" meant "same" or "indistinguishable" in all facets of paint analysis. I was curious about paint analysis. I found an auto supply store and asked the clerk if he could answer some questions about auto paint. "What do you want to know?" he asked.

"Can two paint samples from the same article be analyzed as similar but not the same?"

Sizing me up, he said, "Let's say you wanted to make a cake. You get your flour, sugar, eggs and butter and other ingredients and mix it up. If I took a spoonful of the batter and had the ingredients analyzed and then took another spoonful and had that analyzed, the two spoonfuls would be similar but not the same. Close enough to say that they came from the same batter but not the same."

"Even if I was precise about the measurements?" I asked.

"Even if you did that. A spoonful of any mixture of ingredients will never be exactly like another spoonful of those ingredients."

"Would you be able to say that you had a match? Could you go that far?"

"Absolutely."

"If my friend across the street used my recipe for the cake but her ingredients came from other brands, would her batter test similar to my batter?"

"No. If she used different brands that would make a difference. The cakes could look the same but not test the same. I'm not a chemist but that's what happens to paint."

This lesson in cake batter prepared me to understand paint composition and why scientists used certain terminology.

We were steadily collecting information about the van that had been in the Sheriff's custody for almost a year. Mark, at one of our meetings, suggested that we organize the information and create a notebook to assist future experts.

That evening Andy and I worked at categorizing the material and making decisions about what should go into the notebook. The more we discovered about the van, the more frustrated we felt about the FCSO's inaction. We vowed then that we would have engineering experts look at the van.

"So far, all signs point to this van." I remarked.

"And that's the reason we've got to get this van to someone who can tell us what we've got."

"I don't trust Staggs to give up the van. The last time I was in the office, Mark called Staggs who seemed almost friendly. But all the good it's done us," I said. "They haven't done another blessed thing for almost a year."

"Well, Judge Crawford has denied Mark's motion to have the van examined because the case is still open."

"I heard Mark say that he's re-filing the motion to allow engineering experts to see the van and then he'll call Nationwide since they own the van."

"If Nationwide's attorney says that Mark can have the van, it'll really look bad if Staggs holds it up. They'll have to keep dealing with us."

"What would explain this bizarre investigation? The van was dropped in their laps."

"And they've had more than a year to do whatever they wanted to the van."

How exactly Mark was going to pull off the transfer of custody of the van from the FCSO's impound lot to a private forensic laboratory was anyone's guess. Just because the FCSO reported the case as "open" didn't mean they were investigating. They now knew who owned the van when Andrew was killed, had the red-flag BCI report and yet they had never approached the owner.

Reasonable people would expect a law enforcement agency like the FCSO to have the same goal as the victim's family—to hold the perpetrator criminally responsible for a person's death. But something seemed terribly wrong in our case.

Andrew, 10, fishing, a favorite
pastime at Hoover Dam, Westerville, OH

Andrew,10, climbing trees
and tapping for maple syrup

Andrew in his Peewee football
uniform - No.33, the number
he chose for all his sports

Christmas, 1978:
Andrew, Andy, Betsey, me

Andrew, middle school science class, his favorite subject; he consistently won first place blue ribbons at science fairs

Andrew, first row on left, Westerville baseball

Andrew - Westerville North High School graduation 1985

Andrew - Miami University, Oxford, Ohio, graduation
with Betsey and Aunt Mar and Aunt Deb

Andrew
Ultimate Frisbee Club
Ohio State University
1996-98

Oz, Andrew's great friend and now
ours, took the photos and had no trouble
identifying Andrew in his collection:
"Andrew wore abrace on his left leg"
after he tore his ACL twice

In Michigan, after a day skiing with friends:
Andrew, me, Patty, Bryan, Em and Lo

Andrew next to his signature red Honda.

Our favorite photo of Andrew, taken by Oz

Andrew standing next to me at Betsey's wedding

Andrew's mangled bicycle at the site
of the crash, Central College Road

Dr. John Wiechel, SEA's top
Engineer and Crash Reconstructionist

Our hero and attorney, Mark Adams

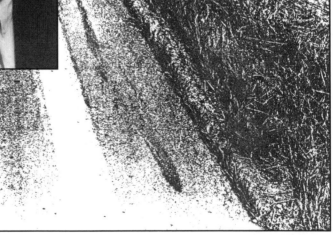

Black tire marks when Andrew was hit.
He had been to the right of the white line.

Van used in posters

Sapp van, 2002, on flatbed from Sheriff's impound lot to SEA garage

SEA Facility that housed and
examined the Sapp/Metro van

Doug Morr, Engineer with
SEA, examining the van

Mark Adams next to
Sapp/Metro van, 2002

Cross that Andy erected at Central College; flowers placed there after a ride by four Central Ohio bicycle clubs

Construction site of Andrew John Drive, 1999

Ride of silence, Downtown Columbus, Ohio, hundreds of bicyclists ride in May in memory of people killed and injured while riding. Roger B. and Mark S., Robin, Paul and Boo rode in Andrew's memory.

2008 Tenth Annual Andrew Starinchak
Memorial Tournament, Beekman Field,
Ohio State University. Organizers: Paul,
Shari, Boo, Tod, Jeff, Julia, Randy, Angela,
Todd, all volunteers to make this a
spectacular event for The Boys & Girls
Club of Columbus, Ohio.

Andy, standing under
"Andrew John Dr." a street named
after Andrew; Tina Miller's brother,
a developer in our area, proposed it.

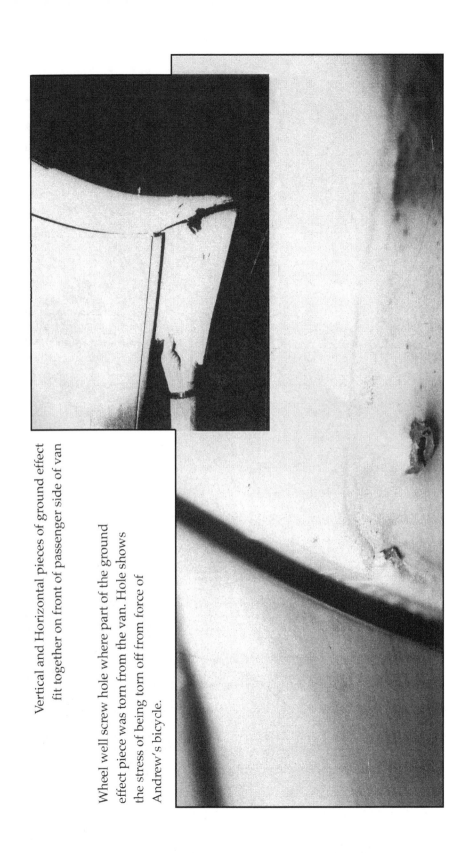

Vertical and Horizontal pieces of ground effect fit together on front of passenger side of van

Wheel well screw hole where part of the ground effect piece was torn from the van. Hole shows the stress of being torn off from force of Andrew's bicycle.

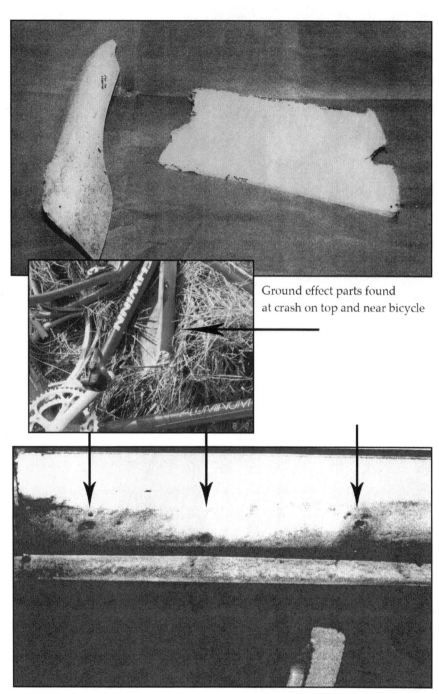

Ground effect parts found
at crash on top and near bicycle

Random drilling of holes in van's rocker panel

2002

32

WHAT WE EXPECTED AND SHOULD have had after the BCI report was a full-fledged investigation of the person who owned the van when Andrew was killed. We expected the van and its owner to become the primary item and person of interest. We expected an interest in solving our son's homicide and in a van that BCI linked to Andrew's death. Yet, the van sat at the Sheriff's impound lot for almost a year. Why? Did someone "tamper" with the van? The opportunity was there for more than a year. Why wouldn't I suspect that after such a delay? And an investigation that made no sense? And when we got nothing from the FCSO, instead of idly standing by and allowing a highly suspicious van—one that could have killed Andrew—to sit month after month at an impound lot, Mark worked the angles to get it released for further examination.

How Staggs felt about Mark's perseverance after a year of the FCSO's stalling, I'm not certain, but when Mark called Assistant Prosecutor Dan Cable to get his approval to release the van, Cable replied, "BCI is so backed up with cases that I'm approving the request and calling Staggs."

That conversation took place in the middle of March 2002. Despite Mark's continual contact with the Sheriff's Office for another two months, not until Mark called Sheriff Karnes directly did he receive word that the van would be released the last day in May. Karnes' primary concern was that all costs for further examination be borne by us. Mark had navigated a major obstacle, and finally we could engage a highly-qualified expert to take another look at the Sapp/Metro van to confirm BCI's report or not.

Although we had doubts about the FCSO ever releasing the van, Mark didn't. As we waited for the van's release, Mark strategized about preparing a private forensic lab to handle the examination of the van.

Under his direction, he put me to work organizing the information we had collected about the van into notebooks. He wanted to have the documents copied and categorized so that the lab would know where to find information.

We met with Mark on a regular basis, and one afternoon in his office, he suggested another task for me—to find an expert lab of engineers who would be willing to take the van and examine it. I turned to the Internet. Several laboratories came up—all of them out of state. I copied a description of a lab in Chicago and gave Mark its address and telephone number.

With one of the notebooks in front of him, Mark called the lab in Chicago and talked to an engineer there. When Mark hung up, he explained some of those problems. "These guys don't come cheap. He quoted $500 an hour for the examination and consultation, and travel expenses would be extra," Mark said. Then he added, "This could go as high as several hundred thousand dollars."

In an earlier conversation with Linda, she disclosed to Andy and me that an examination of the van could run into tens of thousands of dollars. We had been somewhat prepared for the expense but had not thought of hundreds of thousands of dollars.

"Were you able to find any place closer than Chicago?"

"Linda had recommended a crash reconstructionist here in town. I don't know if he has a facility to house a van. Have you ever heard of John Wiechel?"

"I have. I've worked with John on several cases. He's with SEA [a firm of engineers and chemists who do investigative analysis] in Worthington."

"I wonder if he could take the van?"

"If SEA has the facility to house the van and John's available, it'll be a lot less expensive if we can do it all here."

Having the van here with a local crash reconstructionist was the best of both worlds—from the standpoint of expense and our being able to access information. Dr. Wiechel's credentials were impeccable. He enjoyed a prominent, national reputation. His areas of expertise were mechanical and biomechanical engineering, having earned his Ph.D. at The Ohio State University. Now we had to interest him in taking our case.

On April 22, 2002, Mark arranged a meeting for us with Dr. Wiechel, chief crash reconstructionist and head of engineering at SEA. Carrying files and the notebook I had prepared, Andy and I entered the spacious reception area of wood and marble. The SEA facility, a large complex of buildings, is located not more than fifteen minutes from our house. SEA's fleet of engineers, chemists, scientists, and investigators provide the scientific answers to questions about all kinds of accidents and catastrophes.

After we approached the long, crescent-shaped receptionist desk at SEA and were ushered into an office located off the foyer, Andy and I waited for Dr. Wiechel. Both Linda and Mark had called him on our behalf, and he had agreed to do what he could to help.

Minutes later, Dr. Wiechel came through the door. Smiling, he extended his hand and introduced himself. His friendly manner eased my nervousness. Before we left the house, we had listed the items for discussion. "Let's not overwhelm him with all kinds of stories and detail," I said to Andy. "Let's meet him and get an idea of what he's like. Give him some brief background information and what our goal is. Does that sound okay? What do you think?"

"Yeah, but I have some questions," Andy replied.

What I wanted to do before I left the house was to get a promise from Andy that he wouldn't go off on some tangent. And that I, too, would attempt to keep my comments relevant to Dr. Wiechel's questions. When we were paying an expert or an attorney hundreds of dollars an hour, we couldn't afford to ramble.

In preparation for this meeting, Mark had forwarded to Wiechel the crash report and Andrew's autopsy. Before we heard what Dr. Wiechel had to say, Andy emphasized the reasons the van needed further examination. Dr. Wiechel, looking at his notes, confirmed that Andrew was hit squarely from behind—that it wasn't a side hit. Then he went on to explain how Andrew suffered trauma to the front of his head and not to the back.

Toward the end of the conference, Dr. Wiechel looked at us and asked, "What exactly do you want?"

"I want to know who killed our son," I said.

"And for that person to be held responsible," Andy said nodding.

"If you want to find out who did this, you can," Dr. Wiechel said.

"Without the police?" I asked. His comment sounded as though our finding out was not out of the question. But what about justice? I visualize grabbing the coward by the head of the hair, exposing the creep and throwing him or her down a sewer and clamping down the manhole cover. The FCSO was impotent. Someone had to do it.

"You may not get all the answers, but you can find out who killed your son," he repeated.

As strange as this may sound, neither Andy nor I questioned Dr. Wiechel further. This was a startling statement. Was this based on his vast experience as a crash reconstructionist or an intuition?

Mark might have finagled the release of the van, whether it was through his motion filed with the court, talking to the Prosecutor's Office, troubling the Sheriff's Office, or talking with Nationwide's counsel, but no matter what engineers would discover about the van, we couldn't bypass the FCSO. They had the power and we were just plain folks. Still, we could see that Mark knew how to work with the Sheriff's Office, and as long as he worked his magic, we were moving forward. Because we considered Assistant Prosecutor Dan Cable's remark that BCI was backed up, we thought that the FCSO would welcome our help. "Wow, you really are stupid," my inner voice rebuked. "You haven't learned a thing from this experience. Welcome your help?"

We reasoned that BCI's examination of this van pointed a guilty finger to its part in killing Andrew. It's like the kid who emerges from the kitchen with chocolate cake all over his face, and his mother asks after she notices a large chunk of cake missing, "Did you get into the cake I baked for my bridge club tonight?" The evidence was right in front of her. BCI's report placed the evidence squarely in front of law enforcement and us.

SEA's task was to give us an objective, second opinion. Their job was purely to report whether their examination indicated that the Sapp van had been involved. Armed with SEA's assessment of the van, we would go back to the Sheriff's Office with tangible, undeniable evidence to persuade them to act. Or if SEA's examination proved otherwise, we would dismiss the van and get back to working the van list. Andy and I voiced a clear intolerance of anyone, the police or otherwise, who supported an accusation based on unsubstantiated information. Considering FCSO's inaction, despite the BCI's damning report of the Sapp van, we needed a second opinion.

As Andrew's mother and father, we should not have had to fight for the further examination of that van and pay for it! Every deputy in the traffic division knew what the van's BCI report said, and what it meant. By ignoring the evidence, the FCSO summarily dismissed BCI's critical report. And got away with it.

On Thursday, May 30, 2002, on a perfect spring morning, Mark had arranged for the Sapp/Metro van to leave the Sheriff's impound lot to be transported by a flat-bed truck to the SEA facility. At eight-thirty that morning, Andy and I met John Wiechel in SEA's parking lot. He decided to ride with the driver of the flat bed. The plan was for Andy and me to follow the truck.

When the truck arrived at the impound lot, we recognized Mark's car, parked next to Ross Staggs' black Sheriff's Blazer. Staggs escorted the truck through the gates and back to the lot. Mark followed. Just before the job was completed, as the driver was putting the last chains on the van to secure it to the flat bed, Mark came through the gate and stopped by our car.

"We'll follow Staggs to the property room on South Fourth Street to get the rest of the evidence. He'll give John custody of the broken running board pieces, bike, clothing, and anything else."

"Did Staggs say anything?" Andy asked.

"Yeah, he said, 'This is as good as it gets.'" Obviously, Sgt. Staggs was referencing the van as he and Mark looked it over. We took that to mean the evidence was overwhelming.

Leaving the impound lot, the caravan, consisting of Sgt. Staggs in the lead, Mark Adams, John Wiechel and then us, headed out to pick up the evidence pieces and Andrew's bike and clothes. The ride allowed the moment to sink in. Finally, we had the suspect van, and to guide us, two professionals whose counsel we trusted completely. This was a new day and we felt grateful—even to Sgt. Staggs. Yes. Unbelievable.

After picking up the evidence, we followed John Wiechel in the truck bearing the white 1993 Chevy Astro van and headed to SEA. Mark had an eleven o'clock hearing and would meet up with us later. Nearing lunch time, we noticed several deli and sub shops and decided to stop. More than eating lunch, we had to collect our thoughts before arriving at SEA.

"No matter what this costs, this has to be done. I can't think that Chief Jones will ignore SEA," I reasoned.

"He sure as hell ignored BCI," Andy said.

"Incomprehensible. Is Jones in control of the traffic department or are McMannis and his friends still running the show even though McMannis is gone? If you ask me, Jones is covering for McMannis. Maybe orders from Karnes, himself?"

"What I want to know is how long this is going to take SEA."

"Depends on what they find. Wiechel's not going to waste his time."

After lunch on that warm spring day at the end of May 2002, Andy and I pulled into SEA's back parking lot where a hangar-sized garage housed the van. The large doors to the facility were open, allowing the early afternoon's light to showcase the van. At first, we saw no one. Then we noticed some shoes sticking out from underneath the van. Dr. Wiechel was looking at the undercarriage. Stooping down next to the van, a young man with a clipboard was talking to Wiechel and taking notes. Andy approached the young man, extended his hand, and introduced himself and me. Within the next several weeks, Doug Morr, John Wiechel's assistant, also an engineer, would come to know every blemish, every imperfection on that van. Because Morr became the van's constant companion, he was the target of much of our attention. No doubt word of the van's release to SEA traveled through the facility. That afternoon we were to meet most of the team who would test various parts of the van.

After Dr. Wiechel emerged from under the van, he launched into itemizing his initial findings. He first confirmed that the ground effect pieces matched up to holes on the van. He explained, "The pieces match up to holes on the van. Also I noticed the way each of those pieces tore off. Do you see this hole?" pointing to a round hole in the van's wheel well. We nodded.

"This hole is pimpled out. That means that the screw came out with the piece. And that's consistent with the markings of the hole in the ground effect. And what is interesting is that the screw holding the other piece to the rocker panel was not pulled through and that is consistent from piece to van."

"How important is that?" I asked.

"About as important as the holes on the fiberglass pieces matching the van holes. The configurations of the holes have to match."

"Then does the pimpled hole say that some unusual force tore it out? And that the hole would not look like that unless some force was applied?" Andy said.

"Yes," Wiechel answered.

"That happened when Andrew's bike made contact and tore that hole out?" I asked. Briefly, I imagined that terrible collision with a speeding van.

"No question that since the fiberglass pieces are custom-drilled to each van, they have to match up. And since each of those pieces was torn out differently, van and pieces match up as well."

By this time, Doug Morr had climbed on a stepladder, placed next to the front of the passenger side, and looked intently at the roof line surrounding the windshield. Running his fingers over the line and down the post, near the passenger side window, he remarked, "You can feel the uneven surface. All this has been damaged and repaired using Bondo."

"What is Bondo?" I asked Doug.

"It's a bonding agent used to fill dents and cracks. It bonds to the metal and hardens. Then it's sanded down and painted."

Shortly after we arrived, Mark came through the garage entrance and talked briefly to Dr. Wiechel before he left for another hearing. Wiechel commented that when he had to be out of the office, Doug was in charge of the van and it was in excellent hands. Just by observing how carefully Doug plotted the dents on the roofline and post, we could tell that.

"Why don't we let you guys work, and we'll be back tomorrow. If that's okay with you," Andy said.

"Okay with me," Doug said. "I'll be right here."

For the next week and a half, Andy and I showed up at SEA's facility to track Doug Morr and Dr. Wiechel's examination of the van. When Dr. Wiechel was away on assignment, we entered the garage through the back to find Doug Morr with the van. On a table near the van lay the two ground effect pieces and near them was a black plastic bag containing our son's clothes. Against the table, Andrew's mangled bike awaited examination. When I entered the garage,

I made sure I didn't look in the direction of the bike. Almost involuntarily, by just catching a glimpse of it, I would suffer an instant wave of nausea.

Like any true scientist, Doug refused at first to be pinned down to any kind of opinion. When Andy would say, "What do you think?" he would chuckle and answer, "Right now, I'm gathering information."

Andy discovered that Doug had played sports in high school, and he looked like he worked out every day. Greeting us with a smile of perfect, white teeth, he showed a genuine interest in our questions. We watched as he painstakingly scrutinized the van, inch by inch, holding a pair of tweezers or a small brush. His instrument case reminded me of a manicure set.

As the days crept by, we observed the same close inspection of the area near the windshield and the right part of the roof, inside the van and out. Much like a surgeon removing diseased tissue, Doug meticulously dug out the Bondo to see exactly where the dents occurred.

When he finished, the upper right side of the van and across the roofline revealed the dents, right down to the scraped metal.

"Looks like something happened there," Andy said as we observed Doug scrape and dig. "Did you notice the same kind of damage on the driver's side?"

"No. We would expect to see damage on this side of the van and, as you can see, there was. And where we believe impact occurred, those areas have been damaged."

"It seems you've uncovered evidence that the passenger side of this van had been damaged?" I asked.

"Yes, and this damage is consistent with the accident. But what I'd like to find is a connection between the van and Andrew or the bike."

"Have you seen BCI's examination report?" asked Andy.

"Not yet," Doug answered.

"Dr. Kwek of BCI found the link from the van to Andrew. Paint chips in his clothes matched up to the van," Andy explained. "And, consistent with Glaval's information about installation, these ground effect pieces are from that van. One piece was on the bike and the other lay near Andrew."

"What I can say now is this van has had damage that's consistent with the kind of damage involved in your son's crash. You must remember that we're not looking at the van as it was at the time of the accident in 1998. It's been sanded, ground, repainted, parts replaced, repaired. There's no question that everything has been done to this van to obliterate its original appearance," Doug acknowledged.

We left SEA thinking that the examination was inching forward. We could understand why Doug was cautious. Even though SEA's reputation earned it the title of premier lab in Ohio, every report they issued served as a reflection of the skill of their expert professional staff and the organization's integrity.

With the confiscation of the Metro van, we put much of our lives outside of the investigation on hold. One evening as we sat down to a supper of canned soup and whatever we could find in the refrigerator, I wanted to talk about our next step. What we could do while SEA examined the van.

"We have to get to Glaval and look through those invoices to see if a ground effect had been ordered for that van." Andy said.

"You're talking like the guilty driver is a normal person taking his van in for repairs. If a van kills a person and the driver runs, I don't think it's likely there would be a paper trail. But Mark wants us to go back and look through the invoices anyway. Linda's making the arrangements with Vickie,"

"So, we have a damaged van. You can get rid of it but if you do that after the crash, then you become a suspect. Same with reporting it stolen. Or you can repair the van. Only I don't think you can repair the van here in this area. Too much publicity."

"Maybe the owner could find a shop that would do it without asking questions. A cash deal. You can always go out of town. Still you couldn't take the chance of getting parts from Glaval. You'd have to give your VIN, but you can order under another VIN, or go to a junk yard for the part."

"A van costs a lot of money. The best way is to have it repaired under the table and hope that police don't suspect it. In the case of this van, the police show up at the owner's door wanting to take pictures of it. Can you imagine how freaked out you would be? Only you find out that no one is suspicious. They take their pictures and then go away. But then the police come back with another request. To use it for Crime Stoppers. It could never end until the police catch on—at least this is what you might think. Only you don't know the FCSO. That's how I see it anyway."

If we had not had this conversation about the van's title history, I would not have zeroed in on the actual date of the van's sale to Spitzer. What we saw set off an alarm.

Mark subpoenaed Spitzer's records of the Sapp sale. The odometer document which James O. Sapp had to sign when he sold the 1993 Chevy Astro van was dated September 9, 1998, the day after the *Columbus Dispatch* Crime Stoppers' article and the televised interview on WSYX, featuring Sapp's van. The same van that McMannis spotted in his town two weeks after the crash and the same one we unknowingly stood in front of five weeks after Andrew was killed. That sale was not coincidental. I can only imagine Sapp's reaction to that media coverage.

After 9/11, I was listening to NPR discuss with experts how the U.S. was vulnerable to such an attack even with our superior intelligence-gathering tactics and electronics. One expert said that we didn't lack information; we lacked imagination. Allowing one's imagination to consider possibilities of how humans act in certain situations helps in problem solving. What might an owner of a van do after he kills a person with that van?

These conversations at the end of the day took their toll on me. By seven o'clock in the evening I was ready for bed. Here I was alive and my son was gone. I tried not to think about him, to visualize his coming up the walk or hearing his laugh. But I rarely succeeded.

After the first week or so, we didn't feel a pressing need to show up at the SEA garage every day. From our visits to the garage and listening to comments, we could put together the growing suspicion that this was *the* van. Both Wiechel and Morr kept making discoveries, meticulously erasing all doubt.

One afternoon the phone rang. Dr. Wiechel had finished for the day after spending it with his "favorite van" as he put it. He asked, "We've been looking at the windshield. Do you or Mark know how many windshields the van has had?"

"Mark talked to the original owner, and. he said that he replaced the windshield once when he had it in 1995. There were two windshields before Sapp owned it," I said.

"Well, we had an installer here from Safe Auto and by digging around the windshield, he said we have at least three, counting the one in there now."

"We know Andrew broke a windshield. You found windshield glass in his shirt. But can't Sapp say that a windshield must have been replaced after he sold it to Spitzer?"

"He could say that but the windshield in the van right now is the same windshield when Sapp sold it to Spitzer."

"How do you know that?" I asked, amazed.

"Because of the Etchguard logo in the lower corner of the windshield, I called the logo's eight hundred number. I found out that Etchguard sells theft protection. They etch a number in the windshield glass whether you buy protection or not. This number was in a batch of numbers sold to Spitzer in September 1998."

"The van was sold to Spitzer in September 1998," I said. "I'll have Linda call Spitzer to verify the number. You're saying that a number was etched in the windshield when Sapp sold it to Spitzer. And the number is still there. Which means the windshield was not replaced after Sapp sold to Spitzer. Right?"

"Right. There is evidence of at least three, verifiable windshields."

When I replayed the conversation for Andy, he said, "The sooner we talk to Sapp, the better."

"That's what Mark says. Do you think Sapp was the driver?"

"Everything points to him."

"Absolutely. I have no doubts," I agreed.

After some weeks under Dr. Wiechel's direction, Doug Morr's thorough examination of the van was ending. Mark set up a meeting with Wiechel, Morr, and Bob Carbonara, SEA's chemist, to hear what they had to say.

Pending SEA's findings, Mark took the opportunity to assess his role in our case. We had several months to go before our initial case against John Doe, the unknown driver, would come to a close. Andy and I visualized that some evening Mark and his wife, Patty, had a heart-to-heart talk about the growing responsibilities our case placed on him. On top of that, he wasn't much of a fan of the judicial climate in central Ohio. Trial lawyers were continually threatened with new laws that severely limited what they could do for their clients.

We certainly heard Mark as he proceeded to educate us about the kind of judge we potentially could encounter if we filed a civil case against the driver. Judges, like any other political candidate, raise money for campaigns and many of the political contributors are insurance companies. In addition, he counseled that we faced an uphill battle with the typical central Ohio jury.

After everyone settled down in comfortable chairs in SEA's conference room, Mark opened the discussion. What was SEA's verdict? Based on their assessment of the repair damage to the van, Doug Morr said that the van was involved. Morr and Wiechel lost little time in ticking off their findings that supported his statement.

In agreement with BCI, SEA engineers found that the holes in the two ground effect pieces matched up to the van. But SEA found something more. They discovered that each of the two pieces of the passenger ground effect was torn from the van differently. The structure of the holes in the van matched the holes in the pieces at the crash—exactly what engineers would expect to find if the pieces were torn from the Sapp/Metro van.

Still looking closely at the rocker panel, Dr. Wiechel discovered that at the exact spot where the second piece came off, the flange under the rocker panel was bent and that hole aligned with the bent flange.

Next, Wiechel and Morr ascertained that the Sapp/Metro van withstood the kind of damage engineers would expect in a front-end crash with a person on a bicycle, traveling on the right side of the road. The damage had been repaired, but their painstaking examination exposed the repaired damage. After days of digging, Doug Morr uncovered a head-sized dent, filled in with Bondo, on the right side roof near the rim of the windshield. The pillar, or post, separating the passenger front window and the windshield, had also been repaired with Bondo.

Like BCI, SEA found paint chips in Andrew's clothes and those chips matched paint that chemists removed from inside the door.

Lastly, Dr. Wiechel found evidence of at least three windshields. *None of them* could have been installed after the owner sold the van to Spitzer because the Etchguard number was engraved into the van's present windshield when Sapp sold it to Spitzer.

Before the meeting adjourned, Mark asked for clarification on several of the points Wiechel and Morr made. The pieces of the puzzle fit. And let's face it, had the vehicle that hit Andrew not been a customized van with random drillings of those fiberglass pieces, a resolution in this case would have been a miracle. Had Andrew's bike not torn each piece from the van differently, had paint chips not been found in his shirt, had Glaval not provided us with crucial information, had BCI scientists not examined the van, and had we made the decision not to spend the money to allow expert engineers to scrutinize it, we would have remained in ignorance. The van in the SEA garage hit and killed our son. Neither Andy nor I spoke. We allowed the importance of that moment to sink in.

Now we had to see what the owner, James O. Sapp, had to say about his van and its whereabouts on August 1, 1998. Since the FCSO hadn't talked to him, we had to. Mark would send out a subpoena to depose him. After hearing SEA's report, we doubted Sapp's innocence.

Mark was not the police. Sapp, now a person of interest, would not be sitting in an interrogation room under a light with deputies observing through a one-way glass window. No, the deposition would take place in an upscale conference room, tastefully furnished and comfortable with designer chairs under recessed lighting. Sapp might even be offered something to drink as the adjacent closet housed a coffee carafe, a stockpile of cold, bottled water and an array of sodas. The atmosphere and tone of the questioning, civilized and respectful, would decidedly be different from police interrogation.

33

SOME MONTHS AFTER ANDREW WAS killed, we began to take notice of hit-and-run fatalities, principally reported in the *Columbus Dispatch*, and on local and national television news. Several stories stand out, but none more so than a woman, while driving home from a Fort Worth, Texas bar, hit a pedestrian. The victim was impaled in the woman's windshield, but she kept on driving. She parked the car in her garage and entered her house, leaving the man to bleed to death. Friends helped to remove the man and bury him. Did she think that the man would fall off as she drove, thereby shedding her victim and escaping detection? Most hit-and-run drivers are severely impaired, drunken drivers and, in my opinion, impervious to the terrible consequences of drinking to excess and then getting behind the wheel of a multiple-ton weapon. But it is an intentional choice. The victim was impaled in the driver's windshield. Also, unthinkable in this story was the help of the woman's friends.

Ohio laws dealing with hit-and-run fatalities are lenient. If a driver runs and hides and a person dies, that driver, if caught, *could be charged* with a third-degree felony, but ten years ago, the charge was a misdemeanor. The law was changed because of a Columbus police officer's death.

A driver who kills a person and hides is guilty of murder. When Andrew was killed, if the driver sobered up and came forward the next day with his lawyer, the only penalty would have been a nominal fine—little more than a speeding ticket. If the authorities had caught the person, the punishment would have been no more than six months in jail and perhaps, a suspension of the driver's license. Drinking and driving in Ohio, was not a criminal traffic offense in 1998.

It is daunting to think that most people over the age of eighteen operate a dangerous machine, a car or truck. But because most drivers care about the consequences of what might happen to others and to themselves, they obey the laws. Still, this country suffers far too many deaths at the hands of impaired drivers. I'm not aware of any studies that have been conducted to determine whether severe penalties would affect drivers who kill and hide. But I do know that some Ohio legislators think that making it easy for hit-and-run drivers to come forward is better than imposing harsh penalties. These drivers have already made two bad decisions—one, to drive while impaired, by excessive drinking or otherwise, and two, to leave a crash after hitting a person.

It wasn't until a hit-and-run driver killed a Columbus police officer, Lieutenant Claypool, that an editorial in the *Columbus Dispatch* (Nov. 16, 2002) criticized the penalties imposed by Ohio law. "The maximum sentence allowed for a hit-skip charge is one year. The consequences of this gross negligence, the fact that someone was killed, are irrelevant."

Yes, the fact that someone is killed seemed irrelevant in Ohio law. The *Dispatch* editorial continued, "For anyone who might be guilty of any other crimes, such as drinking while driving or drug possession, the quirks of the law encourage a person who hits also to skip. If the skip is successful, such a driver may be able to hide the evidence…. Criminals care not a whit about whether they have the legal right to drive; they will drive anyway. Penalties for leaving the scene when there are injuries and deaths must be severe enough to make people want to stop. The law shouldn't be written in such a way that fleeing helps criminals cut their losses."

Because of Claypool's death and probably because of the impact of the strong editorial in the *Dispatch*, state lawmakers increased the penalty for fleeing the scene of an "accident" resulting in a death from a fifth-degree felony to a third-degree felony, a more serious crime. "A third-degree felony is punishable by one to five years in prison plus a fine of up to $10,000." (Leonard, *Columbus Dispatch*, Mar. 25, 2003, p.1C).

The law still has no teeth; if the crash caused a death, the third-degree felony is *punishable*—which means open to something possible, like a month or a year, for killing and hiding—and a fine of up to $10,000—from $0 to $10,000? As a state highway trooper said to us, "If you want to murder someone, use a car. You can call it an accident."

Generally, the authorities themselves harbor lax, perplexing attitudes toward hit-and-run drivers. I believe a common inclination of law enforcement is to think of a hit-skip as just an accident. And they couldn't be more wrong in that attitude. An accident is an unintentional or unexpected happening, of which the parties involved have no control, often unfortunate, resulting in injury, damage, loss, and so on. Drinking and driving spell disaster. The driver makes a choice. Leaving a scene after hitting a human being is an intentional act. Serious injuries and fatalities, arising from that intent, then become a serious criminal act—worthy of some of the same statutes and punishment as murder.

When forty-year-old Claypool was hit and killed in 2000 as he approached a vehicle involved in an accident in Columbus, and the driver fled, the Columbus Police Department immediately swung into action. Many people noticed the difference between this case with the Columbus Police Department and our case with the FCSO—even though the FCSO had plenty of evidence. CPD had next to nothing.

Without delay, the Columbus Police Department had Lt. Claypool's uniform sent to their labs for evidence examination. Within two days, the *Columbus Dispatch* reported (Narciso, May 2, 2000) "Officer Robert Perry (after his shift yesterday) distributed samples of the paint color that was found at the scene to each police substation." By contrast, the FCSO, as late as three years after our son's death had examined neither our son's clothes nor his bicycle for paint. When we read the *Dispatch* article, we felt not a shred of envy that the right thing was done in Lt. Claypool's crash. We prayed that the police would catch and hold responsible the coward who wrenched him from his family. Whatever it took to find the driver, we totally supported CPD's Herculean efforts and Herculean they were.

We understood that the investigation into Lt. Claypool's death would be unrelenting and had no doubt that the Columbus Police Department would get the offender. But does it not strike any sensible person that a hit-and-run victim's clothes, no matter the person's status, should be examined without delay for evidence?

The CPD in the Claypool case possessed almost no physical evidence—except paint chips – and some eyewitness accounts, which essentially contradicted each other. Newspaper accounts stated the CPD acted on tips. The person of interest was put under surveillance for months before the CPD moved in on him. By that time, the man had sold the green 1970 Buick Skylark—that killed Claypool—to a friend in Texas where the Buick was destroyed. Despite the paucity of evidence, the CPD worked all the angles to get the driver. They followed up on tips.

What prevented the Franklin County Sheriff from paying a visit to the owner of the 1993 white van with the BCI red flags, three years after our son's death? The man was never approached by the FCSO.

In many of conversations Andy and I couldn't help interjecting the kind of evidence we had in our case into the Claypool case. What if the CPD had the ground effect pieces and discovered that the Glaval Corporation manufactured and custom-installed them. In addition, Glaval advised that if holes on a van the FCSO had confiscated, matched up to the fiberglass pieces, they had the responsible van. Then the final piece: the Glaval Corporation had a listing of the VINs of vans with that part sold to Ohio dealerships? How long would it have taken the CPD to solve this case? In our opinion, no more than two days.

After the Claypool fatality, The *Columbus Dispatch* did a story on four other hit-skip fatalities, which have gone unsolved. Ours was not included. I have no idea how many hit-and-run fatalities remain unsolved under the FCSO's jurisdiction. Do they even keep records—records of any kind?

Because hit-skip crashes leave behind such little evidence, they are among the most difficult to solve. If we can call our son's crash lucky in any way, it is because matchless, distinctive evidence was found at the crash. Who can explain why the FCSO ignored their own forensic experts?

Despite the numbers of hit-and-run fatalities, this crime fails to resonate with the public, much like drunk driving twenty years ago. While I was talking to an acquaintance about our case and the lack of public interest, he said, "It's not a very common crime." Surprised by his response, I said, "Oh, but it is. Since Andrew's death, we have collected hundreds of articles involving hit/skip deaths, many local." SafeDriving's web site asserts that a person is killed every 59 minutes in a hit-and-run crash in the U.S. Drunk driving, a common occurrence, and hit/skip deaths are interconnected per Tilde Bricker, Director of the Columbus Chapter of MADD.

On the day, Andy and I left SEA after hearing Dr. Wiechel and Doug Morr's verdict about the Sapp van, we asked Mark, "What's the next step?" Certainly, Mark had known if John Wiechel made a judgment call, that call was indisputable. His reputation was above reproach.

Talking briefly with Mark in SEA's parking lot, we decided to meet the next day. He advised that Linda, our investigator, should once again call the original van's owner, Ed Winn, to ask specifically if Winn had ever replaced the ground effects. Then, as Mark explained to us, we would need to depose every auto body shop and repair garage or dealer that ever touched that van before the sale to Sapp—accurate, documented information of any damage and repair.

"In the meantime," Mark announced, "we need to talk to Sapp and see what he has to say."

"How soon can you do that?" Andy asked.

"Let's get him in the end of August. And please start making note of questions."

Before we parted, Mark pointed out that Linda should call Glaval. We needed to check invoices for ground effect orders in August 1998.

Since Linda had forged a strong relationship with Vickie, she could not have been a stronger ally. Vickie, having an adult son, no doubt, could relate to our situation.

After we talked to Linda, Andy asked, "What are we expecting to find? The owner of the van wouldn't be that dumb to order a replacement part from Glaval."

"Like Mark said, getting the names of anybody who ordered that part around the time of the crash might give us valuable information."

Certainly, some garage would do a repair for cash and ask no questions. But with Vickie's help, we dared to hope that we might be able to track down the repair shop.

34

EVERY MORNING FOR THE PAST ten years I awakened to "Andrew's dead." This wasn't a bad dream. As much as I wanted to deny it, each day began with a dose of reality. Its potency could be diminished for minutes by going over a bank statement, by making that long overdue dental appointment, by sorting clothes for washing, by shopping for groceries—all the ordinary duties to keep our lives orderly. Still, they were done out of habit, automatically. The pot of homemade spaghetti sauce slowly simmering all afternoon, filling the house with the smells of oregano and garlic, drew no more interest than a slice of white bread and margarine. It was just there. Both Andy and I were thinner than we had ever been.

The only real relief came from time spent with Andrew's friends, our friends from The Compassionate Friends, and our daughter and son-in-law. That summer we spent the Fourth of July holiday with Betsey and Scott at their house on Lake Michigan. Since the Fourth of July 1998 was the last time all of us had vacationed together with Andrew at the Homestead, also on Lake Michigan, Betsey knew that I was especially sensitive to the fun and hoopla celebrating the Fourth. The more fun and wonderful the memory, the more I avoided it. I was becoming increasingly aware of the "Before Andrew" and "After Andrew" perception that parents in The Compassionate Friends spoke about when mentioning their own children.

At those times when we were at the lake, she and I would walk down to the beach and without saying much, find a bench, and sit there, with Betsey's arms wrapped around me, looking out at the horizon and listening to the waves as they splashed the shoreline. We would stay until sunset. At one time the shades of pink, pale orange and blue surrounding the sun as evening came would make my heart leap up. At one time, I had known what Wordsworth felt when he saw a rainbow. Joan, a close friend who had lost her son, Luke, observed that one evening she looked to the sky and thought the various colors were beautiful, but she couldn't feel the beauty.

On some of those summer evenings, Betsey would request that I cook some dish that she especially liked and that helped to alleviate my grief. Scott, working late on Friday, usually rode his Ducati from the city to Michigan Saturday morning and would arrive about lunchtime. Feeding him, a young guy with an appetite, was therapy.

In preparation for our arrival at the lake, our daughter cut pink, white and blue hydrangeas from her yard and filled vases throughout the house. She set the table on the sun porch and we ate by candlelight. Evenings we'd walk to town to hear an outdoor concert. All with an effort to run from longing.

We were nearing the end of July. Linda, our PI, had planned a vacation as her boys would be returning to school, and Mark and Patty's children, the youngest of college age, were due to go back to school on the East coast. August presented the last opportunity to spend some time away from home before everyone got back to business in the fall.

After our conference with Mark about our next step, we met with Linda to discuss the items Mark wanted covered. Linda was to call the original owner of the van, Edgar Winn, to get an accident history, if any, of the van. She was also to contact Vickie Stout at Glaval about records for auto parts ordered in 1998.

Days later in talking to Vickie, Linda learned that the only way Vickie could verify an order for parts was through a check of the vehicle's identification number (VIN) or the name of the body shop, garage, or dealership ordering the part. Linda had the Sapp VIN but no other information. Dictating those to Vickie, Linda learned that nothing under that VIN surfaced in August. Then Vickie, not to be deterred, told Linda that orders for parts might be cross-checked, by searching through invoices.

In examining vehicle records, we knew that Edgar Winn had nothing to do with Andrew's death. He had sold the van to a Dayton dealership in 1996, two years before Andrew was killed. To get a more complete picture, Linda called him. She described his tone as curt and annoyed by her questions. As she explained more about the reason for her calls, he warmed up. Winn said that the 1993 van, which he owned from 1993 to June 1996, had been involved in two accidents, one when the van tipped over on the driver's side and the other, when his daughter had a "small accident" on the right front passenger side. The second accident, involving the passenger side, piqued our interest. Winn hadn't saved the paper work of those two accidents, but said that the dealer, Voss Chevrolet in Dayton, had done the repair work.

Immediately, Mark Adams directed his attention to the accident involving the right front passenger side of the Sapp van, and whether the passenger ground effect had been affected. Voss Chevrolet's repair history and paperwork associated with that accident became an item of interest, to say the least.

When Mr. Winn sold his van, he took it to Frank Z. Chevrolet, also in Dayton. And it was from Frank Z., that Sapp bought the Winn van in 1996.

Linda's next call to Voss Chevrolet put her in touch with Pat Kowalski, manager.

Since Voss handled the repair of Winn's two accidents, one in 1995, the other in 1996, they had essential information about the damage to the van. Recognizing the importance of those repair records, especially in the 1995 passenger side small accident, Mark subpoenaed Voss's records. A study of those records, in addition to Pat Kowalski's testimony, revealed that Voss had not replaced the passenger side ground effect.

Mark had thoroughly laid the groundwork for the Sapp deposition. Armed with information Linda collected as well as the BCI and SEA reports, Mark sent out the deposition notice. We had sufficient material relevant to Sapp's van. From the date of the notice to the date of the deposition, Andy and I crossed each day off the calendar—the anticipation was much like those held captive awaiting news of their release.

35

FOUR YEARS AFTER OUR SON'S death, Mark prepared to take the deposition of the man who, at the time of Andrew's death, owned the van confiscated from Metro Chevrolet, examined by Dr. Kwek of BCI and determined by SEA's engineers and scientists to have killed Andrew. Since finding the van, we had sought the help of professionals and experts to eliminate the van. It couldn't be done. Science pointed to it. Facts pointed to it. This was *the* van. Now we had to talk to James O. Sapp, owner.

The FCSO, having more than a year to contact the owner after the BCI report, had failed to communicate with Sapp or follow-up on that report. Sergeant Staggs own words can verify that statement as reported in the *Dispatch* a year after BCI's report that he didn't have enough to waste time out of Sapp's day. Too thoughtless to believe in science or too loyal to oppose a buddy. Based on scientific fact, James O. Sapp should have been criminally investigated as the owner of the van that killed Andrew. Our only recourse was through the civil courts. Under the civil suit, Mark filed in 1999 against "John Doe, the Unknown Driver," we had subpoena power to depose James O. Sapp and others.

James Sapp was notified to appear at Mark's office on August 28, 2002. Mark asked Sapp to bring with him all records dealing with his ownership of the Glaval 1993 Chevy van. I tried to imagine the look on his face when he opened the deposition notice. It must have been a shock—especially since he had sold his van four years earlier—the day *after* the Crime Stopper television interview aired, showing our family standing near his van and the deputy from the Sheriff's Office using it to demonstrate how the fiberglass pieces fit. He owned *the* van August 1, 1998. He was the driver or knew the whereabouts of the van on that day. Undoubtedly, he had to think about how to handle this summons. I don't believe that he had any idea at all about the amount of information we had amassed about him and his van—some of it public record, some through subpoena of documents as well as the BCI and SEA reports. To go forward – to talk to Sapp—we could have no doubts about the van.

The day before Sapp was scheduled to give his testimony, Mark sent us an email. Apparently, Sapp had called him. The gist of Mark's conversation dealt with Sapp's alleged confusion about the reason for the deposition. Certainly, a call about an upcoming deposition could happen simply because Sapp allowed the police the use of his van on several different occasions to publicize the kind of van that killed Andrew. Sapp's association to us publicly was through the police. What happened out of the public eye was yet to be seen, but on the surface, at least, he assisted the police in allowing the use of his van in a vehicular homicide—a serious matter. McMannis had talked to Sapp several times to arrange the use of his van. It wasn't as though an inquiry materialized unexpectedly. Ironically, much happened with that van in 1998. An astounding and memorable set of circumstances.

Immediately, I left the house to find Andy to get his reaction to Mark's email. In the afternoon, if we were home, he could be deep in the woods cutting down a hollow tree, and I welcomed an excuse to go outside, to take a break from the computer.

"Andy," I yelled, while surveying the woods. Following the sound of the saw, I caught sight of his red T-shirt. As soon as he saw me, he cut the motor. "We just got an email from Mark. It's about the deposition tomorrow. Sapp called Mark and wanted to know what this was all about."

"He was notified weeks ago and he's just now calling?" Andy asked.

"And the interesting thing is he told Mark that State Farm, his insurance company, called him asking about the subpoena."

"Mark didn't say anything to us about State Farm."

"Mark told him that he represented us and he was checking up on some local Glaval vans and his was one of them. He made no mention of the BCI and SEA reports for fear of scaring him away. He doesn't know that we have his van. Oh, and Mark said Sapp thought the subpoena was a mistake."

"A mistake? A Sheriff's deputy came to his house and took pictures and videotaped his van for Crime Stoppers. We could be asking about that."

"That's what I thought. How many people named Sapp with a Glaval van did the police approach? In a hit-and-run death?"

"So he said nothing about the police being at his house?"

"Apparently not. And get this. Mark said that Sapp asked to postpone the deposition until one o'clock. He had a noon meeting with some people from the church."

"I don't know about you, but the church card always plays well with me," Andy said, amused.

"So what if the van was being repaired somewhere or someone else used it that day?"

"Then this guy has to know where it was. Either it was in his possession or it wasn't. And if it was in his possession and not some place else, we're probably looking at Andrew's killer."

"We know that Deputy McMannis saw the van about two weeks after the crash and he saw no damage."

"Yeah, which explains why he wasn't suspicious," he said, grabbing his saw to finish cutting a log.

Making my way back to the house, I understood that ignoring the subpoena would put Sapp under a cloud of suspicion. A subpoena is a court summons compelling a witness to show up at a certain time and place to give testimony. Then again, many people know that the long arm of the law oftentimes belongs to a body with no teeth.

I was puzzled. Mark had not said anything to us about notifying State Farm. We saw the subpoena and no copy was forwarded to anyone else. Who had called State Farm and why? Someone who thought that he might need legal representation? Like the owner who thought he could be in trouble? In a case like ours, a hit-and-run fatality, the offender's insurance company bears the legal expenses.

Since BCI's report and SEA's affirmation that Sapp's white 1993 Chevy van was involved in Andrew's death, my anxiety increased daily about Sapp and what he had to say. At Mark's direction, Andy and I had prepared some twenty questions or so based on Linda's research and mine, but we relied on Mark to search out answers to those crucial questions about the van. Science confirmed that Sapp's van killed Andrew, and Sapp was the owner at the time of the crash. But was the van in or out of his possession on August 1, 1998?

Requesting that we arrive a half-hour before Sapp's scheduled deposition, Mark read over our list of questions and advised that Patty, his wife, would be sitting in on the deposition. He trusted her judgment explicitly. No one had the power to persuade Mark the way Patty could. Since Sapp was an unknown to all of us, the more people observing his testimony, the better. Hearing the words of someone's testimony is not the entire story; you should see how the witness acts.

Shortly after one o'clock on August 28, 2002, we waited for James Sapp to show. The court reporter sat at the head of the table with Patty at the opposite end. Mark sat to the reporter's right; I sat next to Mark and then, Andy. When

Sapp appeared in the doorway, Mark greeted him, made the introductions, and ushered him to a chair on the reporter's left, opposite Mark, Andy, and me.

Almost on cue, Sapp apologized for being a few minutes late as he had just come from a lunch with church members. Remembering the conversation the previous day in the woods, I thought "manipulation"—no need to mention church.

The court reporter recognized Sapp as a witness whose deposition she had taken some months earlier involving a grievance by a fellow employee. I kicked Andy under the table to say, "So he knows what a deposition is."

From the minute he walked into the room his manner was jolly—yes, jovial. Somewhat inappropriate. He talked and laughed easily with the court reporter when he arrived, but his later attempts at being funny after he knew the seriousness of the deposition struck me as bizarre. During Sapp's deposition Mark asked him if he fished and Sapp answered, "If the Lord wanted me to fish, he'd have gave me a hook." No one laughed.

In his fifties but looking older because of his gray-white hair, and his short, roly-poly stature, Sapp's appearance resembled a grandpa—just an ordinary aging man. Not the kind of face I would have picked out as a suspect in a line-up.

In almost every book I had read about depositions, from the witness's point of view, the first rule is tell the truth. Of course, tell the truth. You have taken an oath. If you mugged an old lady, admit to it; if you molested the kid down the street, admit to it; if you robbed a bank, admit to it; if you hit a bicyclist and ran, admit to it. Just admit to the offense, no need to elaborate. Who writes these books anyway? If you expect a confession, a damning admission, forget about it.

My thought was if someone in a car hits and kills a person, runs and hides, the chances are he's going to lie about doing it if he's caught. Perpetrators don't confess.

The testimony of a witness, potentially the defendant in a civil suit, suspected of direct culpability in another's death, is something like that of a wayward spouse—one who is thought to be cheating. The wronged spouse should take special notice of the other spouse's actions and words. Are answers to questions brusque? Or excessively explanatory, confusing, and contradictory? An errant spouse, like a potentially guilty witness, will try to guess what the wronged spouse knows. His or her answers will depend on that information, and what the accused spouse stands to lose if he or she is found out.

The point of this deposition focused on Sapp's 1993 white Chevy, Glaval converted Astro van. Mark had to establish Sapp's ownership, August 1, 1998, even though all the official documents supported that. He had to establish where the van was August 1, 1998, and who had access to it. He had to establish who all the drivers had been when Sapp owned the van.

Mark had to establish time and place of any accidents Sapp may have had and where Sapp took his van for repair. Lastly, he had to establish Sapp's whereabouts on August 1, 1998. For more than half of the deposition, the questioning sounded exploratory—just a gathering of information. Up to that point Sapp could not have detected in Mark's tone what we knew about his van.

If Sapp had allowed many people to drive his van and couldn't remember them all, we were going to be in trouble. And if the van had been involved in accidents, possibly repaired by him or garages, in several locations, we were going to be in trouble. Locating people and then deposing them could be a logistical and expensive problem. But that wasn't the case at all. It was exactly the opposite.

Mark asked both questions every which way to make certain that the answers were clear and consistent. Directly and indirectly, Sapp testified who the drivers were.

Q.   In 1998, who besides yourself would have driven the van?

A.   Oh, wow, just me and my wife. [In 1998, the wife was his girlfriend.]

Q.   Okay.

A.   And there wouldn't have been hardly any occasions she had driven it because she had her SUV.

Q.   So there would be you or her… Did you ever let any friends drive it?

A.   No, I don't—no, I don't think I ever let it out of my sight except, you know, unless she took it to the store or something.

Q.   Okay…but if you can, just take a minute and think whether or not anyone else…

A.   Would have ever driven it?

Q.   —could have driven it, any relative, any friends take a trip in it, anything along those lines?

A.   Huh-uh.

Q.   No one else?

A.   I don't think so, no. As much as I liked that van, I'd pretty well remember if I loaned it to somebody for something.

Q.   Okay. And you don't recall ever loaning it to anybody?

A.   No.

The possibilities that Sapp's van had been in a repair shop in August or loaned to someone that weekend in August disappeared with Sapp's testimony. He testified that the van had never been out of his sight. Logically then, that put him directly in the cross hairs as the driver. Circumstantial evidence. Obviously, he was unaware of the extensive examination his 1993 van had undergone.

Mark revisited the issue of other drivers later in the deposition, but Sapp's answer remained the same. Mark's questions and Sapp's answers essentially locked him into being the driver. His girlfriend, who became his fifth wife *after the crash*, had just bought and moved into her own home in June, 1998. On August 1, 1998, she was not his wife, had a job, had just purchased her own house and owned her own vehicle.

Sapp had to admit to being the primary driver because no one else ever drove his van. Then because his van had never been damaged before the crash with Andrew—he would have to produce records—he had to claim that the van was never damaged. No crash. No damage. Because he couldn't have imagined that his van had painstakingly been examined by SEA's engineers and scientists who identified it as the guilty van, Sapp could comfortably admit to being the lone driver. And he knew that by the time the FCSO saw the van, it had been repaired, and the passage of time proved the FCSO hadn't been suspicious. Pieces of the passenger side ground effect of the van had been left at the crash site. So what? I would stake my life on the fact that Sapp did not know about the random drilling of the ground effects. It just so happened that the van's wheel well and rocker panel revealed another secret he didn't know—each ground effect piece was torn out differently from the van's wheel well and rocker panel and the configuration of the holes in the rocker panel matched the configuration of the ground effect pieces. Also,

I strongly believe, that Sapp thought that Mark was grasping for answers, fishing—that we knew nothing.

Mark asked:

Q. How about servicing, repair work, that type of thing, where would you typically take it?

A. Let's see. I don't think I ever had anything go wrong with it, and I have no, you know, like set mechanic or whatever, you know, someone that you trust with your vehicle or whatever.

Q. Can you think back and tell me if you've ever taken it to a friend's house for repair work or somebody who was a mechanic, more mechanical than yourself.

A. No. I still want to say no because there was never anything wrong with it.

Q. Have you had any accidents at all since you've been in Columbus?

A. No.

Q. And it's never been to any body shop in Dayton?

A. No. It's never been to any body shop anywhere.

Q. And...that's also true here in the Columbus area, right?

A. Right.

Q. I'm just trying to jog your memory. Repair work or anything down there? [referring to Kentucky]

A. That's what makes it so easy to answer that question because it's never once—it's never been out of my sight...

Q. Have you ever had the windshield replaced...?

A. No... No, not on the—no, not on the van.

As Mark's questioning related more to the crash, I looked often at Sapp. At no time during that deposition did I see him look at Andy or me, or even glance around, however briefly. His eyes fixed on Mark and they stayed there. It seemed odd that he never took his eyes off Mark.

On the one hand, we had Sapp, who owned a Glaval van on the day Andrew was killed, denying that his van was ever in an accident, damaged and repaired. On the other hand, we had custom-installed parts and paint chips from a Glaval van that matched up to his van. Plus, the Sapp van had demonstrated the kind of repaired damage on the right front passenger side that would have occurred in Andrew's crash.

We had no trouble deciding whom to believe: Sapp, the owner of the van, who denied culpability or Glaval's installation engineers, SEA's engineers, and scientists and BCI's Dr. Kwek whose examination of the evidence pointed to Sapp's van. We also had to consider that Sapp lived within a ten-mile radius of the crash site. His was a local van. No one ever explained to us that it wouldn't have mattered who drove the Sapp van and killed Andrew in a civil case. State Farm insured the van and State Farm had to pay. The owner could walk away without so much as spending a penny or a day in jail. For Andy and me, it mattered.

36

ONE DAY AS I WAS at the library preparing for a meeting with a person who had called with a tip, I picked up Stan Walters' book, *The Truth about Lying,* and several other books that studied the words and behavior of people who lied in serious matters. The ten-thousand-dollar reward signs we had posted around various communities had brought in a number of calls, and I was looking for ways to weed out quickly those who would fabricate stories for money. Walters as well as Pamela Meyer, a Harvard MBA graduate, in her book, *Lie Spotting,* cautioned that a single suspicious behavior, verbal or nonverbal, is insufficient evidence of deceit.

Both discussed the issue of "clusters." Walters defined a cluster as "multiple verbal or nonverbal responses, occurring at one moment when discussing a single issue, indicating a strong possibility of deception." The repetition of a phrase indicates not only deception, but also identifies a matter or problem of concern to the person using the cluster.

A repetition of "Would I lie to you?" is an example of a cluster response that a person might use to deceive another. Some verbal clusters are more obviously deceitful than others. Walters listed other examples, "Trust me," "Why would I lie?" or "I have no reason to" (p.139).

Some months after reading about clusters or certain phrase repetitions to deceive, the repetition of one phrase when Sapp testified about the investigation *leaped* off the page. I was sure that Walters had put that phrase on his list. Checking, there it was: "*I have no reason to.*" Sapp's variation of "didn't have any reason to" was used four times in one area of questioning. The problem the phrase identified? The first time the FCSO looked at his van. This is a textbook cluster, I thought.

Q.   So a deputy came out and looked at this van?

A.   Yeah.

Q.   And you don't remember who that was?

A.   No. *I didn't have any reason to.*

Q.   Were you there when he looked at the van?

A.   Yeah, I was there.

Q.   How did he look at it?

A.   He looked at the passenger side, looked at the front, kind of
      the front passenger part. And he told me why… And he said
      they were looking for a van similar to, you know, similar in
      year and—an Astro van similar in color to mine… And I said,
      there it is…he looked and he said, well, there's no damage to
      yours. I said, *no, sir, was there supposed to be?*

Q.   Did he take any part of your van apart?

A.   No. *I don't guess there was any reason to.* It seemed like he
      was talking about the spoiler…he looked underneath…and
      said…it's not broke or anything, it's not been replaced…I
      told him…there's never been anything replaced on it.

Q.   Other than speaking to the deputy that day, have you ever
      talked to anybody from the Franklin County sheriff's office
      since that day?

A.   No. *Never had any reason to.*

Q.   Did you understand that he (the deputy) was going to
      videotape your van?

A.   No, I don't think so.

Q.   Are you aware that he videotaped your van?

A.   No, I don't think so. And he may have even told me. I mean, I
      wasn't worried about it.

Q.   All right.

A.   And I was trying to remember if the deputy told me…they
      were going to take the picture and say, you know, is it okay
      if we use the van. You know, if somebody was to ask me that
      and it was to help somebody catch somebody, why wouldn't
      I say yes? I wouldn't have said anything about it. *There
      wouldn't be any reason to say anything about it.*

This area of questioning served as one example of the many times Sapp waffled. First, he said that he didn't understand that the deputy was going to videotape his van, but then testified that he may have been told. More than his mind changing, upon rereading the deposition, I was thunderstruck that Sapp, despite only vague, incorrect and no recollection responses, somehow remembered and singled out detail about "the spoiler"—a term Deputy McMannis used, along with the term, "ponyboard," both referring to the fiberglass ground effect. Looking at the above testimony, no mention at this point in the deposition was made of the fiberglass pieces, and yet Sapp felt compelled to mention it: *"it's not broke or anything, it's not been replaced"*—two of the most important details about the ground effect—it was broken and had to have been replaced.

Other parts of the van had also been damaged—the post, the windshield, etc., but Sapp chose to single out the ground effect. First, we contend that by the time McMannis saw the Sapp van, it had been repaired, and second, unless McMannis was packing a screwdriver and took that ground effect piece off, only someone with x-ray vision could tell if it had been replaced. By making that specific comment, Sapp believed he could divert suspicion away from those pieces left at the crash site. Instead, he clearly introduced that item in his deposition.

To cite here the countless numbers of inconsistencies, ambiguities, lapses and contradictions in Sapp's deposition would be overkill.

Mark continued with questions exploring McMannis' visit to Sapp's house.

> Q.   I wanted to go back to when the sheriff's deputy was looking at your vehicle. You have no memory of him videotaping it?
>
> A.   I don't—I don't remember if he told me he was going to or not.

Mark's next question about where the videotaping took place suggested to Sapp that the location was at his house and not at his girlfriend's house—the actual site. Suddenly Sapp remembered emphatically where the videotaping took place—at his house, a wrong answer. If he didn't remember the videotaping, how would he remember where it took place.

> Q.   And in terms of the location, you think that [the videotaping] was done at your home on R-?
>
> A.   Yes, sir, because I remember him [deputy] pulling up—I'm almost sure he pulled straight down the street because he'd have to have been in the circle, and I think he was just straight in.

One minute Sapp testified that he didn't remember the videotaping and in the next, when a location was suggested, he remembered by what manner the deputy pulled up to park on his street. Only his street was as straight as an arrow. His girlfriend's house was located on a cul-de-sac, a circle. Why did he go with the wrong location Mark suggested? Because it was suspicious that he had moved out of his house, days after the crash?

Now (2002), Mark asked Sapp what he remembered about his interaction with the police and the accident. Sapp testified that he heard about it on the news, but he couldn't remember which accident it was. This was the same person who allowed the police to photograph his van. The more he talked, the more he claimed he didn't remember. Most of us remember unusual, significant events that involve us. Mark explored:

> Q.   Do you remember this accident at all, hearing anything about it before the deputy came to see you?
>
> A.   The news…when he mentioned it, it triggered right away it was like, oh, it was the one, it was the thing we'd heard on the news.
>
> Q.   And you mean when the deputy came to talk to you about it?
>
> A.   Yeah. When he—you know, when he said we are investigating because of the accident, and I said, oh, is that the one that was—that you heard—you know, that I heard about on the news. And so I said, you know, they didn't catch that person because I remember it being a hit-and-run type thing. And then knowing I had to come and see you, then I got to thinking about it and I couldn't remember if this was—as sad as it is, *I couldn't remember* if this was the accident—if this was the accident where the two little boys had been riding together or something. But I didn't remember which one was which, because I think this was an accident that happened again sometime—but I always get—you know, you hear these things and you think about them and you think, did this one—was this one that one or is it the same one. I don't remember that one, though.

Listening to that last response especially, I had a hard time making sense of it. When a witness is rattled, the response is often incoherent and convoluted. The videotaping of his van for Crime Stoppers became a sensitive topic?

Knowing answers to questions allows the attorney to test the witness's truthfulness, to confirm from the witness's own testimony what the attorney already knows, or to get additional information. When Mark asked questions about the history of the van under Sapp's ownership, Sapp insisted that he sold the van in 1999—and not five weeks after the crash in 1998.

At first, he said that he didn't remember. But he couldn't leave it at that. He kept volunteering detail to convince us that he sold it in 1999, a year later than he actually did. He had to lead us away from the actual date, but we knew the answers to these questions. We had a complete history of the van, and Mark had all the documents from Spitzer Dodge in front of him. Sapp sold the van on *September 9, 1998.* Trying mightily to direct our attention away from 1998, Sapp settled on 1999. He hadn't trusted us to do our homework.

Before the deposition, most of what we already knew about Sapp and his girlfriend was of public record. What we didn't know was that his then girlfriend and he had taken a trip to Las Vegas. He claimed that he took this trip in 1999 and used this date to verify the time he traded in his van. But we knew he sold the van in 1998. Was he equivocating on the Las Vegas trip, too? The two events seemed tied together.

For anything that can be checked factually, the witness ought to give a straight answer. Of course, that's the right way to answer under oath. Mark asked Sapp about his use of credit cards during the Las Vegas trip. Once again, Sapp's answer didn't match the evidence.

Q.   You had no credit cards in '98 at all?

A.   No. I got in trouble like that once and said never again.

In our civil suit against Sapp, the attorney for State Farm, Sapp's auto insurance company, provided Mark with a statement from one of Sapp's credit cards, which he used in Las Vegas.

When Mark announced a break so that Sapp could call his present wife to get dates about the trip and to ask her maiden name (after almost four years of marriage), Sapp commented that it was the first time he had ever been on an airplane and that they had to stay at three different hotels. Sapp's wife had reported that they left August 7, 1998, almost a week after Andrew was killed, not 1999. She provided the date almost immediately. Four years hence, she remembered the exact date without having to check a calendar or records? I'm positive that both Sapp and wife could not have imagined what we knew.

Two weeks into August when Sapp returned home from Vegas, Deputy McMannis, back on the job after days in training, spotted Sapp's van. McMannis approached Sapp to photograph his Glaval van for FCSO flyers. Abruptly, within days after that, Sapp moved out of his own house and into his girlfriend's house. Then the day after the Crime Stoppers videotaping, he sold his van. James Sapp had a very busy August and September in 1998.

Sapp testified that he didn't remember being told by the police that his van would be photographed and videotaped, that he didn't remember where that took place, but then remembered after Mark suggested it was R-Avenue but it wasn't. Sapp couldn't say he remembered very much about this accident as he confused it with another one involving children. He didn't remember when he traded in his van and then settled on 1999. It was 1998. He testified that he and his girlfriend took a trip to Las Vegas "ten months after they were married." Sapp was batting zero in verifiable facts at this point. The Vegas trip took place the first week in August 1998, days after Andrew was killed, and *before* Sapp and his girlfriend were married in October.

As the questioning was winding down and before Mark advised Sapp about SEA's assessment of his 1993 van, Mark asked him once again if he could remember his fifth and present wife's maiden name. Mark had asked this earlier in the deposition after Sapp mentioned that the only place he would go on the weekends would be to Dayton to visit his in-laws, or to Kentucky where he still had family, or stay home. This was a homebody. This was a person who said his weekends were spent with family.

Since Andrew was killed on a weekend, Mark wanted to get an idea of where Sapp might go. When Sapp wouldn't come up with his fifth wife's maiden name after four years of marriage, Mark looked at him and questioned: "You go to Dayton to visit your in-laws on the weekends but you don't know their last name?" Then, Sapp's story changed. Again. Mark asked, "When's the last time you saw them?" Sapp replied, "Oh, gee, four months, five months…It's been a while. We only see them a couple times a year."

For one response, the answer is "a couple times a year" to explain why he doesn't remember their names, but when asked the question as to how he might spend his weekends, Sapp answered, "Visiting his in-laws in Dayton," as to his possible whereabouts August 1, 1998. He felt compelled to equivocate. An innocent person could have come up with some honest answers as to where he might go on a Saturday evening.

Nearing the end of the deposition, Mark's questioning built the scaffolding to inform Sapp that the van he owned had been in the possession of a forensic engineering lab in Worthington.

> Q.   That van has at least nine or ten different types of damage that suggests that it's the van that's involved in this accident. And so I wanted to ask you and see if any of this either helps jog your memory in any way or helps explain this in any way.
>
> Would you have any explanation for why the broken running board pieces which we've already established are unique to the van by virtue of how they are attached to the van—there's one predrilled hole; all the other holes are custom drilled by whoever put it on—why those two broken running board pieces would have holes that fit the van that you owned in 1998? Do you have any explanation for that?
>
> A.   No.
>
> Q.   Okay. You indicated in testimony that this van that you've— that you owned at the time was in excellent shape and had no problems. We found damage to that van consistent with the type of damage that would be caused by—in exactly the right places where this bike was hit, and there's a paint match between the two. There's dents and damage located exactly where one would expect to find dents and damage when a body is thrown up into the windshield and hitting the roof. Do you have any explanation for why your van would meet all of those coincidences of places that are damaged, of paint transfer, of—
>
> A.   No, because –
>
> Q.   —broken running boards that meet—
>
> A.   Like I said, that was—it was—there was never any damage to my vehicle, to the van, you know, my vehicle meaning the van at that time. I mean, the time that I owned it—*my contacts got dry.* [He offered an explanation as to why his eyes started to rapidly blink.]

When Mark was satisfied that Sapp was in possession of the van at the time of the crash, he leaned across the table and looked directly at Sapp. Speaking in a measured monotone, he told Sapp that evidence found at the crash—the ground effect pieces or running board, custom drilled—had holes that fit his van. And in addition, he told Sapp about the other nine different types of damage, consistent with this crash that his van sustained.

Mark now had all the information. It didn't matter how many times Sapp backtracked, changed his mind, or didn't remember. Mark was in the catbird seat—he had the facts from Glaval, SEA, and BCI. In addition, after examining the van, Jack Holland, veteran crash reconstructionist, retired from the State Highway Patrol, said we had "probable cause." An enormous boost to our case against Sapp would come about six months after Sapp's deposition when Judge Lisa Sadler ruled that the facts and science supported our case and we could go forward civilly. This was the van. Even Sergeant Staggs said to Mark on the day SEA took the van, "This is as good as it gets."

But the authorities were not putting any pressure on Sapp. Mark was a lawyer, not a policeman. The questioning didn't take place in an interrogation room with the evidence sitting on the table. No good cop/bad cop drama. Still, the words Sapp used in denying knowledge and the accompanying body language would no doubt yield some clues in an analysis of his testimony. To file a civil suit against James Sapp we had to be absolutely certain of the information we collected. (See map of crash site on Central College Road to James O. Sapp's house on Rugosa, Reynoldsburg.)

It took a lot to convince us. BCI's report should have been enough. *It was enough* but we wanted corroboration. SEA had no personal stake. No civil suit had yet been filed against Sapp. And would not have been had the FCSO followed through on the BCI report. The van was subjected to a rigorous inspection and the conclusions weren't based on conjecture or speculation.

Mark emailed us several weeks after he received the official transcripts of Sapp's deposition. Days later we replied to his email message: Yes, file a civil suit against James O. Sapp. State Farm's attorneys, a firm that enjoyed a rough reputation according to some attorneys we had spoken to, would represent James Sapp, no matter what the evidence was. They would handle his defense from start to finish. He wouldn't have to worry about a thing. If we prevailed in court, State Farm would have to open its pocketbook, not Sapp.

After Sapp left and the court reporter packed up her steno machine and other items, we sat for a few minutes in the conference room.

"What really bothered me," I said to Mark, "was Sapp's complete lack of outrage or indignation when you told him without mincing words that his van was involved in Andrew's death at the time that he owned it."

"That was an accusation," Andy said.

"Wouldn't you have questions? He didn't even ask how SEA came to that conclusion. He asked nothing about SEA's findings. Here he is accused of being involved in a person's death and he has no questions about the evidence?"

"Wouldn't you expect that he would want clarification as to what this was all about before he left?" Andy asked.

Unless, of course, he already knew what it was all about; unless, of course, he believed that we didn't have any evidence. Unless he thought that we had only suspicions and Mark was fabricating stories to smoke information out of him. Unless he knew a criminal bought his van and was supposed to get rid of it—that the van had gone off paper. It's hard to act innocent, if you aren't.

We no sooner stepped inside the house, when the phone rang. Friends and relatives knew of the deposition that afternoon, and we had told them to call us later that day. Answering the phone, I wasted little time launching into a commentary of Sapp's answers with my friend, Mary Ann. Ending our conversation, I said, "We're moving forward. We have the truth."

"When did that ever lead to justice?" she snapped.

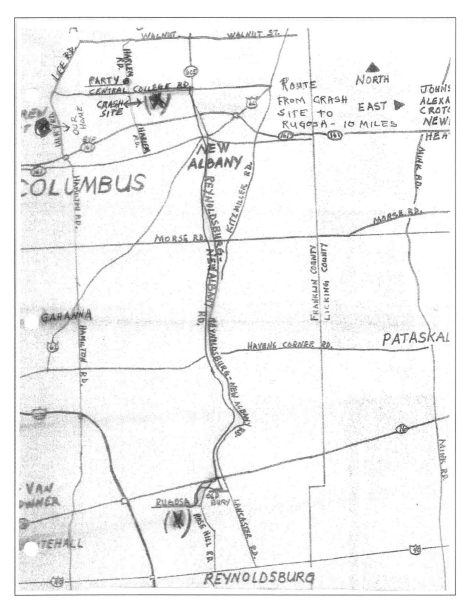

Map of Crash Site on Central College Road

37

SUMMER ENDED, LINDA'S BOYS WERE back in school and she returned after a brief vacation to work our case with her usual energy and efficiency. An email from her in September advised that she had called Vickie Stout at Glaval to plan for Andy and me to visit the Glaval Corporation offices to check van invoices for ground effect orders made to the parts department in August 1998.

Early on the morning of September 9, 2002, Andy and I headed north to Indiana. The Glaval Corporation was a compound of several buildings, and because Glaval no longer converted vans, Vickie's office had been relocated. Linda instructed us to go to a specific entrance where we would have to be buzzed in. After my letter to corporation president Richard Strefling, Glaval joined forces to help us get answers. On that day when Vickie opened the door to allow us in to check for van orders, Andy and I felt such gratitude toward her and Glaval.

She set us up in a corner of a factory area at a long table. Here and there in the large factory area, women were sewing what looked like vehicle upholstery. After settling us in, Vickie explained that the storage room held the boxes of invoices. She would be back in a few minutes with them.

When she left, Andy and I pulled out pencils and tablets. "What's the best way to do this?" I asked.

"We should take down every order for a ground effect made in August in the entire country. No matter where it was ordered from," Andy said.

No sooner had we readied our supplies when Vickie appeared in the doorway pushing a flatbed cart stacked high with boxes.

"I brought the invoices for July, August and September 1998," she said. "These are the August boxes if you want to start there," pointing to a row of boxes.

As Andy stacked the boxes on the table, Vickie removed an invoice from the box to explain the information on it. "You'll want to look for part number, FC2-830P, the passenger side ground effect. If you see an invoice with that number, then at the top you'll see the company that placed the order, address and person who called it in. Below that will be the date ordered and shipped and the VIN. Good Luck. I hope you find something."

"It's hard for us to imagine that a hit-and-run owner would go this route but it's worth a try."

"If you have any questions, my office is at the end of the hall. Don't hesitate. Oh, and do you want to go to lunch? There's a very good Chinese restaurant close by."

We thanked her again and told her that lunch was on us.

We noticed that the invoices were numbered, so to keep track we had to make note of all the numbers. Andy took a batch and I took the next batch of 500. We began with the last week in July, just to be certain. Because most of the invoices listed only one or two parts, we could see within seconds if the invoice ordered a passenger ground effect.

By lunchtime we had found only two orders for the fiberglass part in the entire country. We discovered that the passenger ground effect was not a common order. Working methodically, we were nearing the end of the first full week in August.

Over lunch with Vickie we observed that thus far we had found no ground effect ordered in Ohio. Then, on a lighter note, Andy jested that someone should make a movie about our son and the investigation into his death. With that, Vickie said, "Choose someone pretty to play me."

"And someone very special," we added.

Back at the factory area set aside for us, we were in a race against the clock. The offices and factory closed at five o'clock. If we couldn't get through the month of August in four hours, we would have to stay overnight and come back the next day. Moving through the invoices at a fast clip, Andy found another order.

Then, less than an hour later, I found an interesting invoice. The first item I noticed was the part's number, FC2-830-P; then, the company's name that ordered the part—a body shop with an address in Dayton, Ohio. The order was placed on August 6, 1998, six days after Andrew's death.

"Andy, I may have something. This body shop in Dayton ordered that part on August 6 by a Tyrone*. But look at this, there's no VIN. There's some other number.

I'll take this and show Vickie. My God, what if that's the van?"

"Hey, Sapp lived in Dayton."

Entering Vickie's office, I explained our problem. Puzzled, she looked at the invoice. "That's unusual. That's our production number. It's rarely used. I'll put it in the computer and see what VIN comes up. I can give you that but no other information. Company policy."

"I understand," I replied. "Linda can get us more information. Could you just tell me if the last name begins with an *S*?"

"No, it doesn't," she said.

"Is it a 1993?" I asked.

"No, it's a 1990," she said.

By five o'clock, we were into invoices for the month of September. In the entire country, only five orders for that part were placed in August, and one was for a body shop in Dayton, Ohio.

For the next few days we thought of nothing else but that invoice from Dayton. As soon as I could, I emailed Linda and Mark with the results of our search.

"What bothers me," I said to Andy, "is that the body shop didn't use the VIN. They used Glaval's production number found inside a van door."

"Why wouldn't someone just use the VIN?"

"A VIN is easy to check. A production number isn't."

"Let's take a ride to Dayton and have a look at this body shop," he said.

"And I can get into the library data bases to see who owns this body shop. Linda's researching the VIN on the invoice to see who owned that van. In the entire country, only one ground effect was ordered that first week in August, and it's in Dayton, Ohio. That's beyond strange."

"A hit-and-run driver is not likely to go to a reputable body shop and risk being caught."

"But the shop's in Dayton, not Columbus. No one in Dayton would be suspicious about a crash in Columbus. The Dayton newspaper wouldn't carry our story."

Equipped with the address of the body shop and the name of its owner, we headed to Dayton after breakfast the next day. To get a better idea about the body shop, I knew we had to see it and determine what else of interest was close by.

38

BECAUSE DAYTON IS LOCATED ABOUT eighty miles west of our home in Columbus, we could make the drive in less than two hours. Using MapQuest to get directions to the body shop, we exited Brandt Pike to an address on Taylorsville Road. Once on Brandt Pike, Andy stopped at a gas station to refuel. Parked outside the door of the station was a Glaval converted Chevy van with the same kind of ground effects found at our crash. I jotted down the plates in my notebook as well as the time, place, and circumstances of seeing a Glaval van.

We pulled out of the station and headed for Taylorsville Road. Scanning the buildings for numbers, I happened to look down a residential street off Taylorsville. Parked in the drive of the first house was another Glaval Chevy van with Glaval ground effects. Andy swung around the block and I took down those plates and the address. The information might come in handy. Before leaving Taylorsville Road, we were to see another Glaval van. Because we saw three Glaval vans within a short period, Andy surmised that there must be a big dealer in or near Dayton, and he was right. So Glaval vans were common in Dayton, not so in Columbus. And we knew that the van in the sheriff's custody was bought in Dayton before it was brought to Columbus in 1996.

Once we were near the body shop, we slowed to get a good look at it. We spotted the shop, an ordinary, cement block building, and drove by at least four times. Nothing unusual.

Before we headed back home, I suggested that we stop at the courthouse to check out the owner of the body shop. Retracing our route, we drove up Taylorsville Road to Brandt Pike. I turned to Andy and said, "Why is Brandt Pike familiar?"

"It's not to me." he answered.

Because I always take several files with me, I leafed through them. "Well, what do you know," I said. "Look here. Remember when we came here to check on traffic records? I gave the clerk Sapp's girlfriend's name, too, and she gave me this case number and her address. She lived on Brandt Pike in 1996. Let's see where it is."

We made a right on Brandt Pike from Taylorsville and about a mile or so from the intersection, we noticed an apartment complex. Sapp's girlfriend had lived in that complex when she filed for divorce from her second husband, the one before Sapp, and that address had to have been her last one before she moved to Columbus. During the opening of her deposition taken months later, she would list her addresses but fail to mention that she had lived on Brandt Pike. Our attorney would have to prod her. Did she ever live on Brandt Pike? *She would not answer, "Yes."* She hedged and said she didn't know if her apartment was on Brandt Pike. She filed divorce papers listing Brandt Pike, she filed a complaint against the second husband listing Brandt Pike and had received a traffic ticket listing that address. That address held such significance for her that it was obvious to me she omitted it for a reason.

Our stop at the Dayton courthouse to research the owner of the body shop proved troubling. The owner had been sentenced to prison for attempted murder. Now he was out and operated a garage. On August 6, 1998, he had ordered a passenger side ground effect from Glaval, or someone from his shop had. Was it just coincidental that the only order to Glaval in August came from this body shop in Dayton? Not that far from Sapp's girlfriend's apartment? Or that this order came from Dayton, Sapp's home before he moved to Columbus? Anxious to hear what the owner of the body shop had to say about his order to Glaval, we agreed when Mark offered to subpoena the man's records.

Just days after the subpoena went out, Mark called the house with news of his conversation with the body shop owner.

"I got a call today from Tyrone*. He wanted to know what the subpoena was about. He didn't sound too happy." Mark said.

"That was a quick response," I said.

"I told him about his order to Glaval for a ground effect in 1998 and wanted a copy of his records for that repair. He said that he never ordered a part from Glaval and had no records. He was adamant."

"But we have a copy of an invoice of his shop ordering that part on August 6th," I said.

"That's what I told him. We have an invoice saying that he did make an order to Glaval. He said that he didn't have any records and maybe someone else ordered it. He's not going to change his mind. I saw no reason to insist that he come to the office."

I understood what Mark was saying. An attorney can go only so far. If Tyrone failed to show for a deposition, he would suffer no adverse consequence. Mechanics don't ask why a vehicle is damaged.

When Linda, our PI, tracked down the owner of the van whose production number was on the Glaval invoice, she talked to the owner's son. The son informed Linda that his father was a customer of the body shop on Taylorville

Road and that he had had an accident in that van. "Was there an accident report?" she asked.

"Yes. The Dayton Police came," he answered.

A thorough search of Montgomery County police accident files revealed no report and pursuant to insurance records, no claim had been made then. Letting this information hang there without some satisfactory explanation proved difficult to live with.

2003

39

BY LATE FALL OF 2002, Mark had filed a civil suit in the Franklin County Court of Common Pleas. The suit, a wrongful death action against James O. Sapp, alleged that evidence proved his van killed Andrew. His attorneys representing State Farm Insurance were poised to file a motion to have the case dismissed. Legal minds agree that a criminal trial comes first and then a civil trial for wrongful death even if the jury in the criminal trial found the defendant not guilty. However, we had no choice but to file the civil suit first because of the inaction of the FCSO.

Despite our advising the FCSO of the findings of our investigation, we couldn't motivate them to talk to Sapp. Not even the BCI report motivated them. I wrote letters to Ron O'Brien, Franklin County Prosecutor explaining our dilemma. No doubt the FCSO came up with some doozies as to why they did nothing. Filing a wrongful death civil action against Sapp, we believed, would pave the way for a criminal action. We had done everything humanly possible to eliminate the Sapp van, but couldn't.

The stores had begun to decorate for the approaching holiday season. As I had done for the past five years, I was incapable of appreciating the winter holidays. The anticipation of Christmas with all its fun, joy and traditions was gone. Only Betsey was affected by our dampened spirits. We knew, however, that Scott's parents, and his brother and sisters were picking up the slack and we were grateful to them.

Several weeks after Christmas, in answer to our civil suit, Mark advised that Sapp and State Farm's attorneys had filed a Motion for Summary Judgment. As soon as the plaintiff files a complaint against the defendant in a civil suit, the defendant's attorney usually acts as quickly as possible to have the complaint dismissed by filing a Motion for Summary Judgment. Our case had been assigned to Common Pleas Judge Lisa Sadler. The motion asked Judge Sadler to throw our case out—that no merit existed for the suit. The decision was in her hands to dismiss or allow the case to go forward.

In addition, Sapp's attorney, Mark Gams, argued that the two-year statute of limitations had expired because the crash had taken place more than four years earlier. Mark Adams, responding to the Motion, held that the evidence pointed squarely to the Sapp van, and the statute of limitations in a hit-and-run fatality didn't start running until the perpetrator was identified.

From the time the Motion was filed in January 2003 to the time of her decision months later, Andy and I would fluctuate between arguing and barely speaking to each other. Waiting for a ruling created tension. Andy wanted to preempt the ruling and file a suit against the Franklin County Sheriff's Office for dereliction of duty. I argued against it.

"Why would they ignore BCI's report for chrissake?" he yelled at me. "Those goddamned fuckers."

"Look, you know as well as I do that the Sheriff's Office can do whatever they want and the chance of a jury siding with the victim against law enforcement doesn't happen. Not in central Ohio. Get over it!"

Later we were to hear that Sheriff Karnes said he felt sorry for Andy because he was married to someone like me. From their past performance, I considered the FCSO useless, and all we wanted was for them to do their jobs. I reasoned that they wouldn't care if we took our case directly to the prosecutor. But the prosecutor is tied *securely* to law enforcement and represents them.

"So what do we do? Something is wrong when BCI hands you evidence and you do nothing. I'm calling Ted," he said. Ted was his friend, now practicing out of Akron.

"If you think I'm going to roll over and play dead, you're wrong," I argued. "That maggot took our son's life and the evidence points to his van. For us to turn our backs on what happened to Andrew is to give license to anyone with a car to commit murder. No matter what happens, I'm not going to give up on this. I don't know about you, but right now all I can think about is getting over this hurdle. We have no choice but to wait for the court's ruling on the Summary Judgment."

"I don't see how in God's name the judge wouldn't consider BCI's and SEA's reports," he said.

"This is our first real test with the justice system. We must prove that we have a case against Sapp. The Motion for Summary Judgment basically says that we have no case and asks the judge to dismiss the case."

"What? We have no case?" Andy interrupted, his voice angry.

"The defendant has to say that if he wants the case thrown out. But we bear the burden of proof. We have to show the court that we have convincing evidence on every issue that we plan to raise at trial." I said, reading from notes.

"Sounds to me like Mark has to convince the court of the evidence we have against Sapp's van. Right?"

"That's how I read it, but Mark said it could be several months before we get a ruling."

Sitting at my computer one morning in the early months of 2003, I noticed an email from Mark. "Good News" the subject read. Judge Sadler had ruled in our favor. Instead of coming together and holding each other, Andy went into Andrew's bedroom, closed the door, and broke down. I ran outside and started up the lane, with only the trees and the clouds to hear me cry. I'm not sure why we went our separate ways in times of emotional breakdowns over Andrew's death, but maybe we didn't want to be comforted. We needed to get it all out. Was Judge Sadler's decision an indication that someone believed us? The first call we made was to Betsey and Scott.

Several days later Mark gave us a copy of Judge Sadler's <u>Decision and Entry Overruling Motion for Summary Judgment.</u> Reading her decision, we sat, side by side, at the kitchen table. With pencil in hand, I marked and underlined details—details to share with our daughter in a call to her that evening.

"Bets," I said, "Mark just gave us a copy of Judge Sadler's decision. She ruled in our favor and the overall tone is strong. I'd like to read some of it to you. Are you busy?" Leading her own consulting business, our daughter worked long and varied hours.

"No, in fact, I was waiting for your call. Thank God for Judge Sadler. What was Mark's reaction?" she asked.

"He was happy but like always he doesn't go overboard. In rereading his answer to the motion, the first line that jumped out at me was '*Plaintiffs allege that Defendant was the owner and driver of the vehicle that struck and killed their son.*' The man's own testimony said he was the only driver. And the van was never out of his sight," I said.

"What reason did Sapp's attorney give to have the case dismissed?" she asked.

"They argued that the statute of limitations bars our claims." I said.

"That's it? Did they try to say he didn't do it?" she said.

"I'll bet you they didn't even ask him if he did it. They don't care. They argued that the statute of limitations is two years in hit-and-run and that we didn't bring an action until more than four years after Andrew was killed," I said reading the decision.

"Because it was a hit-and-run. The driver didn't hang around to see whether Andrew needed help after he hit him. He ran and hid. He was drunk or high."

"About the statute of limitations, Mark argued that the Supreme Court of Ohio's decision in *Collins v. Sotka* applies in our case. And Sadler agreed. So, the way I understand it is that the clock on hit-and-run fatalities doesn't start until the perpetrator is discovered. Rightfully, there should be no statute of limitations on hit-and-run crashes because the perpetrators run and hide just like murderers do. So what's the difference?"

"Mom, this is the best news we've had in a long time. Did she say anything about the police?"

"Yes. She restated the point that 'the Sheriff was unable to determine the identity of the driver of the vehicle that struck' Andrew. And she goes on to point out that we 'attempted to assist the Sheriff in this task' and that led to our finding the Sapp van at Metro Chevrolet. She goes into a lot of detail about the Sheriff confiscating the van and the BCI's aligning the holes and the paint match."

"What about SEA and Dr. Wiechel? Did she say anything about them?"

"Her ruling says that SEA's engineers 'concluded, based on a reasonable degree of engineering and scientific probability that the van in their possession was the van that struck and killed' Andrew, and their findings supported BCI's report."

"I wonder if privately she questioned why the police didn't do something after the BCI report? And why we had to go to SEA?" Betsey said.

"Right. But her job was not to question what the police did or didn't do. I think she did a great job. Really well thought out. Almost fifteen pages," I said.

"Maybe we will get justice, Mom."

"And Mark couldn't have put in everything we have that points to Sapp's van. This confirms that we have at the very least, a preponderance of evidence."

"Send me a copy, Mom. Where do we go from here?"

"Mark's talking about deposing all the auto shops and dealerships that had any connection to the van before Sapp bought it. But I should tell you that Mark has been dropping hints about winding down his involvement."

"Does that mean he's not going to be our attorney?"

"That's what I'm beginning to hear," I said.

"How do you feel about someone else taking over?"

"Dad and I are scared. No one can fill his shoes."

More portentous words could not have been spoken.

40

AFTER MARK TOOK SAPP'S DEPOSITION, filed a civil case against him and prevailed against the defendant's Summary Judgment, we met with him to discuss our next move. He had been sending out verbal signals that he thought our case was not within his area of practice. Essentially, our case involved a homicide. His cases involved wrongful death but not homicides. Giving us a great deal of his time without equal compensation, he had put in place a strong foundation for us to move forward against the owner of the van.

"I can refer you to some very good people," Mark offered one afternoon as Andy and I sat in his office. "They're experts in dealing with insurance companies. And you're going to need that. You're not up against another person. You're up against State Farm's attorneys."

"Andy and I were thinking that maybe we should get a criminal attorney to represent us. We're dealing with a criminal," I said.

Unfortunately, not having a scintilla of experience with any kind of lawsuit, civil or criminal, we knew much less about the law than any of our lawyers realized. Ours wasn't a criminal suit. The Sheriff had to bring criminal charges. Ours was a civil suit, primarily asking for money. But we honestly didn't think for a second about money. We wanted a jury to conclude that the Sapp van was involved in our son's death. We couldn't fathom how any amount of money would help us. Money wouldn't bring Andrew back. But that lack of imagination proved to be a huge oversight. Money buys justice.

Mark probably assumed that we knew more than we did. I wish that he had overridden our ignorance and listed all the reasons a civil attorney was the appropriate choice. He certainly tried to educate us. "You have to be careful. Criminal attorneys usually charge by the hour. I would not recommend going that route. It'll be better if you have a contingency agreement," he cautioned.

Here again we completely missed the difference between an attorney charging an hourly wage and one whose fee was based on contingency. Criminal attorneys, because of the nature of their cases, charge by the hour. Civil attorneys, especially those representing plaintiffs, earn their fees based on the monetary award they can garner for their clients. Usually, it's a thirty percent of the reward.

The longer a suit lasts, the more rewarding it becomes for a criminal attorney. If clients pay by the hour, they pay until the case ends. In a contingency agreement, whatever the settlement or money award is, the attorney is paid by sharing the award. Whether the attorney works two weeks or two years doesn't matter. The longer a case drags on with contingency clients, the costlier it is for the attorney. If the case settles quickly, clients may think that the attorney made out like a bandit. But that's the way it's done.

To hear that eventually Mark would not be the one we could turn to was painful. Andy and I had placed so much faith in his abilities; we would have done everything in our power to keep him on. We would have given him anything he wanted.

Since we were dealing with a homicide, it made sense to me at the time, that we should seek a criminal attorney. I went to *Martindale-Hubbell*, a publication that allegedly lists the best attorneys in certain cities and their areas of expertise. Under criminal law, I found Tyack and Shamansky as well as the attorney we chose, David Winters.

When I showed Andy the list, he decided to call Don Sonney to get his opinion. Since Don had taken a private investigation job in Detroit and came home on the weekends, we had not talked to him in months. "If I wanted representation, I'd call David Winters," Don recommended.

And since Mark didn't know David and couldn't say one way or the other, we decided to call Attorney Winters and make an appointment to see him.

Some of David Winters' cases made front-page news in the *Columbus Dispatch.* His clients, the ones who made the news, appeared to be professional people who found themselves in difficult situations. On the morning of our appointment, David Winters left his office and greeted us in the foyer as we were hanging up our coats. My eyes were drawn to a crown of curly brown hair. In one swoop, I looked the man over. Someone's appearance often gives clues about certain personality traits. Attorney Winters cared about his clothes and how he looked. This first impression would hold true. We never saw him as anything but impeccably dressed. And the classic, highly polished tasseled loafers. Later, we would discover that to go with his classic appearance, he owned a black sporty Porsche. What kind of personality is particular about his appearance and pays attention to detail? An attorney who is particular about what he does and pays attention to detail, we reasoned.

During that first appointment, we related the events of our son's death, the FCSO involvement in the investigation and our part in the investigation. Attorney Winters asked questions, took notes, and then expressed an interest in taking our case. Principally, two remarks he made that day convinced us to hire him. "If the evidence shows that Mr. Sapp's van killed Andrew and he owned it at the time, then Mr. Sapp is involved. One naturally follows the other." His other remark involved his connections in the Prosecutor's Office. He was a former assistant prosecutor and maintained friendships with some of the assistants. We anticipated, at the very least, an audience with the Prosecutor.

We never did ask Winters how many plaintiffs he represented. We assumed that he had some of those. We never asked him about his experience with insurance companies. We assumed that he had some of that. All lawyers know the insurance company game. Right?

Had we not been impressed with his affability and intelligence, we would have walked out the minute he announced his hourly charge, a common practice, as Mark predicted, for defense attorneys. Ostensibly he grasped the obstacles that faced us and offered us hope. Leaving his office on that summer day in 2002, we headed for Schmidt's in nearby German Village. Suddenly, we had an appetite for a Bahama Mama and a celebratory glass of beer.

41

REMEMBERING MY LIFE WITH ANDREW—what he did, what he said, who he was—and now living without him, has often made me wish that I had never had him. That isn't a sentiment that most parents of deceased children ascribe to—at least in my experience with parents I know in The Compassionate Friends, a support group for bereaved families who have lost children of all ages. Most will say that to have had their child if only for a little while was a gift. You love that gift more than anything. You can't live without it. Then it's wrenched from you. I would rather not have had that gift than to live without him. The taking of his life at the hands of another struck such a blow to my spirit that the essence of all that's good to be alive left me.

I gave Andrew's eulogy. I couldn't stand the idea that some priest who didn't know him would talk in generalities about him and yet, now, I can't for the life of me understand the words I spoke about him. I even used humor. Recently, I came across a card from Connie, a dear friend and colleague, who wrote to tell me how much she liked the words I had spoken about Andrew. In rereading her card, I cringed. Reality was so horrific I couldn't allow that. *I didn't get that Andrew was dead.* That he could be dead. That our lives together were over.

A year or so after Andrew was killed, his friend, Paul, stopped by the house. As we talked, he said that Andrew had had more courage than anyone else he knew, and yet Andrew couldn't muster up the courage to leave home. Paul asserted that Andrew never backed down from a challenge no matter how imposing the opposition. Yes, this was my son who a month before he died asked if I wanted to watch the *Wizard of Oz* one evening on television. I was preparing to teach summer school and begged off, saying, "Do you know how many times I've watched that movie?"

The next morning at breakfast I asked Andrew, kind of poking fun at him, "Did you stay up and watch Dorothy and Toto?"

"Yeah. Do you think it's just a kid's story?"

I knew by the way he said it that he didn't think *The Wizard of Oz* was *just* a kid's movie. In truth, I did but I sensed a trap. So often he saw meaning where I didn't and after our discussions, I'd be embarrassed that I didn't catch the detail that he did. I was the English teacher. "You don't?" I asked, waiting for him to educate me.

"I think the story appeals to everyone, but I don't think that kids would get the symbolism," he answered.

"Don't you think it's kind of obvious? You have the Tin Man who wants a heart, and the Scarecrow wants a brain because it's all straw, and the Cowardly Lion, the most ferocious animal in the forest, is a coward."

"Yeah, that's what I thought, too, but I changed my mind about what the story was really saying."

"So you didn't think the Scarecrow wanted a brain or the Tin Man wanted a heart?" I asked, a little confused.

"Or that the Cowardly Lion wanted courage," he added. "Each of them already had what they wanted, but they didn't know it."

"OK, and wasn't the Scarecrow always saying smart things to help Dorothy figure out how to get away from the Wicked Witch," I said, trying to remember details.

"His job is to scare away crows and he's stuck in one place, on a pole in the middle of a cornfield. He's frustrated at doing practically nothing all day but wave away crows. He wants to do more with his life, and he's looking for an out. Along comes Dorothy. When he tells her he wants a brain, he ironically shows he already has one simply by wanting one."

"Yeah, you're right," I said recalling that the Scarecrow always seemed smart to me.

"And it's the same with the Tin Man and the Cowardly Lion. They think the Wizard can give them what they want but they already have it. When they rescue Dorothy from the wicked witch, the Tin Man shows his love for Dorothy and the Cowardly Lion his courage."

"That's right," I said, some of the details returning. "Wasn't the Wizard a fake or his reputation was much greater than his power?"

"I think that was the point. No one can give you intelligence, love, courage. We already have them only we need the opportunities to realize it. I see the yellow brick road as a metaphor for opportunities toward development."

"It's almost Biblical," I said. "We have been given all that we need. Now it's up to us."

This wasn't the first time that when we talked about a movie, a play, or a book my supposedly tough guy son was the teacher and I, the student. Along with Lucy, a friend and teacher, he was the one who impressed upon me to notice "the words." Why those words in that particular place in a piece of literature?

While he talked, the thought struck me that I should teach the book and then watch the movie in my summer school class. I wanted my students to know that they had the power within them to realize their dreams. Our conversation that morning was much more extensive than what I have recorded here. And for the first time, through my conversation with Andrew that morning, less than a month before his death, I saw the beauty of *The Wonderful Wizard of Oz*.

"Hey, what about the Cowardly Lion?" I asked.

"If you go by appearances, he had it all – the crown, the roar—and yet he was scared. He knew who he could bully, but when a stronger force challenged him, he'd back down. He had to learn that being scared is not cowardly, and standing your ground, no matter how you feel, that's courage."

As it happened, most of my twenty-three summer school students, having failed English that school year, were a mighty handful. After a few days with them, I decided that teaching *The Wonderful Wizard of Oz* wouldn't be so wonderful. There could be no discussion of love, brains and courage as depicted in the book. Instead, I chose some pop teen novel about a gang of adolescents who steal cars. Engaging this group of students, twenty-two boys and one girl, had me scrambling in the afternoons to find literature that would hold their attention.

When the summer session was over, the school's director met me at my car and handed me a small bag. He cautioned, "Don't open it until you get home." That little bottle of gin mixed in a glass of orange juice was just what I needed. I don't think that I would have thought too much about Andrew's love of literature and his gift for analysis had he lived. Even at an early age he made sharp, insightful comments during discussions of the books he, Betsey and I read together. I expected that from him.

42

ONCE WINTERS WAS ON BOARD, Mark proceeded to scale back the enormous amount of time and energy he had thus far devoted to our case. From the beginning, he had stood by us. He and Patty and their children had been on vacation when Andrew was killed. They cut short their vacation to come home. Mark knew every detail of Andrew's death and the investigation. No matter how many hours we were to spend with David Winters, he could never grasp the situation with the same depth of understanding as Mark, nor have the personal investment.

Our family, all of us, Andy, Andrew, Betsey, and I, loved the Adamses. Even though they were much younger, we had more fun being with them than just about anyone else. And the kids were as witty, engaging, informed and fun-loving as their parents.

Preparing to take the "van" depositions, Mark called one afternoon with an update. "I've made arrangements at the Holiday Inn, May 28 [2003], in Dayton. I've heard from Voss Chevrolet, Frank Z. Chevrolet, and Edgar Winn. Voss Chevrolet serviced and repaired the van for the original owner, Winn, and then Winn sold the van to Frank Z. in 1996. All of them will be there. Come to the office and we'll ride together." The purpose of these depositions was to get an accurate history of the Sapp van before Sapp bought it.

We entered the hotel's lobby. Mark had reserved the conference room, not far from the lobby. Preparing for the depositions, Mark had spoken to each witness, and the two dealerships had forwarded their records to him. After he examined them carefully, we got the impression from Mark that the records held no surprises. Still, in the margin of my yellow note pad, I wrote, "Please give us the truth." To whom did I address these supplications? I wrote these kinds of notes on every pad before and during every deposition.

While Mark was emptying his briefcase and setting up his area, the court stenographer arrived. Most, if not all the time, these people sit at the head of the table. It's imperative that they have an unobstructed view of all the parties and know who is speaking.

We were to meet for the first time an attorney from the firm Gallagher, Gams, Pryor, Tallan & Littrell that represented State Farm. A young woman, Danielle Dunn, entered the room. A thin figure—impeccably dressed—with dark, frizzy hair, she took her place opposite Mark. Next to her sat our first witness, Charlie Roup, from Frank Z. Chevrolet. Roup looked at me and said, "Don't I know you from somewhere? You look familiar." Over the years, I have had hundreds of students, but didn't remember a Roup. Strangely, his spontaneous, friendly remark eased the tension I was feeling.

As controller, Charlie Roup testified that Frank Z. had acquired the Winn 1993 Glaval Chevy van before Sapp bought it in June, 1996. Roup produced the appropriate paperwork. The documents supported Roup's opinion that Winn's van was in good condition. Frank Z. would not put a damaged vehicle up for sale. No surprises there.

As soon as Charlie Roup left, Pat Kowalski, manager at Voss Chevrolet, took his place. His testimony would be a bit more complicated. Voss Chevrolet repaired Winn's van after it had been involved in two accidents, one in 1994 and the other in 1995. The accident in 1994 involved only the driver's side when the van tipped over on its side. Even with extensive repairs to the driver's side, the company did not have to replace the driver's side ground effect. We already knew that because SEA's inspection revealed the driver's side ground effect was the original part. The 1994 accident had no bearing on Andrew's crash.

The damage and repair of the second accident in March 1995 was the subject of our interest, the passenger side. That accident involved the right front fender, the front bumper, and the passenger side "doors and/or sides of vehicle." Mark's questioning of Kowalski pointed out the distinct difference between replacing a part and repairing it. Replacing a damaged part meant installing a different one in its place; repairing involved retaining the part but restoring it.

Obviously, Mark was particularly interested in what had happened to the passenger side ground effect.

> Q.   Is it pretty clear that you have no record of ordering another running board?
>
> A.   It does not appear as though we ordered a running board.
>
> Q.   Just so that I'm straight on this: What I'll call the March '95 repair, there is no evidence that in that particular repair, you had to replace the running board?
>
> A.   That is correct.

Mark also had to ascertain how the ground effects, if they were removed from the van to allow for access to other parts, are reinstalled. When SEA removed the driver's side ground effect to reinstall it, they merely used the same holes in the wheel well and rocker panel. Would Voss have done the same? We held our breaths as the answer was critical.

Q. And let's assume in March of '95 they had to take the ground effects piece off to take the fender off and do all that repair, when the ground effects piece is reinstalled, *would it be typical for the installation to—installer to use the same holes that are already in the running board [ground effect] to reinstall the running board onto the new fender, as opposed to drilling brand-new holes?*

A. *It would be typical to utilize preexisting holes in the running board.*

Q. Because, obviously, the running board, to some extent, is going to be in the same place on that part of the vehicle that was not replaced; correct?

A. That is correct.

Mark uncovered important information about the paint Voss used in the repair of the passenger side. I thought about Dr. Kwek's report on the paint smears she tested and the scope and limitations of the paint examination. And then how it connected to what the guy in the auto body parts shop told me about vehicle paint.

Q. How do you go about matching the paint?

A. Matching the color?

Q. ...do you use a GM paint?

A. We use a couple different suppliers. At that time, we used a company called PPG, it's Pittsburgh Plate Glass and we matched the color taking the paint code off of the vehicle and formulating our own mix of paint.

Q. So, would your mix of paint be different than GM's?

A. Not in regards to appearance or finish.

> Q.   No, I don't mean appearance. But chemically, I mean…
>
> A.   To the best of my knowledge, yes… GM supplies a paint code by which any manufacturer of auto paint can use that paint code to come up with the same material in appearance, sprayability, color.

Reviewing the conversation, I had with the man in the vehicle store about paint, I am positive he would have answered Mark's question the same way that Pat Kowalski did. GM's paint formula and PPG's paint formula would not test the same chemically. His answer would be a resounding, "No, their chemical composition would be different." Of course, the *appearance and finish* of the two paints would have to match in color and texture.

After examining the bicycle and fiberglass ground effect pieces, Dr. Karen Kwek of BCI noted that: "The white paint smear from the top bar (of the bicycle) is similar in color and microscopic appearance, but different in chemical composition from the white paint on the fiberglass in item #3 (the ground effect)." It's possible then that the top horizontal bar of the bicycle could have made contact with an area that Voss had repainted with PPG in the 1995 accident. The Voss repainting was done before Andrew's crash and would have been the paint on parts of the vehicle when the Sapp van hit Andrew. Kwek tested only the ground effect.

Since we know that some of the passenger side had been repaired and obviously repainted in the Winn, March 1995 accident, at least two chemically different paints would be in evidence on that side of the van. (Because the entire van had been painted over at least twice after Sapp sold it, no chemical analysis including those coats of paint was done).

Mark interviewed Edgar Winn last. He remembered scant technical information about the actual repairs. He did provide what personal information he could remember about the accidents which had occurred about nine years previously. When Mark had finished Edgar Winn's deposition and packed his briefcase, he expressed his satisfaction at the outcome of the depositions. The depositions had gone as expected based on the information he had collected in advance, especially the Voss deposition.

On the way back to Columbus, we talked about what we had heard and observed. Andy recounted that during the break he talked briefly to Pat Kowalski and Edgar Winn and both seemed genuinely interested in helping us find Andrew's killer.

Mark's way of operating, his thoughtful strategies gave us confidence in the direction the case was heading. We didn't want to face the day when we had to navigate our course without Mark's wise counsel.

Mark underscored his separation by declaring, "After Spitzer's deposition, the person handling your case needs to take the depositions. He'll want to ask the questions he thinks are important."

Reluctantly, we agreed.

Mark offered to finish the van depositions by sending a subpoena to Spitzer Dodge in Reynoldsburg where Sapp had sold his van. Spitzer sent Richard Masa, general manager of Spitzer, to answer Mark's questions.

Before taking Masa's deposition, Mark obtained copies of Spitzer's documents, and it was then that we discovered the striking occurrence of two events—one likely being the result of the other. The first event—the Crime Stoppers' interview with the FCSO outside the house of Sapp's girlfriend where Sapp's van was used as a sample van (the van had been repaired by that time) and the second event—Sapp's sale of the van to Spitzer, the day after the Crime Stopper's publicity aired on television and appeared in The *Columbus Dispatch*. (See Crime Stopper Article and Spitzer's document). This wasn't just any van. This was *the* van. Later, I could only imagine Sapp's panic—the reason to sell impulsively? Would the police finally catch on and come back? It wasn't until we had Spitzer's documents that we knew when Sapp sold his van in September, 1998, the day after the Crime Stoppers publicity that showcased his van. Circumstantial but still relevant.

We were also especially interested in the Etchguard number, still visible in the corner of Sapp's van's windshield. Spitzer had engraved that number in the windshield glass when Sapp brought the van in to sell it. Since the number was still there, Masa's testimony proved that the windshield had not been replaced after Sapp's ownership. The van depositions were now complete.

Mark, who had so generously helped us, was no longer our attorney. In some ways, we felt that he could not maintain the level of involvement we had come to expect and not be paid the kind of money he deserved. We wanted him no matter what his fee was. We had no choice but to honor his disengagement. His integrity, and his gift for strategic thinking had put us on the correct path. We had been in the best of hands. Still, it was a terrible blow to be without *him*.

COLUMBUS DISPATCH ARTICLE – CRIME STOPPERS

REWARD FOR ANDREW'S HIT-SKIP DEATH: **09/08/1998**

The Columbus Dispatch Online: Archival Article   Page 1 of 1

SEPT. 8, 1998   ANDREW'S DEATH WAS THE CRIME OF THIS WEEK —

The Columbus Dispatch

REWARDS OFFERED FOR INFORMATION IN HIT-SKIP DEATH

CRIME STOPPERS BEGINNING WITH A CHANNEL 6, TELEVISED INTERVIEW.

Tuesday, September 8, 1998
NEWS 06B

The hit-skip death of a Blendon Township man has been designated the Crime of the Week in the Central Ohio *Crime Stoppers* program.

Late on Aug. 1, Andrew Starinchak, 31, of Ulry Road, was riding his bicycle west along Central College Road, east of Harlem Road, in Plain Township.

He was struck by a westbound vehicle. The driver left the scene without reporting the accident. Starinchak's body was not found until 8:50 a.m. on Aug. 2.

Franklin County deputy sheriffs believe the suspect may have driven a 1985 to 1994 Chevrolet Astro van with a Gladiator conversion, or a GMC Safari van with an Autoform conversion.

The van should be missing pieces of the right side body cladding or running board immediately behind the right front wheel. The vehicle also may have some right side hood and windshield damage. The van should be mostly white with a color trim package.

Crime Stoppers is offering a reward of up to $1,000 for any information received by Sept. 16. Starinchak's family is offering an additional reward.

Anyone with information is asked to call *Crime Stoppers* at 645-TIPS (8477).

Crime Stoppers also takes calls about any felony. A coding system protects callers' identities.

Information about *Crime Stoppers* can be found online at www.stopcrime.org

Tax deductible donations can be sent to *Crime Stoppers*, Box 16038, Columbus, Ohio 43216-6038.

Columbus Dispatch Article, Crime Stoppers 9/8/1998

SAPP'S ODOMETER DISCLOSURE STATEMENT

AT TIME OF SALE: **09/09/1998**

ODOMETER DISCLOSURE STATEMENT

Federal law (and State law, if applicable) requires that you state the mileage upon transfer of ownership. Failure to complete or providing a false statement may result in fines and/or imprisonment.

JAMES O SAPP

I, _____ (transferor's name, Print)

78067

state that the odometer now reads _____ (no tenths) miles and to the best of my knowledge that it reflects the actual mileage of the vehicle described below, unless one of the following statements is checked.

☐ (1) I hereby certify that to the best of my knowledge the odometer reading reflects the amount of mileage in excess of its mechanical limits.

☐ (2) I hereby certify that the odometer reading is NOT the actual mileage. WARNING - ODOMETER DISCREPANCY.

MAKE CHEVROLET	MODEL ASTRO	BODY TYPE S/W
VEHICLE IDENTIFICATION NUMBER 1GBDM19Z0PB164414		YEAR 1993

X _____ James O. Sapp
TRANSFEROR'S SIGNATURE
JAMES O SAPP

PRINTED NAME
6490 KUGOSA AVE

TRANSFEROR'S ADDRESS (STREET)
REYNOLDSBURG   OH   43068

the day after Crime Stoppers publicity

CITY 09/09/98   STATE   ZIP CODE

DATE OF STATEMENT

X _____ DOUGLAS K ARCHER
TRANSFEREE'S SIGNATURE
SPITZER COLUMBUS INC.

PRINTED NAME
SPITZER COLUMBUS INC.

TRANSFEREE'S NAME
5100 EAST MAIN ST.

TRANSFEREE'S ADDRESS (STREET)
COLUMBUS   OH   43213

CITY   STATE   ZIP CODE

Sapp's Odometer Disclosure Statement, 9/9/1998

43

MOST OF OUR MEETINGS NOW with David Winters occurred in the morning, and since his office was close to German Village, we usually ate lunch at a deli in the village to recap the meeting.

At these meetings with David, Andy and I did most of the talking—at $250 an hour—but our new attorney was attentive and asked, in our opinion, smart questions. When we left his office, we believed we were moving forward and had hope that the evidence and the foundation Mark laid out for our case would get us some semblance of justice.

Finding a table in the corner at the deli, I took out my tablet with notes. No matter what we did, whether we were dealing with people friendly to our situation or the Sheriff's Office, we were constantly on edge. A hot cup of herbal tea and an egg salad sandwich quieted stomach pains. Along with that anxious feeling, I sensed that something unexpected awaited us around the corner.

"Did Winters say when Gams wanted to take our depositions?" Andy asked, putting his tray down and taking a seat.

"No, just that he wants to depose us. He didn't mention a date. I'm curious as to what things he wants to know."

"Mainly they look like personal questions about our family."

One glaring omission of judgment concerned money. By this time, we should have hired an economist to assess Andrew's potential worth. That's a powerful bargaining tool. A civil suit's job isn't to mete out justice, but we weren't thinking like that.

"It sounded like David is really interested in what the latest Mrs. Sapp has to say," Andy commented.

"Didn't he say she was first on his deposition list?" I asked.

"Yeah. What do we know about her?"

"Well, one thing, she's about twenty years younger than Sapp," I said. "They both worked at the same place in Dayton and both transferred here in 1996 when the Dayton place closed down."

"Didn't she buy her house then?" he said.

"No, she bought her house in 1998, and moved in June or July, shortly before Andrew was killed. Didn't look to me as though she was planning to get married any time soon," I said.

"They must have been dating because Sapp said they went to Las Vegas in August together."

"And then right after that he moved in with her," I remembered. "That was a week or so after the crash. Then, a month after that, they got married."

"If they were planning to get married, why didn't she just move in with him?"

"Maybe they weren't planning to get married. *Something sure changed their minds.* He had the better house. He did say something about a nosy neighbor. Possibly a suspicious neighbor?"

"What do you think of Winters' suggestion to talk to McMannis about the case?" Andy asked.

"He has to. Mark had a way of dealing with the Sheriff's Office and it'd be to our advantage if Winters was friendly. We need the Sheriff's cooperation."

"I like that he wants McMannis to clarify when he saw the Sapp van," Andy said.

"Yeah, McMannis told Chief Jones it was within one or two weeks after the crash. We didn't get the photos of the van until two weeks after. But Winters needs to nail that down before he takes McMannis' deposition," I said.

Picking up my tablet, Andy noted, "So Winters plans to depose Mrs. Sapp, McMannis, Dr. Kwek of BCI, Dr. Wiechel and whatever expert Gams hires to look at the evidence," Andy said.

Sitting in the deli that day with summer just around the corner, we trusted that the investigation would play out as it should when all the material had been collected. And so far, it looked as if we were on the right track.

44

ON THE DAY OF THE fifth Mrs. Sapp's deposition, we gathered in the conference room waiting for her and Attorney Gams. Plump, with brown hair, she wore a plain blouse with slacks. Had I not known beforehand that she was in her mid-thirties and had seen her with James Sapp, I would not have guessed the age difference. In any event, he was an older man who looked his age. And by his own admission, he had trouble managing money. Why marry the guy? The woman had a good job, just moved into her own house shortly before the crash and owned her own car. I did have some theories.

What stood out for me was her lack of emotion. By this time, she was aware of the accusation that her present husband's van was the weapon that killed our son. We strongly suspected that she knew of the van's involvement. Sapp moved in with her a week or so after the crash and they hurried off to a Las Vegas trip six days after Andrew was killed—both events giving Sapp an excuse why the van was out of sight from the prying eyes of neighbors and giving him the opportunity to repair it.

Later we realized that the Crime Stoppers' videotaping occurred five weeks after the crash in early September, 1998, at her house and not Sapp's—we had attended the videotaping but had no idea whose house it was. When Sapp allowed the taping to take place at his then girlfriend's house, he involved her. Perhaps, the sight of a Sheriff's cruiser, once again, and a television van parked outside of his own house might have triggered neighbors' questions and suspicions. Sapp testified that at least one neighbor had asked Sapp about the reason for visits from the police. In any event, Sapp had already left his neighborhood when the police asked to use his van a second time for Crime Stoppers.

Revealing details about their traveling together to Las Vegas and his moving in with her on Oldbury Court in August—although he insisted these events happened a year later in 1999—Sapp pulled the girlfriend into the inquiry. Now Attorney Winters had to explore two additional areas, the Vegas trip and Sapp's move from his house. Knowing what we did about the van, these two events occurring right after the crash were too coincidental to ignore.

Mrs. Sapp didn't appear the least bit ruffled. Accuse any decent person of something horrible that he or she didn't do and 99.9% of the time, you'll get a strong emotional response from the person accused and those related to him. To use a cliché, she was as cool as a cucumber. No daggers were sent our way. In fact, she never looked at us.

I remember thinking during the first part of her deposition how composed she acted and how her answers were "Yes" or "No" with elaboration only where necessary. I would characterize her answers as sparse, telling only what was asked of her—unlike my deposition when I launched into detailed stories about Andrew and our family. I would have shouted from the rooftops what happened to Andrew and to us. During my deposition, David Winters had to kick my chair to tell me, "Shut up!" I wanted the forum. I wanted Sapp's attorneys to know about our family and how Andrew's death destroyed us.

Mrs. Sapp, I assumed, having been coached by State Farm attorneys, was determined to say as little as possible. That strategy may work most of the time but not always. If a witness withholds information that the attorney already knows, then the witness's omission looks intentional and suspicious. Sometimes that omission underscores an important detail.

A case in point entailed a question about her addresses and where she had lived in Dayton and Columbus. If she had not left out the one address we were most interested in, we would not have put that address in the spotlight.

She had a good memory of every place she had lived except for the address in 1996, just before she moved to Columbus. Winters had to remind her about the Brandt Pike address in Huber Heights, a Dayton suburb, which she omitted in her list.

She answered that she had lived in an apartment complex on Brandt Pike, Huber Heights, but wasn't sure whether the apartment's address was on Brandt Pike—the reason for her omission of Brandt Pike. Only the address *was* Brandt Pike and remarkably, that was also the address she used when she filed her last divorce as well the address to which authorities were called about a domestic situation. We first found the Brandt Pike address through court records for her traffic offense in 1996.

Principally, her Brandt Pike Road address jumped out at us not for the above reasons, but because it intersects Taylorsville Road, not far from the auto body shop that ordered a passenger side ground effect on August 6, 1998, under Glaval's production number and not a VIN. Out of five orders for that piece in August in the entire United States, only one order came from Ohio, the Taylorsville Road auto body shop. The body shop and Sapp's girlfriend's address, on Brandt Pike Road, were no more than two miles from one another. That could have been a coincidence, but then, she failed to mention that particular address—one which was personally significant to her.

Attorney Winters asked her the inevitable questions about Deputy McMannis and his request to videotape Sapp's van for a television Crime Stoppers interview. She answered confidently that she remembered when the police came to do the videotaping for Crime Stoppers. It was her recollection that it had happened at Sapp's house. *Only it didn't.* The details of the Crime Stoppers interview as well as the *time* and *place* could have been verified by looking at the video. All they had to do was to view the tape. The taping was at Oldbury Court, her house, in September, five weeks after the crash. Andy and I participated in that Crime Stoppers interview. We knew that event backwards and forwards. When she was asked about that, her answers were riddled with inaccuracies.

Attorney Gams could have checked out her story with the television station and the *Dispatch* before the deposition. But the truth would not have served them. The details had to be distorted to throw doubt on the Sapp van.

By September the then girlfriend and Sapp were living together at Oldbury and worked at the same place. They could have driven to work together, unless he used his second vehicle, a truck. A witness can successfully mislead with bad information only if the other parties don't have the verifiable facts. Boldly, she was trying to lead.

> Q. [Mr. Winters] …There was a Crime Stoppers video made ultimately. Are you aware of that?
>
> A. Yes.
>
> Q. I believe that was done on Oldbury. Do you have any recollection of that occurring?
>
> A. …it's my recollection that no, it was done on Rugosa.
>
> Q. Is there anything in particular that makes you think it was Rugosa as opposed to Oldbury?
>
> A. Because it's my recollection that it was done during the time frame that we had gone on a vacation and the van I believe had been left outside. So that they could do that while we were gone.

Nothing about her recollection was true. The van wasn't left outside at Rugosa while they were gone the first week in August. The van was nowhere in sight then—it was being repaired.

The time and the place were wrong. She said that she was "fairly certain of that."

Winters turned his attention to the trip to Las Vegas.

Q.   What can you tell me about how you happened to decide to go to Las Vegas?

A.   Jim had always wanted to go there and someone that he worked with…in that general area was planning a trip, a couple—several couples, 3 or 4 couples and said would you like to go?

Q.   Who took steps to make the trip happen in terms of making plans and making reservations?

A.   … it was his friend or business acquaintance that we were going to be going with. Jim was really the contact point with him.

Mrs. Sapp claimed that the trip had been in the works for several months before they went in August. In fact, she testified that three or four couples from Sapp's office wanted to go. When she was pressed for details, like their names, her memory failed her. She offered one name, a "Bill" with a common last name, whom she said no longer worked with them and had left Columbus. Sapp in his testimony said that the trip was a honeymoon—actually, they had not been married yet. Their stories collided.

Winters then asked her for vacation documentation from her place of employment.

Q.   What did you have to do to get permission to leave? You are suggesting this came up kind of spur of the moment?

A.   No, no.

Q.   Oh, it wasn't?

A.   No, it was a planned trip.

Q.   What paperwork has to be completed in order for someone to leave, be it a trip to Las Vegas?

A.   Since we have been at this facility…I don't recall ever being required to submit in writing or give a piece of paper that says I request such and such time off

Trying to imagine the logistical nightmare of keeping track of employees of a large government agency strained my ability to believe any organization could operate like that.

Six days after the crash Sapp and the girlfriend flew to Las Vegas. We knew that the Sapp van killed Andrew. What relevance could this trip have to the crash? Unless we had a suspicion that the trip served a specific purpose—like an excuse to have the van out of sight while being repaired—Mrs. Sapp's attorney could have asked, "Why is this relevant?" But Mrs. Sapp's attorney wasn't mystified by Winters' questions.

At this point, Attorney Gams asked for a brief break and when all the parties returned to the conference room, Gams announced that Mrs. Sapp had informed him that she had confirmation of the trip. Not with her, at home. She even told him the exact date—five years ago—of the confirmation! That told me that Mrs. Sapp knew the implication of a spur-of-the-moment trip. Otherwise, she would not have had a clue why the question was asked and neither would her attorney.

Mrs. Sapp did not have any papers with her and, in fact, referred to nothing during the deposition. In any event, any paper having to with the Las Vegas trip had to come from a third source and not her. The die was already cast that the trip was not planned.

Yet her memory wasn't so keen when she was asked whether she had had any auto accidents after 1998 and her answer was, "…yes, just recently. Maybe three months ago."

She could give the exact date of a paper five years old, but she didn't know the date of an auto accident three months ago? No offer of an accident report was voluntarily put forward. An auto accident by anyone having access to the Sapp van was absolutely relevant, but Winters didn't pursue this.

No question—the latest Mrs. Sapp and Mr. Sapp didn't get their stories straight. Mr. Sapp stated that the Vegas trip was a honeymoon and never mentioned that any co-workers and their spouses had planned to go. Mrs. Sapp never mentioned the word "honeymoon" and testified that other people in Sapp's office also went to Vegas.

Coincidentally, both Sapp and Mrs. Sapp during their depositions mentioned church. Winters asked Mrs. Sapp what groups or organizations she belonged to. Along with PTA, she said she was a member of a church. The church card.

Q.   (Winters): When did you start attending church?"

A.   In May of 1998.

She remembered when she started attending church five years ago—in May, 1998 but didn't remember the month of a recent auto accident? Interestingly, she started attending church just months *before* Andrew's crash but two years *after* she settled in Columbus. Curiously, the pastor of the church she and Sapp attended cancelled his testimony as their witness. Again, no objective corroboration.

Of all the depositions I was to witness, only one answer struck me as humorous. I thought Mrs. Sapp's answer to the next question so amusing that I stifled a laugh.

Q.   Do you on occasion consume alcohol?

A.   No.

Q.   No, you don't drink at all?

A.   At communion.

How could she handle these questions without some anger? They were obviously accusatory of her now husband. How could she remain so calm—so detached? How involved was she?

By this time, we had put together enough of the pieces of the puzzle, including the activities of James Sapp and his then girlfriend in August. Listening to Mrs. Sapp's testimony, I was struck by her nonchalance. She didn't remember her Brandt Pike address where she lived when she filed her last divorce and got a traffic citation. She traveled with Sapp to Las Vegas six days after the crash and couldn't remember names of people who traveled with them. She had no work verification that the Vegas trip was planned. She couldn't remember the recent date of an auto accident. She "inaccurately" testified as to the where and when of the Crime Stoppers taping. Her boyfriend, Sapp, moved out of his neighborhood and in with her immediately after the crash.

We had collected more information than these people realized. "Overkill" as Maryanne, my friend, stated. Not to us. We couldn't imagine the horror of accusing an innocent person of killing our son. We had laid the foundation.

As an aside, the Sapps are now divorced.

45

HALLOWEEN WAS OVER AND WE were heading toward another holiday season. David Winters, our attorney now, began preparations to take John Wiechel's testimony, as well as Dr. Kwek's testimony of BCI. Many offices shut down several weeks before Christmas, but Winters and Gams managed to schedule Dr. Wiechel's deposition.

James O. Sapp's attorney, Mark Gams for State Farm, had to hire his own expert to examine the Sapp van, housed at SEA. Attorney Gams chose Greg DuBois, of CTL Engineering. DuBois and John Wiechel are well-known engineering experts in Columbus. But their credentials are different. DuBois earned his undergraduate degree in metallurgy from the University of Cincinnati while Dr. Wiechel earned his undergraduate and master degrees in mechanical engineering from Purdue, and his doctoral degree in biomechanical engineering from The Ohio State University.

Dr. Wiechel's experience in vehicle accident reconstruction is vast compared to that of Mr. DuBois. Dr. Wiechel has certification to practice in approximately twenty states; DuBois is certified to practice in Ohio and West Virginia. Considered the guru of accident reconstruction in Ohio, Dr. Wiechel's reputation and breadth of experience are stellar and far-reaching.

We had arranged to meet Attorney Winters and Dr. Wiechel in the lobby before going up to Attorney Gams' offices. Lining that stretch of East Broad were several businesses and churches festively decorated for the holidays. Outside, small bright lights wrapped around trees and shrubs. Inside, pine wreaths with gold organza bows hung in the expansive windows of the Motorist building. Here, we were about to witness our expert's testimony under oath.

We understood on the most fundamental level that Dr. Wiechel's testimony, based on his scientific and engineering examination of the van, would provide strong evidence implicating the Sapp van. Beyond that, we didn't think about the consequences of Dr. Wiechel's testimony—that because of his professional credibility, this part of our nightmare could have been over before Christmas. And that State Farm's attorney would suggest to Attorney Winters that we talk settlement without admitting to any of Sapp's wrongdoing. Sometimes practicality should triumph over principles—a lesson we still had to learn.

Waiting in the lobby, Andy and I watched Winters and John Wiechel enter the building. They could not have had a more contrasting physical appearance. David, thin and of average height, with dark, curly hair, wore a black Cashmere coat. John, stocky and tall, with strawberry blonde hair, sported a belted tan trench coat. And they were unlike in personality, too—Wiechel, the more relaxed figure of the two. He radiated ease in his professional and personal dealings with people—the kind of person who was easily liked and eminently respected.

Thus far, we had talked to Wiechel enough times to know essentially what he would say in testimony. The deposition went as expected. Besides Dr. Wiechel, Attorney Winters and Attorney Gams, Andy and I were the only other people present. Principally, Wiechel's testimony covered those significant points as to why SEA believed to a scientific, reasonable degree of probability that the Sapp van killed our son. That was the gold standard for science.

His deposition supported those primary items in his report to Mark Adams and us in August 2002: (1) the ground effect pieces matched the holes of the van; (2) in the crash two pieces of the ground effect broke off a longer part—with each of those pieces having been torn off differently; the difference in the torn configuration of the two holes matched up to holes in the van; (3) paint chips in Andrew's clothes matched to the inside door of the van; (4) at least three windshields had been installed in the van—records could account for only two; (5) SEA discovered a head-sized dent on the passenger side roof and windshield line; (6) damage and then repair had been made to the post separating the windshield and passenger window and (7) the flange was bent at the breaking off point of the ground effect.

Also, Wiechel's testimony corroborated Jack Holland's examination of Andrew's bicycle during Deputy McMannis's first deposition in May 2000. Jack, a retired State Highway Patrol accident reconstructionist of excellent reputation, while conferring with McMannis at McMannis' first deposition, stated that the van that hit Andrew had been to the right of white line on the right side of the road—that Andrew suffered a direct hit from the back instead of a more expected side hit. Privately, Dr. Wiechel confided that the hit to Andrew's bike could have been done deliberately. He reasoned that the bike's skid marks indicated that Andrew was riding as far to the right as possible.

The thought that the driver deliberately chose to drive while impaired and left our son after hitting him were all that we could bear. To us, that took this crash out of the realm of an accident and into the realm of murder.

Of course, we knew what Dr. Wiechel's findings were, and what Dr. Kwek's findings were as stated in her report. The unknown was what State Farm's expert, Greg DuBois, for the defendant, James Sapp, would say in his deposition. We had watched enough crime shows and read enough books to know that the experts can spin their findings any way their clients want. If that's true for the defendants, then that's true, you may say, for us too, the plaintiffs.

Only for us, we had the corroboration of Dr. Wiechel's findings from a disinterested third party, Dr. Karen Kwek of BCI, in addition to information from the Glaval Corporation's Dewayne Creighton which pointed squarely to the Sapp van. And after Jack Holland's initial examination at Metro Chevrolet, his admonition, "You have probable cause. Call your attorney." And Judge Lisa Sadler believed we had the evidence. We asked Dr. Wiechel to look at the van not because we had a suit, we didn't. And never considered a suit until we realized the FCSO had chosen to do nothing—nothing—despite the overwhelming evidence that the Sapp van killed our son.

This was information that the FCSO could have used to proceed to investigate criminal charges against Mr. Sapp. This was the sole reason we had asked Dr. Wiechel to examine the van. Deputy McMannis' subsequent testimony—his story as to the events of the investigation—which not one person, not one document corroborated—could not erase the science that this van was involved. We were forced to file a civil suit.

Dr. Kwek, Dewayne Creighton, Jack Holland and Dr. Wiechel—none of them had anything to gain by our filing a civil suit. Each stated factual information, which in turn incriminated the Sapp van. Jack Holland never sent us a bill. His motivation was to help us get the truth. The purpose of Dr. Wiechel's examination was to motivate the FCSO.

We were acutely interested in how Attorney Gams' or State Farm's expert, Greg DuBois, interpreted the evidence. Some facts he *couldn't* deny—like the ground effect pieces matching the van and the paint match from Andrew's clothes to the van. Or would he deny that they matched? How? He would have to negate the Sheriff deputies' findings that the ground effect matched after the van was confiscated from Metro. Those pieces would never have been transported to BCI for examination had they not matched. In addition, DuBois would have to negate BCI's findings. Eagerly, we awaited word of his scheduled deposition. We had no idea how easy it is to convince some people that white is black and black is white. All you have to do is say it.

46

MARK GAMS' OFFICE ON THE nineteenth floor of an East Broad Street building spoke of success. I have no idea how many attorneys work at this firm but clearly, if they wanted to impress their clients and visitors with how successful the practice was, they hired the right decorator to arrange and furnish their lobby, not unlike a small hotel's.

Continually, Attorney Gams fascinated me. As with most professionals I meet, I'd imagine them in my high school classroom and the kind of students I think they would have been. After thirty years of teaching, whether I wanted to or not, I was programmed to observe and evaluate the way people act and speak.

I could picture Gams, a shorter than average adult, giving an oral report in my English class. Standing in front of the class, his stature would not match his voice. He would speak louder than any other student.

Gams' associate in this case was a young woman, Danielle Dunn. The two attorneys, Gams—perhaps in his early forties—and Dunn—in her thirties—made an unconventional-looking pair. Mr. Gams, short, and Ms. Dunn, tall and thin, commanded more than an ordinary amount of my attention. If I had been a casting director for the movies, I would not have chosen either one to play a lawyer.

We attended seven depositions in that office. Two of those were Andy's and mine, a person who called our house about the Barry Snidka tip, Deputy McMannis, Dr. Wiechel, Dr. Kwek and Mr. DuBois, in that order. But I have chosen to recount the depositions of Dr. Wiechel (previous chapter) and Greg DuBois, experts for each side, so that the reader can contrast the two testimonies. And then Dr. Kwek's deposition. Even though Deputy McMannis' deposition came before Wiechel's, DuBois' and Kwek's, I will save the details of McMannis' testimony for last because of *his* stunning revelations about his investigation and the statements he made which, I believe, affected the outcome of the civil trial.

Since we had not anticipated the surprises that were to come with McMannis' testimony, our attention was riveted on Greg DuBois, State Farm's expert—not a mechanical engineer. After we had spent an enormous amount of time collecting information from every possible source connected to the Sapp van and the pieces continued to fit, we trusted beyond any doubt we had the van that killed Andrew. Of course, by this time we knew how things worked. We never entertained the thought that Mr. DuBois would surrender to the facts and to the notion that State Farm would admit to insuring a vehicle involved in a hit-and-run fatality. Yet truth was on our side.

Tall, thin, and rather good-looking, Mr. DuBois took his place at the table next to me. He made a good first impression. He delivered his testimony with confidence and professionalism. At one point in the deposition I found myself listening to his answers, not taking notes. He talked with authority even though it seemed to us he clearly didn't have all the facts, didn't understand them, or didn't want to acknowledge them. We knew what his job was. Then again, we weren't really prepared for this expert's speculative, far-fetched notions characterizing his challenge to the verifiable facts.

His first statement to make me sit up and take notice concerned a question that Winters asked to establish Mr. DuBois' credentials in dealing with a case such as ours. Winters asked him for a listing of his cases in accident reconstruction.

DuBois responded, "I testified in northern Kentucky that involved a case in which there was an alleged hit-and-run, a phantom vehicle allegedly started an accident. And interestingly that is a very similar case to this…"

DuBois used some loaded words in his answer "alleged hit-and-run" suggesting no hit-and-run took place in our case? A phantom vehicle? The use of these incendiary words to draw a comparison between that case and our case assaulted his rationality. Subsequent statements were not as odd but irrational does come to mind. Now DuBois piqued my imagination. What would he say about the ground effect evidence?

DuBois had made two trips to the SEA facility to look at the van. Attorney Winters asked him why he had gone back a second time.

DuBois responded that he wanted to "measure the location of all the drilled holes in the running board on the van. I am talking about on the van itself as opposed to the ground effects device, the portion of the van below the doors."

[Clearly, he had limited vehicle experience and wasn't familiar with "that portion of the van below the doors" termed the rocker panel and not "running board."]

DuBois said that he found three sets of holes [in the van's rocker panel] to which three different ground effects would have been attached.

Q: [Attorney Winters] we are talking exclusive as to the passenger's side of this van?

A: Yes. And if I knew the location of those holes by some measurement, it would be easier to…relay my thoughts about them…and I wanted to verify which of the holes most closely matched the ground effects piece found at the accident scene [and] which of the holes most closely matched the ground effects device currently installed on the van."

During the deposition, DuBois handed over a set of photos and mea-surements he had taken of the three sets of holes in the van's passenger side rocker panel. We all knew that the passenger side had had three different ground effects: the one at the time of its confiscation from Metro; one set that matched the pieces at the accident and a third unaccounted one.

The photos and DuBois' own measurements verified that the ground effect was a part installed without pattern or arrangement as the distance between and among drilled holes could not have been more varied. They were as Glaval reported: drilled randomly, without a jig, wherever the installer wished.

The custom installation of the ground effects on the Sapp van, a critical point to emphasize, was like DNA, unique and one of a kind. At one point DuBois denied that the ground effect pieces matched up to the Sapp van. Then DuBois corrected himself by stating, "and it seems to me that there are other possible explanations for that hole being such a close match."

His scientific explanation? "One, of course, just a coincidence."

And his next scientific explanation was categorically wrong. DuBois: "A second observation…when these ground effect devices were originally manufactured there *may have been* some system in place that consistently produced the same hole locations on the running boards. There would have been marks put on the running board so the installers would put the three screw holes in the same place…so that you've got holes in consistently the same place."

DuBois was fumbling, reaching for some explanation to satisfy Gams. Any child could see that all nine holes were drilled wherever—no pattern even remotely existed. Glaval reported the part was installed by random drilling. But DuBois was not a child. During this part of the deposition, DuBois should have been challenged to explain.

If Glaval had a system to drill each hole in the same place—which it didn't, we wouldn't be here. Would we? The Sheriff's Office would not have sent the van off to BCI for examination to see if the pieces matched. There would have been absolutely no way we could have proven that those pieces found at the scene came from any particular Glaval van. None. In pointing to a specific van, those parts would have been useless had their holes and the van's holes been consistently predetermined. There it was—right in front of us. The explanation the defense planned to use to convince a jury that the holes had not been randomly drilled—that there may have been some system in place.

His own measurements proved that Glaval used no system. Case closed on that idea sticking but that's not how this "expert" chose to deal with the verifiable facts.

DuBois had no wiggle room in testifying how the pieces were pulled out of the van. The van, itself, not Dr. Wiechel, held the proof. If you read the answer carefully, DuBois agreed with Dr. Wiechel that the hole in the wheel well was pulled out. He qualified his answer by stating that he didn't know the size of the screw. What? He needed to know the size of the screw? He didn't hedge, however, at to the other hole.

> Q: Rocker panel screw hole not pulled, matching ground effects
>   piece hole has head pulled through. Agree or disagree?
>
> A: Agree.

The other piece of the ground effect that had broken off was attached to the rocker panel. DuBois had to admit that the way the two pieces were torn off match the configuration of the van holes.

At another point in his deposition, DuBois said that "there had probably not been a ground effect device installed on the right side…or any reason to install one for that matter." Except that it was standard equipment on all Glaval's Gladiator Chevy vans! You would expect that any expert would have known the ground effect was standard equipment. Those were the facts. The only recourse Dubois had was to deny the facts and then muddy the waters.

I listened half-heartedly to the rest of the deposition. I had to admit DuBois' voice, manner and appearance were assets, but to me, had I been Gams I would have been embarrassed. What we knew and thought about DuBois' groundless statements didn't matter. A jury would judge his testimony. An attorney would have to prepare a jury to understand the difficult evidence, often esoteric, in language and illustrations to make the evidence clear to a layperson.

Greg DuBois' deposition was so off base that David Winters should have been ecstatic. Unwittingly, DuBois had demonstrated with his measurements exactly what Winters needed to prove—that the installation of each new or different ground effect is random—at Glaval and any other body shop. Undamaged ground effects already installed but which must be removed for some reason, are reinstalled using the same holes in the rocker panel and ground effect.

DuBois, as State Farm's expert, had to plant doubt about the ground effect pieces matching the Sapp van. His job at the trial was to discredit the ground effects evidence and all that we factually knew about that piece. Yet his measurements of the distance between and among all the holes in the rocker panel proved our case, not his.

A lay person could ask, "What kind of company would install vehicle parts randomly?" Random drilling wouldn't make sense to anyone not knowing about custom van conversion companies. It was up to Winters to deal vigorously with DuBois' erroneous speculation. He would have to educate the jury about the custom installation methods of van conversion companies. Ideally, he would have to take them to the SEA facility and have them examine the van and ground effects.

47

WE HAD WITNESSED WHAT WE thought would be one of the most challenging depositions of all—the opposing side's expert. Realizing that DuBois was creating answers from his own erroneous assumptions, we weren't particularly bothered by his disagreement with Dr. Wiechel's conclusion that the Sapp van killed Andrew. Obviously, DuBois had to say what he had to say. He had to throw misleading speculation and flawed assumptions into his testimony to refute the facts. Having taken so much care to gather, question and re-question the mounting evidence, we listened carefully to every word DuBois said. What struck me was his use of the word "if" when he was hypothesizing about the evidence. And those "if" statements were flat-out factually wrong.

Later that afternoon, when we had a chance to relax, and while the coffee percolated, Andy remarked, "I was impressed when Winters read John Wiechel's list of findings and cornered DuBois into agreeing or disagreeing with John's examination."

"Yeah, because up to that point, it sounded like DuBois didn't agree with anything," I said.

"He agreed with every item on that list but disagreed with John's conclusions," Andy reminded.

"He saw the same things but disagreed that this van killed Andrew," I said.

"He has to say that. That's his paycheck," Andy reminded me.

"Couldn't someone say that about Wiechel?" I asked.

"No. They couldn't. Dr. Wiechel's paycheck didn't depend on his conclusions about the van. He was going to be paid based on an objective examination. His job was to tell us whether we needed to go back to the police or move on. The police ignored the BCI report. Did we or did we not have something here? We had no thought about a civil suit. Gams hired DuBois when we filed against Sapp. His job is to throw doubt on Wiechel's examination."

Several weeks later Brenda, David Winters' secretary, called to tell us that she had a copy of the DuBois' deposition and we could pick it up. In the days that followed the DuBois' deposition, we tried to recreate what DuBois testified about the "second set of holes" as the reason *he said the Sapp van couldn't have been involved in Andrew's death.* At the time of the deposition, I couldn't quite follow what he was getting at, but it had something to do with the "second holes."

We dropped what we were doing to drive downtown to get the copy. Since we weren't far from restaurants in German Village, I suggested that we go there for supper while we looked over the deposition. Sometimes just being away from the house in a different setting helped us to be a bit more civil in discussing what these depositions revealed. It's a chilling thing to grasp that at some point in searching for answers we could have been looking directly at the driver who killed Andrew.

With exposed brick walls and tables in front of windows overlooking the village streets, Schmidt's is a favorite restaurant for diners in search of authentic German food and music. No matter what time of the late afternoon or early evening, the rooms in this Columbus landmark are busy with patrons looking for Schmidt's signature sausage sandwiches and peach strudel.

Seated in a booth across from Andy, I opened the envelope and removed Greg DuBois' deposition. Scanning the deposition, I looked for his testimony explaining why he didn't think the Sapp van killed Andrew.

Reading quickly to get the gist of DuBois' testimony—key testimony— that detailed State Farm's expert's speculation that the Sapp van was not involved in our son's death, I let out a sigh of disgust. As discussed before, three sets of holes had been drilled in the van's rocker panel. The first set belonged to the pieces found at the crash, from the original part, and the third set belonged to the ground effect on the van at the time of its confiscation. The second set, Wiechel asserted, belonged to a ground effect installed *after* Andrew's bike had torn off the original part. What happened to that ground effect, we don't know. Maybe it was borrowed temporarily.

"Listen to this," I said to Andy. "Listen to what DuBois said about the second set of holes and why he believes this isn't the van.

DuBois: "…a possible explanation for the second installation would have been when the damage to the right side of the van occurred before Mr. Sapp owned the van. Because there was painting…I would expect that they [Voss Chevrolet] may have removed the ground effects device and then reinstalled it. When they reinstalled it, it's possible they could have redrilled new holes right next to the original holes…because it would be hard to match up every hole exactly right."

The opposite is true. It's harder to attach by redrilling. Pat Kowalski testified that Voss Chevrolet uses the same holes if a ground effect is reattached. And every single mechanic will tell you that the part is reattached by using the existing holes. Andy and I witnessed the removal of three ground effects at Goodyear. Mechanics screwed off the ground effects to look for additional holes. None of them had any. In reattaching the ground effect, mechanics aligned the holes in the ground effect to the rocker panel using the same holes. Screwing back the part took no more than a few minutes. Dubois' speculation as to why the Sapp van couldn't have killed Andrew made no sense.

"I wonder if Winters was following his thinking? At least Dubois figured that the second set was the suspicious set.

That evening, we paid our bill and left Schmidt's without eating the rest of our food. If this was the way the law worked—no accurate probing of the information, no real search for truth—that an expert could say whatever—we should have had some inkling then what was going to happen.

48

WHEN WE ENTERED THE LOBBY of Attorney Gams' office that winter morning, the only other person in the waiting room was an attractive Asian woman. We assumed she was Dr. Kwek of the Bureau of Criminal Investigation and Identification (BCI)—the official forensic laboratory used by most Ohio law enforcement agencies like the Franklin County Sheriff's Office. Some of the larger police departments have their own in-house forensic facilities.

As much as I thanked her silently for her examination of the Sapp van and her report, all I could think about was her description of Andrew's socks as smelly, dirty and ragged when she pulled them out of the black plastic bag at the BCI lab. These had to be the socks he had worn to Ultimate Frisbee practice that afternoon. Raggedy, I would accept. That was Andrew. He never threw a pair of socks away. If I needed a rag for dusting or cleaning, I went to his sock drawer. But with the dirty and smelly part, I took issue. This young man was finicky about cleanliness. I think he washed a load of clothes every day, and in the summer, he usually took three daily showers. On the morning of his death before going to practice, he was taking a shower when I left to buy groceries.

Dr. Kwek's description of Andrew's socks helped me, however, to estimate the time he left the house on August 1 to take that terrible bike ride. Obviously, he hadn't showered or changed clothes. He had planned to go to Cincinnati after practice. It had to have been early evening.

When we were called into the conference room for Dr. Kwek's deposition, the young woman headed with us in that direction. Mark Gams would question her.

Of special interest to us was Kwek's testimony involving the paint chips found in Andrew's clothing and the smears on the top and bottom tubes of his bicycle. It was up to Dr. Kwek to offer her professional opinion about paint.

From the onset, Dr. Kwek's melodic, light British accent captivated me. Still, I listened critically and took notes, especially in those areas of her deposition where we needed more information.

During her postgraduate work in France, Dr. Kwek studied the synthesis of biomolecular compounds. Later, she specialized in paint analysis at the Center for Forensic Sciences in Toronto. She testified that she concentrated on paint analysis but as a trace analyst, she examined other kinds of physical evidence, "such as paint, glass, hairs, fibers and impression evidence and miscellaneous other physical evidence."

After she listed her academic achievements, she rolled through a list of her accreditations. No doubt she was well-qualified. We knew what her initial report to the Sheriff's Office said, but we hadn't yet seen her final report. To explore the kind of experience Dr. Kwek had in crashes like ours, Gams questioned her:

> Q: Before being involved in the Starinchak matter, had you been involved in any other bicycle /motor vehicle hit-and-run type forensic testing?
>
> A: Yes, I have previously, in Toronto, Canada—involving a bicycle, maybe two other times…I've done many cases involving hit-and-run type accidents involving pedestrians and cars, other types of motor vehicles.
>
> [Unlike DuBois, Dr. Kwek demonstrated a fair amount of experience in hit-and-run crashes.]
>
> Q: Let's talk about the Starinchak case…Based on your recollection and notes how do you recall this file coming to you?
>
> A: I'm first making reference to our submission sheet…that law enforcement would bring with them upon submission of items to the Bureau…
>
> Q: Okay.
>
> A: What you see on the bottom is a list of the items…actually submitted and the examinations requested. So what was delivered to the lab on July 18th of 2001 was a 1993 Chevrolet Astro van… A 1998 Schwinn bicycle…two pieces of what was described as right side rocker panel cover recovered from the crash scene…a black plastic bag marked as…Starinchak clothes.

The submission sheet directed Dr. Kwek to determine if the above van struck the bicycle and rider on the right side which resulted in the death of the rider: She was to look for paint transference from the van to the bicycle and from the bicycle to the van and ground effect. She was also to check damage on the bicycle to determine if it is consistent with repaired areas on the van and to determine if the windshield had been replaced.

Puzzling to us, Attorney Gams at this point in the deposition did not follow up on the all the instructions and what her findings were. Conceivably that was Winters' job.

Not until after Dr. Kwek's deposition did we see those instructions submitted by Deputy Fickenworth. For some reason, given what she said in testimony, she didn't complete the list, like checking the windshield. She was a glass expert. Was she ordered to terminate her examination? Yes, that's what had happened.

Dr. Kwek interpreted some of the instructions to mean that DNA testing should be done but that because the case investigator, Ross Staggs, communicated with the serology examiner that "no work was necessary in this case because it was submitted so much later there was no relevance in doing DNA analyses." What was going on there? We agreed that because the Sapp van's exterior had been rigorously altered—painted and repainted, striping removed, decals placed on the side, back windows, and rear lights—almost no chance existed of Andrew's DNA still being in evidence on the exterior. But an examination of the van's exterior for DNA was not the issue; it dealt with a hair that a mechanic from Metro had pulled out of the rubber gasket from the passenger side door. Jack Holland, our accident reconstructionist, took the hair from the mechanic and put it in an envelope. We gave the envelope to Staggs. He commented to us, "We don't have the money to test this." We accepted that. And in response I said, "Then, we'll pay for it, but let's get it tested." It takes years for DNA to deteriorate.

The Sheriff's Office had the hair from the van at the time the van was transported to BCI. Apparently, from Dr. Kwek's testimony, she knew nothing about testing a hair for DNA.

Staggs had the hair that Jack Holland had witnessed a Metro mechanic remove from the van. Staggs pulled the plug on its being tested. The reason: the time factor. DNA can survive for years and it's likely that the hair's DNA had not degraded in three years. The chance that the hair was Andrew's, I thought, was remote. We wanted the hair tested anyway. Send us the bill. I was disgusted when Dr. Kwek testified that Staggs scratched the DNA testing from Deputy Fickenworth's list, *especially, since Dr. Kwek testified that she was a biological expert only in testing hair.* Staggs made no mention of a hair to her.

In examining the fall-out from Andrew's clothes, Kwek observed "tiny glass fragments and tiny white deposits" and "one tiny white paint chip that was collected from an apparent bloodstained region" of the t-shirt. She observed that if "the paints appear similar or the same in color" she would "proceed with chemical analysis."

When Kwek compared the chips in Andrew's clothes to the chip taken from around the taillight from the van which had escaped the two paintings done after the crash, she stated, "I found that the three-layer paint from item number 4 (Andrew's clothes) is indistinguishable in layer sequence, color and microscopic appearance and similar in chemical composition to the original three-layer paint removed from item number 1" (the van). Dr. Kwek had a match of van paint to chips in Andrew's clothes.

After Kwek verified that the paint chip had adhered to the blood stain, Attorney Gams asked her if she thought the chip was the result of this accident. She was noncommittal. At this point, she knew absolutely nothing about the crash—nothing, not even if blood was involved. Without any background information, whatsoever about the crash and the van, she answered questions based solely on what was in front of her at the time.

That morning Dr. Kwek testified that she had found white paint smears on the top and bottom bars of Andrew's bicycle. The smears from the top tube of the bike appeared similar in color and microscopic appearance to the white paint on the fiberglass pieces. A white smear on the bike's lower tube was different in color and different in chemical composition—much like house paint. Andrew had been painting our house and garages when he was hit and killed. We needed more facts about the paint on the top bicycle tube and how it matched the van.

Interestingly, Dr. Kwek had testified earlier that she had extensive experience in testing glass. She found glass in Andrew's clothes. She conducted no tests on the glass shards. Deputy Fickenworth's instructions told her to examine glass. Had someone from the FCSO obstructed the testing of the hair and glass?

Also, I recalled that Dr. Kwek was told nothing about Glaval vans, specifically. In fact, she stated something very telling about the information she received from the Sheriff's Office that just about sums up the entire case. "They [the Sheriff] couldn't tell me—we had no synopsis of this case as to what happened. *I don't think the Sheriff's Office even knew what happened...*" An incredible assessment of the FCSO's knowledge of this case by a smart forensic scientist.

Considering the above, Gams then asked her if anything in her *paint* analysis pointed to this specific van "as opposed to any other van that would have had similar paint?" And of course, she didn't.

Toward the end of her testimony, Gams inquired what other testing had she done? She answered that the last items she had looked at were the two fiberglass pieces. She had been instructed to determine if these pieces originated from the Sapp vehicle.

She testified that she took one piece, 3A and "lined it up with that rear edge of the wheel well area and found that the two holes present on that piece lined up with holes that were there. Then I took the second piece…fitting behind the first piece… And the hole present on this piece lines up with one of the two holes in that region of the rocker panel."

Most of Dr. Kwek's testimony involved her tests and scientific examination of the materials the FCSO had given her. She had no idea that this was a customized van. She was given only a request sheet of items to examine – half of which never materialized because someone at the FCSO pulled the plug on those. Had Glaval not informed us of the random drilling and that if we found a van with holes to match the ground effect holes, "we had just won the lottery," we, too, would not have known. If we had not had that critical information, finding the vehicle that hit Andrew would have been impossible.

The van the FCSO confiscated from Metro in 2003 looked nothing like a custom, converted Glaval van. By the time we found it, it had been painted a stark white, had no striping, and looked generic, like a utility van. This was what Dr. Kwek saw and the Franklin County Sheriff gave her no other information about the van.

The deposition ended with a question about the windshield. Deputy Fickenworth's request sheet listed "examination of windshield to determine if it had been replaced." Dr. Kwek said that she "did not determine whether the windshield had been replaced." Our attorney didn't ask Dr. Kwek why the hair, glass and windshield were excluded. Given what we knew about the totality of this investigation, we assumed with suspicion that Staggs had his reasons for aborting the examination.

As that winter morning turned to noon, we hoped that Dr. Kwek's curiosity about our case might compel her to do some inquiry.

49

BRACING OURSELVES AGAINST THE BRISK November day in late 2003, Andy and I left our parked car in the open lot and headed up the side street to the main entrance of the Motorist Mutual Building on East Broad Street to witness the dramatic and bizarre deposition of the Sheriff's deputy, David McMannis—the proverbial fly with sticky feet who feasted on honey before flying into the spider's web.

This stunning performance—his deposition—cast him, undoubtedly, as a hostile witness. We had put him on *our* witness list. Neither Andy nor I had an inkling before the deposition of the extent he would go to cover his tracks and ultimately hurt us. Gloss over the details? We expected that. Recognizable lying under oath? No.

Our attorney, David Winters, never talked to McMannis before deposing him. Common sense dictated that Winters should have had an idea as to what Deputy McMannis was thinking. Obvious to all, McMannis had been livid when we asked the State Highway Patrol to take our case. His response, "I'm not going to ask the Patrol to do my job," replayed in many of our conversations. I merely thought that he would be ecstatic to be rid of us. Had I disrobed him of his costume uniform?

Winters had to explore McMannis' statement to his supervisor, Chief Deputy Gil Jones, that he saw the Sapp van "within one to two weeks after the crash" [stated in the letter from Jones to Attorney Benson Wolman]. We had maintained that it was not one but two weeks after the crash. Linda, our private investigator, discovered that McMannis took Polaroid photos. No work document existed to confirm when McMannis took those photos. *No work document existed to confirm any part of the investigation.* He brought two photos of the van to our house on August 14, two weeks after the crash. Neither Attorney Winters nor we had anticipated that McMannis would change his story.

Given the lack of his participation in an investigation with plenty to go on, McMannis' behavior confounded us. He had the list of Glaval vans but failed to use it. He had Andrew's clothes, but failed to have them examined for evidence. He had the bike. He had the pieces from the vehicle that killed Andrew. None of the evidence was tested until we found the Metro/Sapp van in 2001, three years after the crash and after he was no longer assigned to our case. Three years later.

At the time of the crash, he never asked BCI to run any tests. The clothes lay untouched in a plastic bag in the evidence room where the bicycle also lay on the floor. How he got away with it—ignoring damning evidence left at the scene was as perplexing. Just as puzzling was the inaction of his supervisors. Reports were non-existent.

As with McMannis' first deposition in 2000 when we were gathering evidence and knew almost nothing about the FCSO, we anticipated that McMannis would request this deposition in 2003 to take place at the Prosecutor's Office. "He's not going to consent to a deposition unless it's at the Prosecutor's Office," Andy reminded me. Except that McMannis didn't make the request. This time, in November 2003, the deposition would take place at the offices of Mark Gams, the attorney for Sapp and State Farm. The only plausible explanation was that McMannis felt that he was in friendly territory. The law office of the attorney representing the man whose van that experts determined killed our son was a safe haven for this deputy. At the close of that deposition, we stood aghast, speechless, at the level of deception and dissembling we had just heard. We might have been incredibly gullible in 1998, but not five years later.

Going into the deposition, we genuinely believed that McMannis would report events as they happened, peppered with excuses, and that as poor as the FCSO's investigation had been, we did not expect fabricated testimony. McMannis was under oath.

McMannis' deposition had been scheduled for one o'clock that afternoon. David Winters drove his black Porsche not more than a mile from his office to the Motorist Mutual Building. We met him briefly in the downstairs lobby to talk before taking the elevator to Attorney Gams' offices. "I think we're going to hear a lot of excuses," Andy said.

"And worthless explanations," I added.

But Winters was suspicious. "You need to paint the witness into a corner and give him no wiggle room,"

Winters had to show that McMannis didn't do his job, and that McMannis' negligence allowed a criminal to go free.

No question—Sapp's van killed Andrew. If Sapp denied being the driver, then the authorities had to explore other possible drivers. The owner of the weapon is the obvious person of interest. But the FCSO never talked to or contacted Sapp after the BCI report. Sapp had testified in his deposition at Mark's office that he was the only driver.

By this time, we thought that we knew the extent of the failure to investigate Andrew's death. We were wrong. We were soon to discover it. I expected McMannis to maintain that he had seen the Sapp van within the first or second week after Andrew's death—just as he told Jones as evidenced in Chief Deputy Jones' letter to Attorney Wolman. That letter should have been thrust in McMannis' face. It never was.

Neither Andy nor I expected McMannis to take sides. McMannis couldn't allow this van that he only "eyeballed" [his word] to be the killer van. Not the van that he procured for the Crime Stoppers' publicity. Not the van that he photographed. Would the truth—that he missed the smoking gun pointing directly at this van—a symptom of his professional apathy—confirm the reason for his demotion?

Exiting the elevator, we approached the large glass doors of Gams' office. Pushing against the doors, we no sooner entered the waiting area when all three of us glanced at the couple sitting on the couch. If they saw us, they didn't look up from the magazine that both were supposedly reading, periodically talking, and laughing. The Sapps. Mr. and the fifth Mrs.

Andy and I looked at each other in disbelief. What the? I said under my breath. There were eleven depositions, not counting their own, and this would be the only deposition that the Sapps attended. The testimony of Deputy David McMannis. Apparently, they weren't all that interested in what BCI had to say. *Only McMannis.* Someone Gams could manipulate? The weak link.

Stopping by the front desk, Winters gave our names and announced that we had a one o'clock appointment. It was precisely one o'clock. The receptionist responded, "I'll tell Attorney Gams. He's in a meeting." Winters nodded politely and we moved to a little alcove to stand and talk. The office foyer spoke of success—tufted leather furniture, paintings, and large ceramic lamps with just the right wattage to cast a glow over the show.

"Why are *they* here?" I asked Winters, nodding toward the Sapps.

"We'll soon find out."

"I don't see McMannis. He must not be here yet," Andy said.

"When he left the traffic office, what job did they give him?" I asked, making small talk.

"He stands in the back of the court room in case there's trouble," Andy responded.

As we were making an effort to talk, David Winters kept glancing at his watch. He was a model of punctuality. "It's almost one-thirty. Let me see what's going on. Maybe McMannis is a no-show."

Approaching the desk again, Winters asked, "We had a one o'clock deposition scheduled with Deputy McMannis and I don't see him. Could you check with Mark Gams to see if he cancelled?"

"Oh, he didn't. He's here. He's in a meeting with Attorney Gams," she offered. "I'll remind him you're here."

Turning to us, a look of disgust on his face, "McMannis has been here all along. He's in a meeting with Gams."

Winters' words hung in the air for a moment before sinking in. Immediately, all three of us knew that something was up. McMannis and Gams had been planning McMannis' testimony?

A few minutes later a staff person appeared to lead us to a conference room. As we approached the conference room, a door to an adjoining office opened and out emerged Deputy McMannis and Attorney Gams. During McMannis' deposition, the story they cooked up would become evident.

At the head of the long, polished table, the court reporter set up her equipment. To her right, Deputy McMannis took a seat. Winters sat next to him. I sat next to Winters and then Andy. Gams sat across from McMannis, an empty seat, and then the Sapps.

Days later in thinking about the deposition, I wondered if our attorney, David Winters, could have predicted that McMannis was going to testify on behalf of the Sapps. Meetings and conversations before McMannis' deposition smelled strongly of collusion between him and Attorney Gams. In this way, McMannis didn't miss the obvious and State Farm didn't have to pay up. Going into this, we had little doubt that McMannis wouldn't find a way to frame his apathy around some kind of creative excuse. We did not expect lies. He didn't have to lie. We weren't out to get him.

50

WHAT I THOUGHT WAS A routine deposition, the gathering of information, suddenly felt repulsive. The Sapps showing up only for this deposition besides their own? Neither came to the other's deposition. And the defendant's attorney meeting with the first investigator of our son's homicide, Deputy McMannis, before his deposition? What was wrong with this picture? As we were to learn, *plenty.*

Only Gams could not have anticipated the drama that would severely compromise McMannis' credibility after Winters got hold of him. Gams questioned him first. Simply reading the deposition would not give the reader full appreciation of this performance. A court reporter records only the words—not the body language or tone of the witness or the stunned faces of those present, having to listen to false testimony.

Attorney Gams' early questions dealt with McMannis' training as a deputy and then he moved on to questions about McMannis' part in the investigation of Andrew's death. McMannis arrived at the crash scene on that Sunday morning while Andrew still lay in the ditch. The deposition had just begun when we heard astounding information that we hadn't known in these five years. It explained why nothing was done in the investigation of our son's crash until the sixth day after his death. This exchange took place between Attorney Gams and McMannis.

> Q: Let's fast-forward a little bit after the scene had been
> secured and you left. What was your plan of investigation
> from there?
>
> A: Yes… During the period of time that the crash occurred, I
> was in the process of completing a training session at the
> Ohio Peace Officer Training Academy, on Monday, Tuesday
> and Wednesday, I believe of that week after the crash to
> complete that.

McMannis had done no investigating on Sunday when Andrew was found in the early morning, nor on Monday, Tuesday, or Wednesday of that week! No one had been appointed in his place to investigate Andrew's death; therefore, the investigation didn't begin until six days later. McMannis confirmed that he had no idea what measures were taken in his absence. No investigation. No measures. No sense of responsibility. No thoughts. No activity. I sat stunned.

> Q: And what do you recall was your plan to do first when you got back to the office?
>
> A.   Initially we would complete a crash report... And then start the process of trying to determine what vehicle these pieces would have come from in the attempt to locate a suspect.

Now McMannis just admitted that on Thursday morning, six days after Andrew's death, on his first day back on the job, he would "start the process of trying to determine what vehicle those pieces came from" proving he didn't have the remotest idea about those pieces at the start of the work day on Thursday. But he'll change his story.

> Q: And what did you do in that regard? [to determine what vehicle those pieces were from]
>
> A: Several things. We went to aftermarket places. That's how we determined they were most likely Glaval parts [and] to see if anybody had been looking for one. Of the businesses we talked to, none had [and] then to several dealerships...to determine first of all, what make or model of vehicle are we looking for.

On Thursday morning, August 6, McMannis' own testimony confirms that he had to determine make and model. He had no idea before that.

> Q: What did you do... to locate a van that matched this description?
>
> A: [W]e eventually obtained a list of vans from Glaval...we sent out faxes and notices to body shops.

The FCSO did eventually send faxes to area body shops with a brief description and it did receive a list from Glaval—both events happening near the end of August. The Glaval list contained the VINs of Glaval vans in the Central Ohio area—so vital that had it been used, it would have placed the Sapp van in McMannis' lap.

Q: What else did you do?

A: We went to the media... [McMannis arranged a media conference on Friday, August 7 in the afternoon.]

Q: Did you take photographs of any vans?

A: Not right away. I mean we—I didn't have—we had the pieces in our possession, but I—took a picture of, I think, a van that we had gotten from Byers [a dealership] to show...how they fit right onto a GMC van...without a conversion package...

When asked if he took photographs, McMannis answered—"not right away." His testimony in 2000 and now in 2003 established that he didn't know on Thursday morning what make and model vehicle was involved when he returned to the office after training. By Friday, August 7 (seven days after Andrew's crash), he had the make and model because of his investigative work on Thursday. He arranged a media conference Friday afternoon to announce the make and model. Hence, because he had not seen a Glaval van as yet—not right away—to demonstrate to the media where those pieces fit on a Glaval van, he borrowed a new Chevy van [not Glaval] from a dealership.

McMannis continues: The other van [Sapp] I photographed was the one that I found in the neighborhood [same town but not his neighborhood] in which I live. That was the first van, I feel, that I photographed.

McMannis did take Polaroid photos of the Sapp van in Reynoldsburg, but not on the date McMannis will testify he took those photographs. On Sunday, August 2, he left the crash site. No investigating. On Monday, Tuesday, and Wednesday of that week he was out of the office training in London, Ohio, and did not begin investigating until he returned to the traffic office on Thursday morning, August 6.

Interestingly, however, as his testimony progressed, he claimed that he had seen the Sapp van on Wednesday, the day prior to his return to the office. Conversely, in his first 2000 deposition, not yet two years after Andrew's death, McMannis specifically stated that during the period he was trying to determine the make and model, he saw **no** Glaval van, despite an effort to find one. He visited several dealerships to see if they had one. He saw none. He forgot about that detail in this deposition. In 2000, he volunteered that detail in an answer. He shared no Polaroid photos of the Sapp van with the press that Friday, August 7. The purpose of the photos was public dissemination. He had not seen the van yet and therefore, had no photos. Yes, he and Gams believed we were unable to detect this blatant discrepancy.

Gams and McMannis now had a problem. McMannis didn't work our case—indeed no one from FCSO did—from Sunday, August 2 to Thursday, August 6, when McMannis returned from training. Sapp and his girlfriend went to Las Vegas on Friday, August 7 and didn't return until Wednesday, August 12. From August 1 to August 12, he saw no Glaval van. The facts support that he did not see the Sapp van until after Sapp returned August 12 from Vegas. Probably August 13 or 14th. When McMannis gave us the Polaroid photos on August 14, he said that he had just spotted a Glaval van, stopped the driver and asked to take photos.

So, if McMannis wanted to contend that the Sapp van didn't kill Andrew—that, indeed, he did not stand next to the smoking gun—he had to say that he talked to the owner and saw the Sapp van on Wednesday before Sapp left for Vegas Friday. Were these dates the subject of the Gams/McMannis' conference just before McMannis' deposition?

Seeing a Glaval van August 5, with the ground effect piece would have been monumental. Emblazoned on the sides of their vans is "Glaval." That's information he would have had to share with other deputies—as others were involved on Thursday. But he didn't. If he had, he and other deputies would have had a starting point, an actual Glaval van! But McMannis had no substantive information on Thursday morning. That's why McMannis and other deputies canvassed shop owners and dealerships with those fiberglass pieces to find the make and model of the vehicle. By the end of the day on Thursday, McMannis knew the make and model. Still he had not seen a Glaval converted van as confirmed by his testimony in 2000 and the lack of photos and/or video footage of the Sapp van at the Friday, August 7, 1998, media conference.

The delay of six days before an active investigation began gave the owner time for repair—emerging two weeks later with his van intact. McMannis wasn't on the job the first week, from Sunday to Thursday.

No one in the Sheriff's Office knew about McMannis' alleged van sighting on Wednesday, August 5, and the media never saw the photos McMannis said he had on Friday. Now we had a good idea where this was heading.

The LEADS report is a critical document, containing date, time, deputy number and information about vehicles that are being investigated. This is a data base that law enforcement can access about vehicles. Where was the Sapp LEADS report? *McMannis will testify that it was missing.* His modus operandi. McMannis was directed to bring relevant documents to the deposition. He brought nothing. FCSO files—that they shared with us—contain nothing, not a scrap about Sapp's van before we found it in July 2001. Experts had only to examine the Sapp van to affirm how loud it screamed, "I'm the one. I did it."

Gams then wrapped up his part of the deposition. Listening to McMannis' testimony, riddled with inaccuracies, inconsistencies, and contradictions, Andy and I sat stunned. The honest thing for McMannis to do was to repeat the approximate time frame he reported to his supervisor, Chief Deputy Gil Jones. He would not have had to expose his negligence. It would have made his fabrication unnecessary. But he was used.

Before the deposition, I wondered why James O. and the fifth wife were there. They attended no other depositions except each's own. I imagined their attorney, Mark Gams, telling them, "You gotta be here for this one. McMannis is going to back up the wife's story." All lawyers know that the law is not about truth or justice. It's about money — truth and justice be damned.

The strangest observation I made was the occasional smile McMannis would accord the Sapps—as if we weren't there to see this? Wisely, I swallowed the expletives that appeared on the tip of my tongue.

But the best of this deposition was yet to come. Now it was Attorney Winters' time to question Deputy McMannis. Enter the dramatic and the bizarre.

51

SINCE ATTORNEY WINTERS WAS SITTING between McMannis and me, Winters moved into Attorney Gams' spot on the other side of the table to face McMannis. When he did that, I moved to his seat next to McMannis. His testimony claiming that he saw the Sapp van just days after Andrew was killed clearly contradicted not only his own words to his supervisor, Gil Jones, but unwittingly, his own testimony.

Over the years, I had read several books on body language and was not a staunch believer, but I knew that certain actions speak louder than words. Rolling the eyes, wringing the hands, and pacing back and forth, are common acts of body language. I saw McMannis' smiling at Sapp. It floored me—demonstrating a symbiotic relationship? I turned toward him, sitting at an angle, staring unflinchingly at his profile. My stare shot out in rapid succession a barrage of terrible words.

Winters began questioning by asking who, besides McMannis, was involved in the investigation? McMannis answered Deputies Wassmuth and Booth.

Winters:	[I] called you 'corporal' a minute ago. Is that correct?
McMannis:	It is not. I am a deputy at this point.
Winters:	[D]oes that suggest that at some point you were downgraded or demoted?
McMannis:	I took a voluntary demotion to take the job that I am currently in. It was not any punishment of any sort. [Our private investigator believed McMannis had a choice: voluntarily quit or voluntarily take a demotion.]
Winters:	[W]hen you would work a shift investigating on this case, what did you do to memorialize the actions that you had undertaken on that day?
McMannis:	The three of us would individually keep a log book to show what—not specific to any one case. Just that at 8:00 o'clock I was at the office, what I did, may have worked at the office and then where I might go during the day.

Not specific to any one case? The log book really had nothing *specific* to do with this case. McMannis truthfully admits that this "log book" contained no information useful to this or any other investigation.

Winters:	All right. That would tell me if I looked at the log book now, assuming it still existed, where you were physically, correct?
McMannis:	It was very general. It wasn't—we didn't carry it with us and write down, it's 11:45, I am here... *The exact times may not have been noted.*
Winters:	Okay. Do you know whether or not such a...log book is still in existence at the Franklin County Sheriff's Department?
McMannis:	My *personal log books* are in my possession. They weren't something that was reviewed or said, Okay, the year is over, give me that and file it.

I was stunned at the word "personal." Apparently, these log books were personal calendars and not work calendars. I have one. We needed official records with dates and details he kept in the pursuit of his investigative duties with the FCSO. We should have locked on to this detail and made a very big deal out of it.

Winters:	If someone else were to take over an investigation that you had been conducting, what in the file of that investigation would one be able to look to...educate one's self? Did you keep any information like that in the Sheriff's Department investigative file in the Starinchak case?
McMannis:	Not on a daily basis.
Winters:	All right. Did you do that on an every other day basis then?
McMannis:	I don't know exactly where you are going, counsel.
Winters:	I am trying to find out what documents you kept that would show what you did and when you did it.

Continuing, Winters asked:

Winters:	[D]id you then, in fact, review a document in that file [Starinchak] that told you that on August 7, 1998 you went to the Rugosa address and photographed this vehicle?
McMannis:	That was in my personal log book.
Winters:	So that was not anywhere in the sheriff's investigative file then that you reviewed today?
McMannis:	No, sir…it's nowhere in that file that I went to Rugosa on that day.
Winters:	[I]s it in any other file in the sheriff's department anywhere?
McMannis:	No, sir.

Persisting, Winters pressed McMannis for a look *at this personal log book.* Winters reminded McMannis that his subpoena instructed McMannis to bring all documents relating to this crash. No excuse. Every deputy knows this. McMannis responded, "There was no summaries or any exact details of any part of the investigation in those [the personal log books.]"

That statement supporting the utter worthlessness of this personal diary was never expressed to the jury at trial or to the visiting judge who allowed this useless calendar in evidence as an exhibit.

Winters clearly established that the Sheriff's file contained no report, no verifiable evidence as to *when* McMannis saw the Sapp van. And where was the LEADS report McMannis supposedly ran to check out the Sapp van? Not in the McMannis/Sheriff's file at the time of McMannis' first deposition in 2000. Not a scrap of paper in the 2000 file with James O. Sapp's name on it.

We had met McMannis for the first time on Monday, August 10, ten days after Andrew was killed. It was not until this second deposition that we learned for the first time that the investigation didn't get underway until Thursday, six days after Andrew was killed. Had he not realized how critical time is in a hit-and-run fatality?

Winters then asked McMannis what sort of conversations he had with his successor, Sergeant Staggs about the case. McMannis answered, "I don't recall any specific conversations."

No documents, no specific dates, no reports, and no conversations with a successor. How lucky could Sapp get? How lucky could any perpetrator get? We're talking about someone killing another person. Not omitting the sugar in a batch of cupcakes.

Staggs, McMannis' friend, wasn't particularly happy about inheriting our case—a case he believed caused a buddy's demotion. Staggs stated bluntly aloud in the office that he was not going to work our case. Everyone in the traffic office heard him. Surely, the Sheriff, himself, knew that Staggs was just a figurehead replacement.

Winters hammered McMannis about his memory and his adversity to keeping track of an investigation. Sitting next to him, I saw him wringing his hands in his lap. He had nowhere to go except to admit that he kept no records and made no reports. Although no signs were visible above the table, they certainly were under the table. Angered, McMannis spoke.

McMannis:	Mr. Gams, Mr. Winters, can we go off record and the three of us have a conversation for a second, please, outside?
Winters:	No. Why don't we just have the conversation right here on the record.
McMannis:	*Okay. If we are going to continue with things that I did or did not do as a result of this crash investigation…*
Winters:	We are.
McMannis:	I am going to ask that we postpone my deposition until I can again be represented by someone from the Franklin County Prosecutor's Office.

When McMannis walked into what he thought was friendly territory—the office of the attorney representing the man whose van killed our son—he had no problem with venue. He had no problem when Attorney Gams questioned him about his investigation. What in the name of God did he think this deposition was about if it didn't concern his investigation? A tangible tension filled the room. His conspicuous irresponsibility was tantamount to dereliction of duty.

Winters:	Why is that?
McMannis:	I just would be more comfortable.

This is a twenty-five-year veteran deputy. Why was he uncomfortable? Had this inquiry exposed his brand of investigating so much so that he felt embarrassed, distressed, unnerved, or uneasy—all definitions of *uncomfortable*. He had announced how he felt answering questions about his investigation of Andrew's homicide. *Uncomfortable.*

Winters:	Are you telling me that you are not going to proceed with this deposition unless you have counsel?
McMannis:	No, sir…I came here…upon the subpoena to talk about the item of this crash, not – you know, obviously I'm not prepared to answer a lot of your questions.
Winters:	I don't know what the circumstances that brought you to this deposition pursuant to the subpoena that was issued by Mr. Gams or Ms. Dunn [Gams' associate] were. I know that you met with them before we began the deposition. I know that you must have had some communications with at least Ms. Dunn on occasions prior to this.
McMannis:	That's correct.
Winters:	When you produced the copy…of the then Sheriff's department file for Mark Adams on May 3rd, 2000, you did not produce a single piece of paper that had the name James Sapp anywhere on it, did you?
McMannis:	I don't know. I mean *if* it was in the file, it would have been copied and given to him.
Winters:	Nothing in that file would support your representation that you went out and looked at the van under certain circumstances, though, correct?
McMannis:	More than the photos of it, no sir.
Winters:	Did you ask Sergeant Booth if there were anything else…

McMannis:	I don't specifically recall. ...
Winters:	...And when would that conversation have occurred with Sgt. Booth?
McMannis:	Sometime in the last week. I don't have an exact date.
Winters:	...think back for a moment. You say you have a good memory.
McMannis:	I just did think back. I cannot give you an exact date.
Winters:	Can you give me an exact day of the week?
McMannis:	No, sir.

Returning to questions about the first five days after the crash when McMannis had been in London, Ohio, for training, Winters asked, "What hours was the course being held?" And as with previous answers, McMannis said, "I don't recall specific hours. It was daytime." Daytime. That narrows it down.

His deposition huddled under a melting igloo. The drip, drip, drip of "I don't have an answer," "I don't know," "I don't know if it happened that day," "I don't have an exact number," "I would not want to guess. I don't know," and on and on landed with an incessant ping on his head. That would be mighty uncomfortable.

Despite our poor opinion of Deputy McMannis' investigation, Andy and I could not have anticipated that he would play such a part in his own humiliation. Attorney Winters had to ask those questions. Too bad that a jury had not been a witness to this deposition.

Clearly, Andy and I weren't surprised that McMannis had written no reports. We were surprised that he had admitted it. Without a shred of doubt, we believed that if there had been reports in those first few weeks, those reports would have supported that McMannis saw the Sapp van after Sapp had returned from Vegas. Also, the facts and his conversation with his supervisor support that McMannis took the photos after Sapp and girlfriend returned from Vegas, in plenty of time for the van to have been repaired while Sapp was away—the reason for being away.

We also believed that if any kind of official paper, such as a LEADS report, existed that indicated a date, we would never see it. Alas, as circumstances would have it, McMannis testified that the LEADS report was missing or lost! Did he ever run one?

Everyone in the Sheriff's traffic department, knew that McMannis blew our case off. We had the audacity to notice that his apathy was an obstacle to justice. We needed a bar to lift the boulder, this stone, out of the pathway blocking justice.

The pieces were coming together. To protect himself, McMannis had to support Sapp's defense. Would a jury accept the word of a deputy who wrote no investigative reports, but instead claimed information in a personal diary? Unwisely, we dismissed McMannis' weak performance as absurd. We underestimated what Gams would have to do to shore it up.

52

MCMANNIS' DEPOSITION WAS AS MUCH of a disaster as Dr. Wiechel's testimony was a stellar presentation. Those two contrasting depositions had prompted an offer from Attorney Gams to talk to our attorney. Stupidly, we didn't fully realize that a civil action is always about money, always. And that even a settlement, despite Gams' protests that a settlement was not an admission of wrongdoing, would have been a kind of victory—no matter what the money figure was.

Attorney Winters, prior to our case, represented defendants. Attorneys representing plaintiffs, like us, have a different mindset, especially about settling. When Attorney Gams asked, "What do these people want?" Winters answered, "Sapp tarred and feathered and run out of town." We sat in Winters' office that day and smugly shook our heads in agreement. Didn't they understand that Andrew's life meant everything to us? We wanted the finger to point scientifically and publicly to Sapp's van.

Our attorney should have explained that the guilty driver, his insurance company, and their attorneys couldn't care less about Andrew and us. The driver left the scene. A person, who can leave after hitting a human being and then take great measures to hide, is a criminal. For the attorney and the insurance company, however, this was just business—another crash. Whether the insured was guilty or not didn't matter to them. The idea was to get out as cheaply as possible. If that meant not having to prepare for trial, all the better. Conversely, a plaintiff's attorney working under a contingency fee agreement would have done everything in his power to get us to settle. Prolonging a suit is usually not in the best interests of that fee arrangement.

We would have had to swallow a bitter pill to settle. We seemed to have mindlessly obeyed a course of action that made little sense. When the arena is entirely new—neither Andy nor I had any experience at all with civil or criminal cases—what's happening doesn't look as obvious as it does in hindsight. Then, too, we were in a game where we were playing it straight up. That's not how the game is played.

53

THREE YEARS AFTER THE VAN'S discovery, we had looked under every stone, asked every question we could think of, listened to the testimony of experts, compiled the evidence, and harbored no doubt, absolutely none, that the Sapp van killed Andrew. Consequently, we were ready for trial. Our standard wasn't a matter of possessing a preponderance of evidence or even evidence beyond a reasonable doubt. For us, the standard had to be *no doubt* that this van killed our son.

The weekend before the trial in late March 2004, David Winters barricaded himself in his office—away from his family and the world—to prepare nonstop to convince the jury of eight people that we had identified the right vehicle.

Our civil case was built on facts. We had our expert witness, Dr. Wiechel, and the supervisor at Glaval, Dewayne Creighton. Dr. Kwek, I anticipated, would present her findings—the alignment of the ground effect pieces to the van and the match of paint chips from Andrew's clothes to paint samples from the van. Like her deposition, I didn't expect any surprises from her testimony. I was wrong. It was better than Christmas morning.

Dewayne Creighton's testimony represented to us all what a witness's testimony should be—one that was objective and credible. He had no stake in the outcome of our trial. He wasn't a friend. He wasn't a colleague. He was an employee of the Glaval Corporation and knew their ground effect parts inside and out. He could tell the jury exactly how the ground effect parts were installed and anything else anyone wanted to know. We paid him nothing. Not even his travel expenses. This purest of witnesses, this unassuming man with his straightforward, factual testimony would become the target of one juror's ignorance.

Witnesses need to be evaluated as to their motivation for testifying and their credibility. Andy and I were both called to the witness stand. After BCI's and SEA's reports, we believed strongly that the Sapp van was involved in Andrew's death. Since we were not automotive experts, we couldn't have offered any credible evidence ourselves that the Sapp van, in particular, was involved. But we could tell the jury what we did in the investigation, and what we discovered.

Then, too, we all know about expert witnesses. If I served on a jury, I would listen to an expert's testimony with a critical ear. Our jury didn't know that we asked Dr. Wiechel to examine the Sapp van *after* BCI's report. If Wiechel's examination had revealed nothing suspicious, we would not have filed a suit against Sapp. Dr. Wiechel's involvement came about after we realized that the FCSO was not going to act on the red-flag BCI report.

As we neared the trial date, Mark Adams, our friend, and attorney who handled the first half of our case, voiced a lack of confidence in our jury system. The flaws in the system are enormous. Every attorney and judge know this.

The outcome of any trial depends upon many complex issues. Besides the expertise of the attorneys, the most obvious are the jury's cultural backgrounds, their beliefs—often tied to religion—experiences and levels of education. The voir dire process could only scratch the surface of who the jury members were.

We had the facts. We would not have filed a suit against this man if we had any doubts about his van. Despite all that, certain unknowns caused us anxiety—the most prominent being Deputy McMannis' testimony. Would he repeat his claim that he saw the Sapp van on August 5th, and would the jury accept his claim without any kind of official documentation? Without factual support? My other concern was how a jury could understand in three or four days the important information about the fiberglass pieces. If the jury didn't understand the essential facts, how could they critically evaluate Dr. Wiechel's testimony as opposed to Greg DuBois' testimony—State Farm's expert? The jury had to listen attentively to the objective testimony of automotive witnesses, not hired as experts. Then our attorney had to clarify the facts and emphasize the differences between the two experts.

Few people knew our trial date and we didn't announce it. Even if we prevailed, and we believed that we would, we would not gloat. Our son was dead. How could we celebrate? We might feel a sense of relief. That was all.

Essentially, Andy and I with our attorney were now in this alone. Our daughter, living and working in another state, remained on standby in case Attorney Winters had to call her as a rebuttal witness. Her testimony would involve her visit to Deputy McMannis after Christmas 1999, when she brought him a basket of snacks. We wished desperately, nonetheless, that she could have been with us.

One afternoon as Attorney Winters sat in his office preparing for trial, he called to make a request. "I could use an assistant during the trial. Someone who can keep track of exhibits, make calls, see that I have equipment—that kind of thing. Do you know of anyone who is capable of helping me the week of the trial?"

After I had hung up, I described Attorney Winters' request to Andy. "The only person I know who would meet David's expectations and isn't working is Teresa," I said.

"Call and ask her. We need someone exactly like her."

Feeling somewhat sheepish, I called Teresa. She had been a top programmer at Bank One and was on sabbatical. This request meant a huge act of sacrifice of time and energy on her part. Having no idea how long the trial would last or the demands placed on her, Teresa, nevertheless, consented. We knew that this pretty, smart, young woman in her starched white blouses and business suits, would assist Winters with perfection and efficiency. What we didn't know was that at the end of each day of trial, she would become the moral and emotional support that kept us going that awful week.

2004
THE TRIAL

54

TALK ABOUT UNKNOWNS. WE WERE to get a few surprises even before the trial began. And those surprises no doubt cost us. Did they occur because of scheduling changes at the courthouse? Possibly. But unlikely. That's my opinion because I know a little more now about how things work. The first shocker was that the courtroom to which we were assigned was a rarely used one, all by itself on the second floor. Adjacent to the main Franklin County Sheriff's Office.

The second shock came when we learned that a visiting judge from Fairfield County had replaced Judge Guy Reece. Reece inherited our case from Judge Sadler after she was elected to the Court of Appeals in 2002. How lucky for Attorney Gams that this visiting judge, Judge Martin, who presided over our trial didn't know squat—unless he read the files. This elected Republican judge was somehow maneuvered to preside over our case. Two very lucky breaks for Gams: the rarely used courtroom next to the FCSO's Sheriff's offices and a judge who was rumored to be sympathetic to insurance companies. Probably not luck. Attorney Gams was one formidable and creative lawyer. His reputation preceded him. We had been warned, but dismissed it.

It might have been gossip but someone who knew this visiting judge said that he had no consideration for plaintiffs who didn't settle. His tone was unfriendly to our attorney. Perhaps he thought we were wasting the taxpayers' time. A judge's attitude toward one side or the other—when it can be detected—is a huge factor in influencing the jury.

Here we were, Elaine and Andrew Starinchak vs. the real defendant, State Farm Insurance, who was paying the legal bills. Do insurance companies make hefty contributions to judges' campaigns? Yes, of course.

The first order of business was to decide who from the pool of jurors would participate in our trial. By looking at these people or even by hearing their answers to questions, I couldn't tell which ones could follow the mechanical evidence and think critically or which ones would be bored and sleep. Having voted in every November election since I was eligible, I was never called to jury duty. The actual experience was new for Andy and me. In the next five days, I was to learn much about juries, the influence of judges in using a certain tone when speaking to one lawyer or the other, and the method or non-method of lawyers in handling jury members. Being a trial lawyer is like leading a symphony orchestra—technical skill and art combined.

Our attorney had to make it abundantly clear to the jury that our case was not a criminal case—even though it involved vehicular homicide – but a civil case brought about by us (plaintiffs) against the owner of the van with evidence that supported the fact that his van killed Andrew.

Generally, the standard for verdicts in favor of the plaintiff in civil trials is different from the standard in criminal trials. In civil trials the standard of proof is termed a "preponderance of evidence." In criminal trials the standard of proof is guilt "beyond a reasonable doubt," a higher standard. In a civil case, preponderance is based on the more convincing evidence and its probable truth. We would not have been sitting in that courtroom had we not had "clear and convincing evidence"—a standard far more stringent than a preponderance of evidence and stronger than beyond a reasonable doubt.

The attorneys picked the jurors. I can see some of them today—especially the ones who slept throughout the trial. And without shame. I wondered if Attorney Gams noticed. Our attorney didn't, and my commenting about it only caused him to lose concentration. Apparently, sleeping jurors are common. Someone told us that reacting emotionally would not win us any points with the judge or jury, so I kept myself in check. I wouldn't make a scene in front of a crowd anyway, but I'm sure my face revealed signs of distress when I heard lies or half-truths.

I remember little about our attorney's opening statement or Attorney Gams'. Both gave an overview of background material based on their client's perspective and how and why we were in the courtroom that day. I'm sure that everyone in the courtroom noticed the difference between Attorney Gams and Attorney Winters. I'm not certain that Gams wore a suit as he always seemed to be in khakis with his jacket hanging on the back of his chair. Short and small in stature, Gams was in his early forties or maybe late thirties. His smallness made him look younger. Out of this undersized body bellowed a voice that commanded attention. A voice that the jury could hear.

Winters, on the other hand, was at least ten years older than Gams, and taller than average. He wore expensive suits, white shirts, and ties—and could have stepped out of GQ magazine. You couldn't miss his cloud of brown, curly hair. Articulate but soft-spoken, he was not easily heard.

One statement by Attorney Gams during his opening jumped out at me, and I still remember the gist of it. He said, "I would submit that the evidence will show that there is no evidence, not even one single thing that connects the two [the crash and James Sapp] together." A magician, I thought. This guy is so good, he can make the evidence and facts disappear. He had *nothing* to support Sapp's innocence. Lucky for the magician that the burden was on us.

What we had beyond any doubt at all were *facts* that James O. Sapp's van was involved in killing our son. And James O. Sapp owned that van on August 1, 1998. Because he wasn't married at the time of Andrew's death, lived alone, had no children, and testified in his deposition that no one else drove his van except his girlfriend occasionally to the store, the finger pointed squarely at him. Still, the hard evidence dealt with his van and for Andy and me the standard of evidence had to be nearly perfect.

In Winters' opening comments he affirmed to the jury that we would prove with many evidentiary factors that the Sapp van killed Andrew. And then he made several statements about the Franklin County Sheriff not doing its job. At times Attorney Winters surprised us with his no nonsense, bold declarations about the FCSO.

So much that goes on at a trial is not about the law and courtroom procedure. Does a law student know that during a trial, he should make eye contact often with jury members? That he should look kindly at them at times when he talks? That he should notice them? That he is essentially courting these people in the jury box? That he needs to cultivate a voice projection so that the jury's ears are always on notice—"pay attention; you could miss important detail." That his audience is the jury. He is the teacher as well as the entertainer. And most importantly, no lawyer should assume that juries can put two and two together. Because so much detail is thrown at them, the lawyer must emphasize those vital points they need to understand in case they missed those points. Having been a teacher, I could put myself in the jury's place, and since I knew the information, I could tell where the information needed repeating.

After the jury selection and the opening statements, court was adjourned until the following day. As we exited the courtroom, we saw Teresa, sitting on a wood bench outside the room. As she gathered up her equipment, we filled her in on our observations. Having that extra ten minutes or so with her at the end of each day buoyed our confidence. She was there to assist David Winters. But us even more so.

55

ON TUESDAY, MARCH 23, 2004, Andy and I entered Court Room No. 2, next to the Franklin County Sheriff's office. Making our way to a long table in the front row we sat next to Attorney Winters. I came with tablet and pencil. I would have written furiously every day, but Mark Adams warned me not to do that. The jury would see that as a negative.

Our seats in the front row allowed us, at times, to hear the sidebar conversations between the judge and the attorneys. Attorney Gams didn't want the jury to know that James Sapp's present marriage was his fifth. Also, he thought it unnecessary for the jury to see photos of Andrew lying in a ditch soon after he was discovered. If Winters allowed those concessions to Gams, then Winters wanted no mention by the coroner of the trace amounts of marijuana in Andrew's system. It was an amount so small, the toxicologist couldn't quantify it. Curious, we asked our family doctor—a young guy himself—to read the autopsy report. Smiling, he said if we walked into a room where people were smoking, we'd breathe in the contaminants from the cigarettes. Our blood would show traces of nicotine.

When the coroner's first report came out and toxicology tests revealed traces of nicotine and marijuana, Andy and I spoke to our daughter about it and to some of his friends. Our daughter, attempting to stifle a laugh, responded, "Mom, please. You can't be serious. Anyone who's been to college has smoked marijuana. Even Al Gore in college. Al Gore, Mom. And you know what a nerd he is."

"But where would Andrew have been?" I asked her.

"You gotta be kidding me," she said. "He's a grad student. He hangs out with grad students on campus. High Street," Mom, "Just walk out the door and get what you want."

After our conversation, I would not have bargained away that bit of information. Ironically, though, I was thankful that Attorney Winters granted Attorney Gams' request not to show photos of Andrew.

Reading Winters' notes, we checked the roster of the day's witnesses. He would begin by questioning Terry Wassmuth, Deputy McMannis' partner at the time of the investigation. Frankly, we had formed no opinion of Deputy Wassmuth, since promoted to Detective Wassmuth. I don't believe we exchanged more than twenty words in our two visits with him, and that was to invite him in for something to drink. He never got out of the squad car.

Winters established that McMannis was Wassmuth's supervisor. Since then Wassmuth had been promoted to detective while McMannis had been demoted to deputy status. Wassmuth testified that McMannis was the lead investigator in Andrew's crash. Winters questioned Wassmuth's part in the investigation.

Winters: And did he [McMannis] tell you what to do each day, after you had initiated the investigation?

Wassmuth: Basically, yes.

Winters: How did he communicate with you the Monday… Tuesday and Wednesday…after August 2nd? [Winters is referring to August 3, 4 and 5th, when McMannis was out of the office in London, Ohio for three days after the crash.]

Wassmuth: I am not sure that he did but I believe he was in school for three days

Winters: [I]f he was in school, how did he tell you what to do?

Wassmuth: [I]t all didn't happen the three days there. Mostly, the three days, I did reports, and that was all that was done. [Confirmation of no investigation those critical days.]

Then Attorney Gams cross-examined Detective Wassmuth.

Gams: Again, how long were you on this investigation?

Wassmuth: We worked it almost nonstop for months and months, and then the leads kind of died out, and I would say we worked on it for over a year.

Whenever I heard a statement like this, I had to compose myself and look down at the table. McMannis never had the bike, clothes, and shoes tested for paint or other evidence. With the unbelievable luck of a list of Glaval vans, no one in the FCSO traffic department checked to see which Glaval vans on the list were registered in the Columbus area in August 1998. Testifying that deputies on the case were working nonstop for months and months, but not doing the most basic tasks in a vehicular homicide served as a gross contradiction. If the FCSO didn't even bother to have the paint tested or the Glaval list updated, what did they do for months and months?

After Gams finished, Winters had some additional questions. He asked Detective Wassmuth what he thought of James Sapp as a suspect.

Winters:	During the period of your investigation, did you ever have reason to believe that Jim Sapp was somehow involved in this hit-skip accident?
Wassmuth:	We had no information.
Winters:	And why is that, sir?
Wassmuth:	We had no information of him ever being a suspect, and Corporal McMannis inspected that van, I am not sure of the exact days, but not too many days after, you know, *a week or so after the accident*. It had no apparent damage.

I interpret "a week or so after the accident" to be at least seven plus days. We totally agree that McMannis spotted the van after Sapp returned home on August 12th—a week plus five or six days after the crash.

Then Winters moved on to questions about the Polaroid photos that McMannis took of the Sapp van.

Winters:	Would you show me, detective, the Polaroids, that series of four there…
Wassmuth:	Yes, sir.
Winters:	All right. On the originals in the sheriff's file, there are no markings, are there? …just the four photographs put in there?
Wassmuth:	I don't know what you mean.
Winters:	[T]here is nothing on either of those pages to indicate when those photographs were taken, is there?
Wassmuth:	Not that I can see, no.
Winters:	Well, look carefully then. The answer is either yes or no.
Wassmuth:	No, sir.
Winters:	So in other words, from looking at the Sheriff's Department's file, we have no idea when those photographs were taken, correct?

Wassmuth:	Corporal McMannis knows when they were taken.
Winters:	The question…was from looking at the Sheriff's Department official file, we have no idea when those photographs were taken, do we?
Wassmuth:	From the pictures, no.
Winters:	Correct. There is no other information in that file which would indicate when those photographs were taken, is there?
Wassmuth:	I can't tell you that. I haven't had time to read the whole file.
Winters:	There isn't any information in that file…during the period of time in which you worked on the case, that would indicate when those photographs were taken, is there?
Wassmuth:	I can't say that for sure.
Winters:	All right. Let me make a suggestion. We are going to recess. I will suspend the redirect examination and [you] look through the file and see if you can find something that substantiates when those were taken.

At this point, Attorney Winters asked for a recess and the judge declared a 15-minute recess. After the recess, the court ordered Winters to continue his examination of Wassmuth.

Winters:	Detective Wassmuth, …we just had the court reporter confirm that we recessed at 10:23… You have been sitting there for 16 minutes, looking through the files?
Wassmuth:	Okay.
Winters:	Have you found anything that confirms when those photographs were taken?
Wassmuth:	The exact date, no sir.
Winters:	[A]nything that shows the inexact date?
Wassmuth:	Well, we did a press release. Crime Stoppers came out and filmed this.

Winters: In September?

Wassmuth: I don't know when it was. But that would give you an idea.

Detective Wassmuth testified that the Crime Stoppers' event, taped the first week in September and five weeks after the crash, "would give you an idea" of when the photos were taken. His testimony again contradicts McMannis' testimony of the date he took the Polaroids.

56

ALTHOUGH I BELIEVED SOME OF Detective Wassmuth's answers were disingenuous, I didn't want him to be humiliated, especially after he testified that McMannis saw the van a week or so after the crash—the "or so" was "two weeks" that McMannis told his supervisor. And then he had to sit on the stand for fifteen minutes, leafing through files to find a date—a date we knew didn't exist. I feared that someone on the jury might think that Attorney Winters' treatment was demeaning, but Winters' intent was to show the jury that McMannis prepared nothing official to document when McMannis took those photos. To prove our point that no date existed, he had to press the issue with Detective Wassmuth.

After Wassmuth, Winters called several witnesses—the coroner, and managers of the dealerships that dealt with the repair and sale of the van before Sapp bought it. The testimony of the service manager at Voss Chevrolet where the original owner, before Sapp, took it for repairs was consistent with the manager's deposition taken almost a year earlier. Voss had not replaced the passenger side ground effect.

We ended the second day of trial with my testimony. The big moment occurred when Attorney Gams asked me about our suspicions dealing with Barry Snidka. When Don Sonney, our PI, was investigating the tips about him, I had compiled a list of reasons why the Sheriff's Office should consider him a serious suspect. Even though we didn't and couldn't connect him to a Glaval van, Attorney Gams had me read to the jury that list of items we gave to the Sheriff. The strategy for Gams, of course, was to create doubt that James Sapp's van killed Andrew.

We were all waiting for McMannis. After him, we wondered how Greg DuBois, expert for the defendant, would handle himself. Our big guns were John Wiechel and Glaval's supervisor, Dewayne Creighton. Much of our case rested on their testimony about the mechanics of the van. BCI's witness, Dr. Kwek, would confirm that the ground effects matched the van as did paint chips in Andrew's clothes. Would this jury be interested and capable of understanding difficult, mechanical testimony?

57

TO ME, DEPUTY MCMANNIS WAS the lynch pin in the Sapp defense. Of course, we didn't know about the rogue juror. Once McMannis took the stand and stated that he had seen the Sapp van on Wednesday, five days after Andrew was killed on Saturday, the jury had to be affected by his declaration. His words provided the hole through which the other witnesses for Sapp could slip. "Whatever could be the reason for Deputy McMannis to testify that he saw the van on Wednesday, August 5th, if he didn't?" a member of the jury could possibly ask. I would answer in the words of a friend, "Because he stood next to the smoking gun and missed it. He could lose the respect of his department."

McMannis' declaration that he saw the van on Wednesday and that he had photographed it Friday, August 7, contradicted the facts of what he actually did those days—from his own mouth—and from news tapes as well as his previous testimony under oath. Without official records, how could McMannis support his claim as to when he first saw the Sapp van? On a personal calendar that was "not specific to any case"? Those were his words at his deposition in November. A calendar, or log as he called it, that only he saw and kept at home. His story would change at trial. In his November deposition, McMannis never pretended that his log was an official record of his work day. In fact, he stated that the log was never a part of our investigation, or any investigation. It was *personal*, a word he used several times to denote its uselessness at work. By trial, however, the useless *personal* diary was spun as having some legitimacy.

Winters:	Did you prepare a written report about your photograph of the Sapp van on what you say was August the 7th?
McMannis:	No…I did not.
Winters:	You had the finished product of the photo…because it was a Polaroid.
McMannis:	That's correct.
Winters:	The purpose of the press conference that afternoon [August 7th] was…to get out information to the public through the media…
McMannis:	Yes, sir.

Winters:	During the course of the press conference, there were TV cameras present…
McMannis:	I believe there were…
Winters:	In order to check your memory, we would either have to refer to a report that doesn't exist, or a memorandum that doesn't exist, or look at the video, which does exist?
McMannis:	I would assume so.
Winters:	I am sure that you are familiar with the expression that *a picture is worth a thousand words.*
McMannis:	I have heard that.
Winters:	You claim that you had a picture [Polaroid] that you had taken that morning of the kind of van that you were looking for, don't you?
McMannis:	That's correct.
Winters:	And the morning that you claim you took the picture was before the press conference in the afternoon?
McMannis:	To the best that I recall, yes, sir
Winters:	You have a picture of what you are looking for. You have the TV cameras from the media there. You have a big audience to see what it is. And you don't show them the photograph on camera that demonstrates this is what we are looking for, ladies and gentlemen of the public?
McMannis:	Yes, sir.
Winters:	You chose not to use that opportunity to show that photograph to the watching public, correct? You didn't show the photograph, correct?
McMannis:	I don't believe we did.
Winters:	Or you didn't have the photograph?
McMannis:	If that is your statement, that's fine.
Winters:	The video shows what the video shows.
McMannis:	That is right.

No other reason existed why McMannis would not have shown the Polaroid photos other than he hadn't seen the van as yet. And that detail has been corroborated by a seemingly innocent remark McMannis made to Deputy Ken Wooten. Several days after the Sapp's van confiscation in 2001, Wooten talked to McMannis at a bingo hall. McMannis disclosed to him that this was the same van featured in our reward flyers and the one in the Crime Stoppers television interview. At the time of this revelation, we were speechless. During that conversation, McMannis said that he saw the Sapp van two weeks after the crash. That coincided with the time McMannis' brought the Polaroid photos to the house on August 14th.

Later, I reminded Wooten of his conversation with McMannis. "Yes," Wooten confirmed, "he said two weeks." Wooten had no idea that after McMannis met with Attorney Gams, McMannis would change his story.

Winters:	Another deputy named Ken Wooten also picked up some responsibility for that case…correct?
McMannis:	That's correct…
Winters:	As a matter of fact, you had at least one meeting with Deputy Wooten at a bingo hall where you were working a special duty job…at that location you had a discussion with Deputy Wooten in which you told Deputy Wooten that you had seen the van in those photographs two weeks after the accident. Do you remember making that statement?
McMannis:	I do not.
Winters:	A couple of weeks later you deny telling Deputy Wooten that?
McMannis:	I don't recall saying those words…If Mr. Wooten recalls it differently, that is his opinion.

Undoubtedly, Attorney Winters was going to use Chief Deputy Gil Jones' letter to Attorney Wolman to prove McMannis said "two weeks." Attorney Gams asked the court to disallow the use of the letter as hearsay.

After some argument, the judge allowed Winters to continue his questioning.

Winters:	Deputy, I am now placing before you an item which I wish you to review to see if it refreshes your recollection about any discussion that you may have had with Deputy Chief Jones.
McMannis:	Okay, sir. [Reads the letter.]
Winters:	The question is did you at any time before July 21, 2001, tell Deputy Chief Jones that you had eliminated what we now know as the Sapp vehicle within a week or two after the accident?
McMannis:	I may have said that.
Winters:	*There is a big difference between a week after the accident and two weeks after the accident, isn't there?*
McMannis:	*Not to me.*

A Sheriff's investigator just testified that he believed there was no difference between a week after an accident and two weeks after an accident. Maybe I had misjudged the man. Instead of contempt, I should have been more sympathetic.

The circumstantial evidence—his conversation with Deputy Wooten, his remark to Chief Deputy Jones, his aversion to official reports, his not sharing the photos with the press because he didn't have them as yet, his testimony in his 2000 deposition and then in 2003—that he spent the day on Thursday trying to determine the make and model of the vehicle based on the ground effects—all point to his lack of knowledge of the make and model of the vehicle until the end of the first week. Not until Sapp and his girlfriend returned home from Vegas after August 12th did McMannis spot an actual Glaval van—the Sapp van —giving it plenty of time to be repaired.

58

ATTORNEY WINTERS PROCEEDED TO QUESTION McMannis about our unhappiness with his part in the investigation. McMannis admitted that we were disappointed with the job he did but that we showed no antagonism toward him. No one explored how he felt when we requested the State Highway Patrol take our case. If our attorney had, Winters might have been able to give the jury much more insight into McMannis' animosity towards us. When I spoke to McMannis on the phone about relinquishing our case to the State Patrol, he responded, "That's not going to happen." At trial, Winters asked him about that statement and McMannis denied saying it. He lied.

One of the problems, for me, involved the Glaval list and why no one in the Sheriff's traffic department thought to utilize that list. Without having updated registrations, we went out for weeks after Andrew's death to look at vans on the list. Not one van owner said the FCSO had already been there. Now, at trial, we were anxious to hear for ourselves why McMannis ignored the van list.

Attorney Gams: Tell us, again, just in your own words, what else that you did…

McMannis: Once we determined that we felt the investigation had indicated these pieces were from …Glaval Corporation, I contacted the Glaval Corporation. They provided us with a disk that had a list of vehicles that they had placed these pieces…

And we started working on that list… From that list, we created a list of vehicles by the VIN number. We had all those VIN numbers run through LEADS [a law enforcement vehicle data base] to determine the present owner of the vehicle.

When I heard this, I thought I would leap out of my chair. If he "had all of those VIN numbers run through LEADS," he had made no mention of doing that in his 2000 deposition, nor was there any evidence in the file that he had done so. Not even for central Ohio. And he sure as hell never worked it or talked to any of the van owners.

Gams: With regard to looking at vans specifically, tell me what you can recall about being able to do that?

McMannis: I, myself, went to a lot of the residences that were the present owners of the vehicles [still referring to the Glaval list, I believe] in an attempt to find the vehicles and look for damage, anything consistent, or fresh repairs, until we exhausted the list.

I had to report this brazen response. One van, the Sapp van? This man lied. In his 2000 testimony, he never pretended that he went around to "a lot of the residences." He found out from the Delaware police that we were visiting van owners. He knew that we knew he was not checking the Glaval list

McMannis came to the house in October, several months after the crash, and gave us one VIN from the Glaval list to mark "checked" and that ironically was Sapp's van. Why hadn't we been instructed to mark all those other vans "checked" as well? We had the list right there on the table.

Gams: Do you think that Jim Sapp's 1993, Astro van was involved in the Starinchak hit-skip?

McMannis: It is my opinion it was not.

Gams: Why?

McMannis: Based on observations I had of the vehicle, there was no damage consistent with what I would have expected to find on the vehicle involved in this crash with this bicycle.

By the time, Deputy McMannis saw the Sapp van two weeks into his investigation, it had been repaired.

Winters: [our attorney] You just rendered your opinion that the Sapp van was not involved in the Starinchak hit-skip death, haven't you?

McMannis: My contact with Mr. Sapp and the investigation and
              the evaluation of his van was early on, *very limited.* …I
              gave my opinion based on the information I knew…

Yes, McMannis' evaluation of the Sapp van was early on, "*very limited,*" based on what he knew. Yes, he didn't know it had been repaired.

I never accepted the theory offered by friends and even professionals that McMannis might have known Sapp because McMannis described the Sapp van as in his neighborhood. The same town, but not the same neighborhood. I believed in a simple explanation. When McMannis spotted the Sapp van two weeks after the crash, enough time for repairs, he saw no damage. Important also to remember is that for almost the entire first week after the crash, he did no investigating and was out of the office in training. He testified in 2000 that he was not someone who could readily tell if a vehicle had been repaired. He was not suspicious of the Sapp van based on what he saw two weeks after the crash. We would have had no problem if he had said that. It was the cover-up that caused the problems.

In view of all the information we had amassed about the van by the time of trial, our attorney questioned McMannis about whether he could be wrong in believing the Sapp van was not involved.

Winters: You will not agree that if the experts are right, you are
              wrong if you have got the date wrong?

McMannis: …I don't have the date wrong.

McMannis could not admit that he was wrong. Not in the face of scientific fact. Not in the absence of any document proving a date. Not in the face of his partner's testimony. Gams, Sapp's attorney, had propped up McMannis' claims to help his client, State Farm. Gams didn't care about McMannis. No official document of any sort exists to validate McMannis' claim. He wrote no official reports. The so-called personal log he mentioned in his deposition was not specific to any case—his words. *Personal* papers like journals, calendars and logs could easily be fabricated

Winters: Did you prepare a written report about your photograph
              of the Sapp van on what you say was August 7th?

McMannis: No, sir. I did not.

There it is. Period. His investigating six days after the crash—almost a week—involved exclusively determining the make and model of the vehicle. His partner, Wassmuth, confirmed our two-week time frame. I'm being kind when I say that he has a poor memory. I hate to belabor the Pinocchio image with a mustache and badge.

In resuming his questioning, Winters, our attorney, asked McMannis what was in the crash file.

Winters:	There is nothing in this crash file, and there is nothing in this official file at all, is there, other than the photographs and the license number?
McMannis:	Not at this time…I recall running a LEADS strip on the Sapp vehicle. That appears to be no longer in the file.
Winters:	Then, the…official file that you were active in the generation thereof, has no documentation about the Sapp vehicle other than photographs…
McMannis:	No, sir.

Remarkably, documentation of the Sapp van exists only after Andy and I found the van at Metro which was after McMannis was demoted. Also, he implied that somehow the LEADS report he claimed to have run on the Sapp van was missing.

As Winters questioned McMannis about reports, even I winced. The point was clear beyond any doubt that the man failed to do the simplest of investigative duties.

Winters:	Let's talk about what work you did on the case from December 28, 1999, to your departure from the case essentially May lst of 2000…would it refresh your recollection for you to look at your file…?
McMannis:	*I don't have any specifics on any certain date what I did.*
Winters:	Because there is nothing in the file to memorialize anything that you did that you could read to refresh your recollection.
McMannis:	Not on a specific day-to-day basis, no sir.

Winters:	How about on a specific week-to-week basis?
McMannis:	No, sir.
Winters:	How about on a specific month-to-month basis?
McMannis:	No, sir.

Andy reminded me, "Don't feel sorry for the man. If there's no documentation, he can say whatever he wants." The thought crossed my mind that Sapp had been incredibly lucky that this particular investigator had been assigned to our son's crash.

To explore Deputy McMannis' feelings toward us, Attorney Winters broached the subject of our asking the State Highway Patrol to take our case

Winters:	I am asking you why you didn't want the Highway Patrol to help?
McMannis:	It's not that I didn't want them to help… I think what the Starinchaks were after was more detailed informational things that the Highway Patrol could provide…
Winters:	My God, we are a year plus into the investigation—if there is one going on—in the death of their son, but you don't think you can use any help. Is that what you are telling us?
McMannis:	That is not the way I said it.
Winters:	No, that's the reality of the situation.
McMannis:	If there was some specific item that the Highway Patrol could have assisted us in the investigation, we would have certainly asked for their help.

There was *one* specific item. We asked the State Patrol to update all the Glaval owner registrations. That was a specific direction. That would serve to narrow down which Glaval vans were owned in the Columbus area in August 1998. The State Patrol would work off the Glaval van list. No one from the FCSO nor McMannis asked the Patrol to do that one simple thing.

Attorney Winters summed up without mincing words our contacting the Patrol by saying, "They wouldn't need to call the Highway Patrol if you were getting the job done." To which McMannis answered, "Those are your words."

Our requesting help from the State Highway Patrol cast a spotlight on McMannis' brand of operating and caused his demotion. We hadn't realized this. It's no wonder he hated us. And we learned on the day of his testimony at trial, he was performing his last duty. His career with the FCSO was over.

I'll never forget the conversation that took place when Betsey climbed into the car that cold winter day after seeing McMannis. We had expected her to drop off the holiday basket, say a few words to McMannis and we'd be on our way. We were baffled when she repeated her conversation with McMannis—his demotion, therapy, and then the question, "Are you wearing a wire?" Offering a holiday basket, but wearing a wire? Preparing to sue him? Sitting in stunned silence that day in the courtroom, we had heard enough.

Winters:	You had a meeting—I think...at the...bureau offices on West Mound Street on December 28th 1999, with Betsey Starinchak...Do you recall meeting her?
McMannis:	Yes...
Winters:	You expressed your views of the situation to her.
McMannis:	I don't recall the exact content of the conversation.
Winters:	Did you tell her you were taking a demotion and going to some other job in the sheriff's department because of this case?
McMannis:	No, I did not...
Winters:	I will ask you point blank. You told her: For all I know you are probably wired, didn't you?
McMannis:	I don't recall saying that.

Later that evening as we discussed McMannis' testimony, Andy observed, "McMannis was not going to say that he was in therapy because of our case or admit our case caused his demotion. That makes him sound weak."

"But he did. He said that to Betsey."

Ending our comments about what we had heard that day, we thought that Betsey's visit underscored the blame McMannis placed on us for his demotion, a serious consequence of his ineptness. And would the jury pick up the contradictions and hedging? Maybe not, if as a juror, you find the trial so boring that you use it to catch some shut-eye.

59

IN MY MIND, DEPUTY MCMANNIS and State Farm's engineering expert, Greg DuBois, comprised the primary two-pronged plan to oppose our affirmation that James Sapp's van killed Andrew. McMannis' testimony couldn't be corroborated or verified—Greg DuBois, didn't understand the mechanical facts and had based his testimony on "*ifs*". Deputy McMannis' testimony was tangled up in psychological factors having to do with his job performance. He then added that a personal date book was authentic evidence was beyond the pale.

Furthermore, the testimony of Greg DuBois, the metallurgical engineer hired by Attorney Gams as their expert to examine the Sapp van came off as expected. After all, his job as a hired expert was to shoot holes in our expert's conclusions about the van. But his testimony underscored his uncertainty with things mechanical. He was a metallurgist.

Despite the disparity in credentials, John Wiechel had earned an undergraduate degree in mechanical engineering and a doctorate in bioengineering and was licensed in seventeen states—Greg DuBois had an undergraduate degree in metallurgy, he spoke with authority and confidence on all things mechanical. As he had testified in his earlier deposition, his experience included only one other alleged hit-skip crash. Possessing a distinct air of professionalism, Mr. DuBois looked and sounded like the ideal expert. Before trial, I had read closely his deposition. I had a good idea what he would say, but you never know at trial.

Briefly, Attorney Gams questioned DuBois about those areas targeted by our expert, John Wiechel. Beginning with the number of dents DuBois discovered on the roof of the van, he testified that Andrew's head could not have hit the roof. Given Andrew's height, DuBois didn't believe that Andrew's head hit the windshield/roof line of the van or that he was tossed into the air. His testimony was in direct contradiction to Dr. Wiechel's deposition and the FCSO police report. Andrew was tossed some 200 feet from the point of his bicycle's impact. Dr. Wiechel's doctorate is in biomechanics; he can offer an opinion. But DuBois' had no expertise whatsoever in what happens to live beings in crashes.

To Andy and me, the matter of the windshield was a critical piece of evidence. DuBois concurred that the van in this crash sustained a broken windshield. Without any kind of examination, he believed that the Sapp van had two windshields, based on records before Sapp's ownership. Dr. Wiechel did examine the windshield and found three different layers of caulking that had encircled three windshields, the second of which shattered during the crash. Since the third windshield showed an Etchguard number put there by Spitzer Dodge, the windshield was not replaced after Sapp sold it.

DuBois also had trouble reconciling the fact that a mark on the flange, which is observable at the exact place where one of the pieces of the ground effect tore off, had been made by the bicycle's handlebars as Dr. Wiechel had contended.

Still to come was a discussion of the most crucial evidence—the pieces of the ground effect part found at the crash site. Would the jury understand all the information about the ground effect, its holes and the corresponding holes in the van's rocker panel? What would DuBois say about those pieces found at the crash?

In his December deposition, DuBois conceded—although reluctantly—that one set of van holes (of the three sets) matched up to the pieces torn off the van. He also knew that the holes were random, custom-drilled at Glaval—making the holes from ground effect to van unique. Yet he explained that the matching was a coincidence.

Now in court, would he stick to the same creative theory posed in his previous deposition that the Sapp van could not have killed Andrew?

When Linda, our PI, contacted the first and only owner of the van before Sapp, Ed Winn* described an accident involving a fender bender on the passenger side, the side of Andrew's hit. Voss Chevrolet's manager testified that neither the passenger side nor the driver side ground effects had been replaced with new parts. The manager also testified that if the ground effects had to be removed to repair other parts, the same ground effects would be reinstalled using the same holes. Therefore, there would be only one set of holes. Nothing could be simpler.

DuBois predicated his theory on speculating that *if Voss* Chevrolet, in repairing a right front fender bender, had reinstalled the undamaged ground effect *by drilling new holes instead of using the existing holes, there would be a second set.* DuBois maintained, that *if* these ground effect pieces found at the crash did not have a second set of holes, they could not have come from the Sapp van. No *ifs*—new holes weren't drilled—the old ones suffice.

The jury would have to remember that Voss's manager testified that the shop didn't drill new holes; mechanics merely used the existing holes to reinstall the original ground effect. No need for a second drilling, and the jury would also have to remember that DuBois said *if*.

To demonstrate his point about a second drilling, he asked for a blackboard. Juries, I was to learn, like blackboard demonstrations. So, do I. DuBois drew a series of nine circles to represent the three sets of holes in the Sapp van rocker panel. He noted the measurements, from one hole to the next one. What struck me about this demonstration was that no continuity in measurement existed between or among holes. DuBois could have written numbers ad infinitum, but the fact remained, intact ground effects removed from a van are reinstalled using existing holes and those holes are randomly drilled. DuBois' demonstration showed exactly what Glaval said—ground effects are installed using random drilling, no pattern. Confirmation of random drilling with random numbers on a blackboard came directly from the State Farm expert!

DuBois represented himself as an expert about what was typically done to reinstall a Glaval ground effect—a person whose testimony proved he didn't know the difference between a running board and a rocker panel.

DuBois finished his testimony by affirming that the metal around the hole in the wheel well had been pulled out, but he quickly made the point that he didn't know the reason for this and that there could be several possibilities—like a crash with a bicycle, when the bicycle handles pulled it out?

Unquestionably, the most important evidence involved those two pieces that had broken off from the passenger side ground effect. And that evidence wouldn't have been significant if Glaval had not advised that the piece had been custom installed with random drilling and that the pieces found at the crash would have to match the guilty van.

Not until Attorney Winters wrapped up his questioning did we realized how little DuBois knew about the ground effects. Like many people, we thought that experts if they were called to testify at trial knew as much as we did and probably more. That was an erroneous assumption. Winters said to DuBois, "Let me give you one additional bit of information which you did not have or I think you did not have. The body shop manager from Voss Chevrolet took the ground effects piece off to put the bumper on. And he put it back on through the same holes. It was actually the same holes. There would not be additional holes as a result of that."

"You are talking about the right side?" DuBois asked.

"Correct," Winters said. "That would have an effect on your conclusions, as well, would it not?

"It may, yes," DuBois replied.

61

THE TESTIMONY OF DEWAYNE CREIGHTON, the man who knew more about Glaval's ground effects than anyone else at Glaval, continued to be a key factor of our case. All parties were aware that his testimony would provide *the* critical component in the collection of our evidence against the Sapp van. If you're on the other side, somehow, in some way, you must discredit Creighton. How could you cast doubt on his straightforward, factual testimony? By any means necessary. Interpret that any way you want.

In 2000, Don Sonney, our then private investigator, obtained custody of the ground effect pieces from the Sapp van from the FCSO to have Glaval personnel in Elkhart, Indiana, examine the pieces and confirm their origin. Don Sonney, Andy and I met with Mr. Creighton, along with Glaval's customer service rep and its legal counsel in 2000. Creighton led the discussion. Essential to the information we had gathered about design and manufacturing of their ground effect part was Glaval's method of random, customized installation. At the meeting, Creighton pointed out that if we found a van with holes to match the pieces, we had the van that had killed Andrew. On that day, those pieces shot to the top of the chart in importance.

After our meeting with Creighton, we spoke with him on the phone to arrange his coming to Columbus to testify. He presented himself in court as the same man we had met almost four years earlier. If one's demeanor or a way of speaking engendered confidence in a person's truthfulness, Dewayne Creighton possessed it. Accomplishing much in his work life, Mr. Creighton not only designed parts, and supervised manufacturing but also managed a company. At the time of trial, he was the President of the Charleston Corporation, a subsidiary of Glaval that built fiberglass components. He showed no hint of self-importance.

Winters established Creighton's credentials. He helped to design the manufactured fiberglass parts for Glaval, including the ground effects. Importantly, he supervised the installation of the pieces. He ascertained that the parts found at the crash site were Glaval manufactured and Glaval installed.

Winters: I am going to show you what have been previously identified as…exhibits [photos of the ground effect pieces.] If you would…identify them for me.

307

Creighton:	This is a ground effects for the passenger side of an Astro van.
Winters:	How can you tell that it is for an Astro van?
Creighton:	Just merely the style of it. I recognize the shape of it, the way this is concave here…I know that nobody copied us out there.

The jury should have no doubt that these parts were Glaval manufactured as Creighton assisted in their design and manufacturing.

Winters:	Can you give the jury some sense of how the installation process traditionally occurred?
Creighton:	Yes. I am holding this [a ground effect part], it goes this way with the same way on the other end going from wheel well to wheel well. They would lift it out, put it into position, and put these two screws in first.
Winters:	The same guy screwing it that is lifting it up?
Creighton:	Yes. Then they would throw a screw in in the front and the rear, and from underneath they would just lay on the floor beside the van, reaching underneath, and then they would just start putting screws in, self-tappers, you don't need to have a hole drilled. *They just randomly put them any place they wanted.*
Winters:	You are standing here at about waist level…people probably visualize this process as occurring where the installer is holding it up and the van is up on a lift and he is carefully putting the screws in. That is not the way you are saying it worked?
Creighton:	No. They were going down the line pretty fast.
Winters:	Assembly line?
Creighton:	Yes.
Winters:	Are they bending over or lying down?

Creighton:	Laying on the floor. They just roll the van to the next position, lay on the floor behind it, beside it, with a screw gun, and would just reach underneath any place in this flange. It is about a three-inch area, all the way down, just matching metal on the rocker panel. They would just randomly put screws in.
Winters:	What I am wondering. Is that the way it happened, they are not even looking, doing it by feel and poking?
Creighton:	That is right.
Winters:	Did you ever try to do anything to get them to be more uniform in where screws were put?
Creighton:	No.
Winters:	No marks, no pencil lines, no measurements, no nothing to guide it?
Creighton:	No.
Winters:	So in light of that...what do you think about the odds of a second guy matching up and getting exactly the same holes?
Creighton:	Probably would be like hitting the lottery. It would be that difficult.
Winters:	So a double set of holes somewhat near each other would suggest that there had been a second installation then?
Creighton:	To me it would, yes.

To Creighton, the designer and manufacturer of the ground effect, and a plant supervisor who observed the installation of the ground effects thousands of times, a double set of holes meant a *new* second installation of a different ground effect. But Greg DuBois, metallurgical engineer and expert for State Farm, speculated that a double set of holes meant the *reinstallation* of the same ground effect. Factually dead wrong.

Jack Holland, retired State Highway Patrol crash reconstructionist, Don Sonney our PI and former State Highway official, and the mechanics at Goodyear, as well as Andy, Jeff Adams (another PI) and I *all* have witnessed mechanics removing a ground effect and then putting them back on the van, merely using the same holes and screws.

We heard through one of the jurors—that another juror proposed during deliberation that Dewayne Creighton, expert in the installation of the ground effects in 1998 for Glaval, was one of our (the plaintiffs') paid experts. Mr. Creighton was not our paid expert. He had no connection to us whatsoever.

This juror not only planted doubt about Creighton's credibility, but also, he proceeded to negate the trustworthiness of Creighton's testimony. This juror announced that working an assembly line for years, every task was precisely predetermined. Yes, but this was a different assembly line—one that customized vans. Another juror who reported this to us said that the juror who worked on the assembly line effectively convinced even the doubters. It seemed this jury, even if members had made note of the words "customized" and "random," believed that Mr. Creighton, an associate of Glaval, would perjure himself for us.

How did such an erroneous idea take hold in the jury room? Could one juror hold that much sway over the others? And if that juror convinced most the other jurors that the ground effects were not, in fact, installed randomly as customized pieces, and that Creighton's testimony was not truthful, then what happens to the factual validity of the evidence that the Sapp van killed Andrew? Did Gams just get lucky?

62

ALTHOUGH OURS WAS NOT A criminal trial, Dr. Wiechel suspected that Andrew was hit purposely. Andrew's bike was as far to the right as possible. No vehicle skid marks smudged the road. Dr. Wiechel expressed to us more than once the strong possibility that Andrew was targeted. But that was premeditated murder and the best we had was this civil case. During Dr. Wiechel's testimony, he described in graphic detail Andrew's injuries. One injury was so horrendous, so awful in its detail to Andrew's body, that if bicyclists were more aware of this injury, many of them might reconsider serious biking. The injuries our son suffered were as bad as any terrible murder.

The problem we faced at trial dealt with Dr. Wiechel's schedule. He and his family had scheduled a much-needed vacation to South Carolina the same week as the trial. He agreed to fly to Columbus from South Carolina, give his testimony and then fly out again on the same day. Not the best scenario, but Andy and I thought that postponement would just prolong the agony.

Almost everything about John Wiechel, our expert, was the antithesis of Greg DuBois, State Farm's expert. DuBois has an engineering degree in metallurgy. Our case was about mechanical engineering.

Wiechel, an adjunct professor at The Ohio State University and researcher for the National Highway Traffic Safety Administration, had given testimony as a witness hundreds of times. He is licensed nationally. No other engineer in Ohio could match Dr. Wiechel's credentials or experience in crash reconstruction.

From our experience in dealing with Wiechel, he was not only the consummate professional but also a person of impeccable reputation. As his clients go, we were insignificant. Most of his clients were large companies wrestling with safety issues. If he had not detected reasons to continue his examination of the Sapp van, he would have cut us loose immediately.

A key, significant point in Dr. Wiechel's testimony was the reason for his examination of the Sapp van. If the jury had not been listening closely, they could have missed this key testimony. After BCI's report, we had many questions about the Sapp van that went unanswered. We were looking for more information. The FCSO wasn't helping. On our PI's recommendation and with Mark Adams' help, we asked Wiechel if he would look at the van after the the red flags in BCI's report. If Dr. Wiechel found additional information or confirmed BCI's report, we believed his investigation would compel the FCSO to act. He did find additional information, but the FCSO did nothing. They strung us along for a year after the BCI report. Whatever they were doing, it wasn't to help us.

Filing a civil suit against the van owner never occurred to us until the FCSO's failure. We hired Wiechel, not because we had a law suit, but because we were looking for information to prompt action by the FCSO. We needed his expert assessment. To that end, at trial Attorney Winters clarified the reason for Wiechel's involvement.

Winters:	And what was the purpose for which SEA undertook the investigation of the van, the bicycle, the ground effects piece, and other items of evidence related to the Starinchak's son's death?
Wiechel:	The purpose of our involvement was to determine if we could identify a connection between the van and the other things that were clearly part of the accident, the bicycle, the broken pieces of the van, the clothing, the paint chips…
Winters:	You had no preconceptions in that investigation then, I take it?
Wiechel:	No, I did not.
Winters:	How did the van and other items of evidence come to SEA's possession?
Wiechel:	From the Sheriff's department. They had been in the Sheriff's property room and on the vehicle lot, their impound lot.
Winters:	You acquired it the end of May 2002, is that correct?
Wiechel:	Yes.

From the middle of July in 2001 to May 30, 2002, the van sat outside the Sheriff's impound lot—almost a year.

Winters asked Wiechel to tell the jury how he and his team of engineers and scientists at SEA, Doug Morr, Bob Carbonara and Bob Moss, went about their inspection.

Wiechel:	We started off by looking at the bicycle…When a bicycle is struck by a car, the first point of contact is going to be evident, and if that is on the rear wheel, then I would expect to see some kind of an indentation or bending of the rear wheel, just like we have here.
	In a rear-end accident like this, and he gets hit from behind, the bike is going to get thrown forward. He is going to essentially fall backwards, and the seat is getting shoved out forwards and as he goes back, he is going to rotate back, exposing his left side or his front side of his head to impact on the windshield… on the roof.

You almost had to be an engineer to grasp all the finer points he was making. Clearly, he was the expert here.

Wiechel confirmed that the Sapp van had been painted several times. Anyone could see the difference between the Sapp van in the August 14, 1998 photo and the Sapp van in the 2001 photos. Because Wiechel inspected this van four years after the crash, whatever damage was there from this accident had been repaired or parts replaced.

His findings confirmed that the holes in each of the two pieces of the ground effect matched up to the holes in the van's rocker panel. First, he discussed at length how each piece was torn out. In referring to the hole in the vertical piece, "we know it [the vertical piece] got pulled off and if we look at the screw hole [in the vertical piece], it is not big enough for a head [screw head] to fit through…it wasn't stressed far enough that the hole actually got big enough [that] the screw pulled through…In addition to that, the hole is pulled out on the sheet metal [the van] but not pulled through on the ground effects piece. So that is a similarity. If we go to the holes on the rocker panel [for the horizontal piece] those holes are not pulled out. That says to me that when the ground effect piece separated on this one, the screw stayed with the van. So we have a match there."

How much of this was the jury understanding? What was needed here was an actual demonstration. Or pictures. Regardless, the way these two pieces were pulled out of the van was different and the pieces as well as van showed that.

Wiechel: So…when this damage occurred [the pulling out and the breaking of the pieces of the ground effect] there was something that contacted the inside of the ground effects piece and pulled it outward, and as a result of that pulling it outward, it pulled these two pieces off the van at that point.

What that says to me is that we do have an object that is the right size to make that kind of damage, specifically the right handle bar so what happens then is during this accident, the right handle bar is up. The left handlebar is down, gets into the pavement, and as a result of getting underneath the van…the right handlebar catches hold of the ground effects part [and] pulled it off [in two pieces.] [We] now understand how the ground effects piece was broken and we understand how it relates to the accident.

At this point, Dr. Wiechel turned the bike over to demonstrate to the jury how the right handle bar tore off the parts of the ground effect found at the crash.

Then Wiechel, resuming his explanation, explained his reason for believing that a bend in the flange was related to this crash. In using a picture exhibit, he directed the jury's attention:

Wiechel: You also see this flange here. This is where two pieces of rocker panel come together…and this flange here is where they are kind of spot welded together."

Up here at the front, we have a piece of flange that is actually bent outward. It turns out that if we put the ground effects pieces back on, that that location matches the gap [see picture of ground effects showing the gap] and that makes sense because we got the handle bar that is coming in, and it is getting shoved down from above…and that [bend in the] flange is the point where I would expect that to happen…

Greg DuBois, State Farm expert, confirmed that the flange was bent exactly where Dr. Wiechel had pinpointed. He also agreed that the handlebars pulled out the ground effect pieces from the guilty van. But he would not agree that the bend occurred because of this crash.

"Now what about the dents?" Winters inquired. In Wiechel's list of condemning the Sapp van, he focused his attention mostly on one dent—a head-sized dent on the roof line, near the windshield on the passenger side that had been filled-in with Bondo.

Wiechel believed that the head-sized dent—at the time of his examination—revealed a shoddy repair with Bondo and to him, Andrew's head made that dent.

Winters:	…Let's talk about paint for a few minutes.
Wiechel:	One of the things we did find was that we took a sample, the paint chips that were found with the clothing and we compared that with some paint off the back of the passenger's door. If we take identical samples and we do a comparison, it is uncommon to get a 100 per cent match, because of slight variations in thickness [and] the local composition of the paint. But anyway, an 84 percent match says that that is really the same paint.

As Dr. Wiechel was talking about vehicle paint, I thought about my conversation with the clerk at the auto paint shop. The clerk explained how two paint samples from the same batch could never be exactly the same but could be called a match and termed "similar." I imagined workers, standing over stainless steel vats, stirring the contents with large shovels. A recipe for vehicle paint or for cake batter—the principle is still the same. In testing two teaspoons from the same mixture, you would not get the exact same results, but similar enough to say that they are from the same batch.

BCI's analysis strengthened Wiechel's testimony. The paint chips found in Andrew's clothes were characterized by BCI and Wiechel as similar in chemical composition, texture, and color. To experts, this means that the van chip and clothes chip are a match.

For the jury to understand how Andrew's body hit the van, Wiechel began a detailed explanation of rider kinematics:

Wiechel	...to sustain a skull fracture here requires a force of, oh, in the range of about 4,000 pounds. And that would be consistent with this kind of impact... where the bicycle gets shoved forward, the pelvis gets pulled forward, it essentially settles back, he rolls off, goes over to his left and hits his head up on the roof.
	We have got a variety of injuries...the sternum injury...the left chest...severe abrasions on his legs... on his head and...other lacerations here and there. He is being pulled off the bike...where his right leg is being pulled...and essentially his pelvis being pulled apart at that point...and a femur facture...

Listening to Dr. Wiechel list Andrew's injuries, I blocked out his testimony. Of all the information shared in the courtroom that week, this was information I didn't want to hear. When Andrew was killed, I wanted out of this life. I didn't have the strength to face what had happened to our son.

Much of the rest of testimony was formality. The crux remained—the deciding points were that the ground effect pieces matched up to the Sapp van, and the way the pieces were torn off, matched the van according to the configuration of holes in the van's rocker panel and pieces themselves.

Additionally, crucial parts of the examination to mark this van guilty dealt with the paint match, the third windshield and the bent flange.

Finishing, Attorney Winters asked:

Winters:	Can you think of anything that you guys didn't do that could have been done...?
Wiechel:	[W]e tried to be very thorough...we have identified that there are a number of matches... But we have got like 15 or 20 matches here, and it is difficult to say that we have that much coincidence in matching this bicycle to this van in this accident.
Winters:	Doctor, I have one final question, and that is based on the efforts of you and your team, did you

collectively…come to an opinion as to whether or not the van you examined, the bicycle you examined, the ground effects pieces that you examined, to a level of a reasonable scientific probability involve the van that was registered to Mr. Sapp August 1, 1998?

Wiechel: Yes, I did.

Winters: And what is that opinion?

Wiechel: *That opinion is that this van was involved in this accident.*

63

ATTORNEY GAMS FOR STATE FARM Insurance and its insured, James O. Sapp, would now have his opportunity to cross-examine Wiechel. Gams had to find some weak point in Dr. Wiechel's testimony. After all, it was his job, his duty to make certain that his primary client, the insurance giant, State Farm, came out of this unscathed.

But by this time, Attorney Gams had successfully maneuvered a motion past the visiting judge to take money off the table. All civil cases are about the money reward. How Gams, et al, managed to pull that trick—yes, trick—is astounding in retrospect. When I testified, I said that I didn't need money. This was about money and not about justice? Not justice? For Gams and his client, State Farm, of course, money was *the* issue. Gams assessed their chances of a sustained motion ruling by visiting Judge Martin, who knew nothing about our case. The motion to take money off the table meant that Gams was scared. He could lose the case but it can't cost State Farm big money. How in the name of God did he get away with that stunt? I have a plausible theory.

If anyone noticed my reaction to this motion that Gams filed mid-trial, he saw that I was visibly distraught. I thought that the motion was about dismissing our case against Sapp, not money. Luckily for Andy and me, Mark and Patty Adams were sitting in the courtroom that day and explained what was going on. Winters, without any experience in plaintiff civil cases, conferred with Mark Adams, but Attorney Gams prevailed. Ignorantly, I breathed a big sigh of relief. Neither Andy nor I cared about the money. We were too naïve to understand that removing a money award from the suit immediately weakened our case. It also meant we would be facing enormous legal expenses. Punish the victim's family.

Even though the big client was essentially off the hook, Attorney Gams had to make his points. The trial wasn't over. No jury member could have remembered all the pertinent information. Each important point needed to be repeated again and again. And I saw no juror taking notes, I did see jurors sleeping.

When we had found the Sapp van in 2001, it looked nothing like it had in 1998. By 2001 it had been painted and repainted a stark white and resembled a utility van. The outside appearance had been seriously altered. If there had been any transference from the bicycle to the van or from Andrew to the van, that evidence was long gone with the repainting. Absolutely paint transference from the bicycle to the van would have happened, but three years after the crash and with the van's repairing and repainting, who would believe that any trace of the bicycle paint was still on the van?

However, automotive paint was on the bicycle. This involved one smear of white paint on the top bicycle bar. Cleverly, Gams *never* asked if van paint was found on Andrew. *There was and it matched.*

Gams hammered Wiechel about the difference in results between BCI's paint match and SEA's—BCI's results were better, more precise. Here, Dr. Wiechel could have explained how even taking paint samples from various parts of a brand-new vehicle can't match exactly but are considered a match. Gams also attempted to get Wiechel to say that the paint sample from the Sapp van could have matched any GM van. Considering all the other matches, including paint, Wiechel answered with a resounding, "No."

In questioning Wiechel about the holes in the ground effect pieces, Gams pointed out to Wiechel and the jury the various measurements of distance among the holes. Since no pattern existed between any of the distances, those measurements proved our point that installation was random and unique to this van. And disproved Gams' own expert's testimony that Glaval might have had a pattern for installation. If the jury didn't understand the *significance* of those haphazard, arbitrary measurements between and among holes, it was up to our attorney to emphasize that.

Sapp's defense would not have been complete without some mention of Raymond Farris*, the guy who bought Sapp's van at Spitzer. Farris ended up in jail after attempting to kill a girlfriend and breaking and entering in a separate crime. Gams broached the subject of Farris buying the Sapp van on November 21, 1998.

Continuing, Gams reported that the van was stolen while in Farris' possession, months after Farris bought it following Sapp's sale. "And then no one knows anything about it until it is discovered that a John Brown* takes it in to Metro Chevrolet, correct?"

Incorrect. We knew a great deal about this van from November, 1998, to the time we found it. The van had a criminal history. Four months after Farris bought the Sapp van, he filed a theft report with the Columbus Police, claiming a female hijacked it. After that, the 1993 van took on a 1990 identity with a number of owners, all with criminal histories, passing it around like a hot potato—no single person, owning more than two months. This history was unusual and suspicious. Then the Sapp/1993 van posing as a 1990 van went off paper.

Finally, Dr. Wiechel testified to the same conclusion that he expressed to our attorney, David Winters.

During a trial a witness or attorney could make a remark that would cause those in the courtroom to chuckle, had they been listening. That kind of remark occurred when Attorney Gams and Wiechel were handling the third intact dirty ground effect part recently removed from the van.

> Gams: I will give you [referring to a towel after Wiechel
>   handled the ground effect], if you need something to
>   wipe your hands with.
>
> Wiechel: I am an engineer. I am used to this. *The law is a dirty
>   business.*

Fitting words to end Dr. Wiechel's testimony.

64

WE CALLED ONLY ONE WITNESS, our daughter, whom the defendants might characterize as having a personal agenda. Her testimony involved Deputy McMannis himself, who admitted at trial to the late December 1999 meeting with her.

The glaring difference between our daughter's and Deputy McMannis' versions of the meeting happened when he denied telling her that because of our case, he asked for a demotion and that he was in therapy. We never considered connecting the details of Betsey's conversation to our request to have the State Highway Patrol intervene. But we later surmised that request put his job performance in the spotlight. Our case probably wasn't the sole reason for his demotion. There must have been a pattern. And we learned that deputy reprimands often involve two choices: resign or be demoted.

When anything unusual happened, we called our private investigator and attorney. And I made mention of that Christmas visit and its details countless times in conversations and emails.

Initially, we didn't realize what that visit meant. We didn't know that we weren't considered friendly when McMannis asked our daughter if she was wearing a wire. Why does someone wear a wire? To get information covertly. The question itself implied McMannis' guilt—that we could gather evidence against him. But we never intended to sue the FCSO. Betsey wasn't wearing a wire. Frankly, we weren't interested in McMannis—only as far as he could help us find our son's killer. All we ever wanted from the FCSO was a reasonable investigation into Andrew's death. We never expected anything but that. And as to McMannis' demotion. That move didn't help us—in fact, it hurt us. McMannis' anger was misdirected at us.

Several personal witnesses were called to testify on James O. Sapp's behalf. One of those was the fifth Mrs. Sapp whose testimony repeated her deposition. Another witness, Sapp's supervisor at his work place, testified that Sapp and friends had talked about going to Las Vegas; hence, in her opinion, the trip was not last minute. No work document or request supported her opinion. Sapp's minister was supposed to testify, but he pulled out—no reason given. And two other women testified on Sapp's behalf, having to do with personal, unverifiable issues.

For me, the most attention-grabbing witness for Sapp was his golf buddy. His story was so untenable that Winters could easily have excoriated him. Parts of his testimony tested the limits of absurdity. He and Sapp golfed every Monday in a work-related league. Now in March 2004, almost six years later, Sapp's golf buddy claimed that on Monday, August 3, 1998 (Andrew was hit August 1), Sapp showed up to play golf in his undamaged 1993 Glaval Chevy Astro van. Did the golf buddy realize that Sapp had another vehicle? Or that he could have borrowed his girlfriend's car?

How did the buddy know that Sapp drove his Astro van on that Monday, August 3, so many years later? Because he testified that he met Sapp in the parking lot every Monday to carry Sapp's clubs for him. One hundred per cent of the time over several years? And what if Sapp got there first? Did Sapp go to the buddy's car? What if Sapp drove his other vehicle? Or his girlfriend's? Would the buddy have noticed? Did the buddy really meet Sapp in the parking lot to carry his clubs? Women carry their own clubs or have those metal carriers on wheels. Did he realize that to say that he saw Sapp's van at the time, he had to have some excuse to see his vehicle in the parking lot? But I could see the look on Winters' face that said no one, not even the most gullible, would buy that story.

After the buddy relayed how helpful he was on Monday golf league day and that he saw no damage to Sapp's van, Winters asked, "What color was the van? A large photo of the Sapp van was propped up against the podium. The colors—because of enlargement or copying—were distorted. The Sapp van was white with red striping but the enlargement made the stripes look blue. Of course, the buddy witness answered, "Blue." Winters baited him, "Dark blue or light blue?" "Blue," was the reply. In the movies, the audience would know the van was white and red. The lawyer would say nothing and walk away, having exposed the witness, and heightened the drama.

Conversely, in a real courtroom, for all the jury knew by looking at the picture, the witness was correct. Winters never challenged his answer. I sat there frustrated. When Winters walked back to the table to take his seat, I started to remark about the color. He gave me this look as if to say, "Don't you dare bother me with that now." I thought the jury should realize that this guy, who claimed he met Sapp every Monday in the parking lot, didn't remember the color of Sapp's van. But he remembered August 3, 1998. Sometimes you should help the jury and say the obvious.

We did have an ace up our sleeve, or so we thought. We had one last witness to call, but putting that witness on the stand was fraught with problems. As much as I assumed I knew about police culture, my insight, then, of the consequences of not totally supporting a fellow officer came close to zero. If a policeman tells the truth under oath about an investigation—trying to put the best spin possible on the truth, but still telling the truth—and it contradicts another policeman's testimony, he will become a pariah with fellow officers.

Essentially, we backed Deputy Ken Wooten against a wall. When a FCSO supervisor handed him our file in November 2000, a little more than two years after the crash, he read the file and met us the next day. Amazed by his energy and candor, we dared to envision that he might be the one to solve our case. Today, I can't think of one criticism of him. No doubt lurked in our minds that this young man was going to get some answers. We were struck by his transparency. He attempted at every point to keep us advised about what he was doing and what he learned. If we called him with a question about the investigation and he knew the answer, he would tell us. If he had a negative opinion about this investigation, he kept it to himself. His approach was to move forward and get answers. That was just fine with us because that's what we wanted, too.

The problem came about after the Sapp van had been examined by BCI and its subsequent report. Deputies in the traffic office recognized that the report meant the van had to be investigated. Since Wooten had worked our case six months previously and knew that McMannis handled the case during the first months, Wooten wasted no time talking to McMannis. At a visit with McMannis at a bingo hall, he talked to McMannis about the van. In that conversation in 2001 and long before the trial in 2004, McMannis told Wooten that he had seen the Sapp van two weeks after the crash. Because that squared with McMannis' initial remarks to his supervisor, Gil Jones, of McMannis seeing the van "within two weeks" of the crash, this information was merely confirmation when McMannis viewed the Sapp van. Wooten delivered the information as ordinary detail in a conversation. And that's how we received it.

Now at trial, McMannis testified differently, but we had made note of Wooten's conversation with McMannis in 2001—for no other reason than McMannis had revealed a stunning discovery: our reward flyers featured the Sapp van, the van that killed Andrew. Our attorney subpoenaed Wooten as a witness to verify what Wooten told us in a conversation he had had with

McMannis. At trial, witnesses aren't allowed to hear the testimony of other witnesses. Wooten had no idea what McMannis' said. And he had no reason to think that his testimony would be different from McMannis' testimony. He had no knowledge of McMannis' November deposition wherein McMannis alleged that he saw the Sapp van on Wednesday, August 5, 1998.

Winters moved to question Wooten about his conversation with McMannis at the bingo hall after the Sapp van inspection.

Winters:	Did you have an occasion, Deputy Wooten, to be on the Westside of Columbus seeking information from Deputy McMannis while he was working…at a bingo hall?
Wooten:	Yes, I did.
Winters:	Were you given any specific information by Deputy McMannis at that time in terms of whether he had seen what turned out to be the Sapp van?
Wooten:	Yes.
Winters:	Did he specifically tell you he had seen the vehicle two weeks after the accident?
Wooten:	Yes, he did.
Winters:	Any question in your mind about that?
Wooten:	Not at all.

Like Detective Wassmuth, McMannis' former partner, Wooten testified truthfully. That was the extent of the conversation in question. McMannis offered nothing further in that conversation about seeing the van earlier.

65

JUST AS IN THE MOVIES, a television show, or in a Grisham novel, something spectacular happened during our trial. But this wasn't the kind of display that aroused some members of the jury out of their drowsiness. One juror sat with head tilted back, mouth opened and slept. I can still see the same three people sleeping at some point in the trial. One juror's ample bosom rested on the rail in front of her as she dozed. Too bad what happened wasn't obtrusively dramatic. You had to be awake and listening.

Attorney Winters called to the stand Dr. Karen Kwek, forensic scientist with the Bureau of Criminal Investigation, an agency under the Attorney General. After we found the van at Metro Chevrolet in July 2001, Deputy Fickenworth of the FCSO transported the Sapp van to London, Ohio, for her examination. Her investigative report in 2001 sent up red flags: The ground effects pieces aligned with holes in the van's rocker panel and paint chips stuck to blood on Andrew's shirt matched paint samples that she scraped from the van. She testified that deputies reported that they had a suspicious vehicle that might have been involved in a hit-and-run fatality. With that, Deputy Fickenworth handed her a list of tasks to perform in her examination of the van. She testified at her deposition that deputies gave her no additional detail. The FCSO absolutely knew the significance of her findings.

We first met Dr. Kwek at a December 2003 deposition. Pretty, with a light British accent, she earned her doctorate in chemistry in Canada, did post-doctoral research in France and had an extensive work history in Canada before moving to the United States. Clearly, in her deposition before the trial, she had not been given any information other than that the van was suspicious and therefore, some items needed examination. Her report to the FCSO's traffic department, described her examination.

From her perspective, the van looked like a utility vehicle—one of a thousand plain work vans seen on the roadways every day. She didn't know that at the time of the crash, this van looked very different. Originally this van was a custom-converted vehicle, and that this van had special features found only on a Glaval-converted van. That bit of information would not have altered her findings—it just would have told her *the significance* of her findings. When the FCSO was advised of the results of her examination, they knew the significance. Dr. Kwek didn't know what the alignment of those pieces to the van meant. No doubt, that valuable bit of information eventually became a topic of discussion.

Lawyers ask certain technical questions of witnesses even though they know the answers or the answers are self-evident. Winters had to ask Dr. Kwek exactly what items Deputy Fickenworth delivered to her. She listed the van, the bicycle, the two pieces of the ground effect and a black plastic bag containing Andrew's clothes. I thought it strange that his shoes were not in the bag. Why strange? When the policemen came to the house on that terrible Sunday afternoon, the first thing they asked about was his shoes. Where were the shoes? Automotive paint could well have been on those shoes.

After a brief look at the van and the bicycle, she began her examination by looking at the clothing. In describing the process, she testified, "I would take a drop sheet, a big brown sheet of paper, put it over an examination table, take the clothing out of the bag and conduct an examination. I have documented...that the blue T-shirt had apparent bloodstains... I observed tiny glass fragments and tiny white deposits that were collected from the apparent blood-stained regions...two tiny white paint chips were found in the debris shaken from the clothing."

Taking the white paint chips from the clothes, Kwek examined them under the microscope to get layers. Then she took paint chips from the van–around the tail light and inside the right-side door to get samples of the original paint because the van had been repainted several times. These chips from the original van paint had the same three layers as the chips from the clothes. To see if she had a match, she set up a comparison microscope with the chips from the clothes and the chips from the van on two separate slides.

Winters:	The first thing you look at is color?
Kwek:	That is correct.
Winters:	If the color isn't the same, then you've eliminated the unknown from being the same as the known?
Kwek:	Correct.
Winters:	You go on to the second test?
Kwek:	Yes...we also look at microscopic features like texture, graininess, the inclusion of particles and we also look at the relative thickness of each layer...if the paints appear the same in color and microscopic appearance, I proceed further with chemical analysis of each layer.

Winters:	Going back to your conclusion with regard to color, layering, and microscopic appearance, the sample from the van matched the same from the clothes, correct?
Kwek:	Correct.
Winters:	So now we move on to chemical analysis.
Kwek:	[T]he method I use in the lab is what we call free transform infrared spectroscopy…an instrument that analyzes the components in the paint.
Winters:	You are about to say what your findings were …
Kwek:	I overlaid them. I superimposed them and I deemed that all sets of the spectra from the questioned [chips from the clothes] and the known [chips from the van], that they were all similar respectively in chemical composition. [T]he reason why I use the word similar instead of same, I did see some slight variation in the relative peak heights, but that is to be expected in paint, because paint is not of homogenous material.
Winters:	It would be possible then to get samples from two different places off the same vehicle and get slightly different wave readings?
Kwek:	Yes. It is not the wavelengths that are different. It is the relative intensities of the peaks.

So far so good. We expected her to confirm what she said in her initial report—that she found a paint match from van to clothes and clothes to van. Now what about the alignment of the ground effect pieces to the van?

She testified by referring to her report: "the vertical piece fits along the rear of the front wheel well of [the van] and the two holes present on this fiberglass align up with holes present in and around the wheel well area. The second piece of fiberglass…as fitting behind the first piece. Pieces and portions, however, are missing between the latter two pieces, and the hole on this second piece aligns up with one of two holes in that region of the rocker panel of the van."

Witnesses aren't allowed to hear other witnesses' testimony. Somehow, Dr. Kwek must have learned that the ground effect piece was custom installed by random drilling. After Dr. Kwek's December deposition, did she ask questions about the van? In wrapping up her testimony, she dropped a bomb on the defense.

Winters: Dr. Kwek, you have put in your report some conclusions or opinions. I ask you if, based on your education, your training, your background, your experience, your examinations of the items in question, your conclusions and opinions reach the level of a reasonable scientific probability?

Kwek: My conclusions in this case, I summarize in one sentence, that these findings indicate that the three-layer paint found in the debris from the clothing, could have come from the white Chevrolet van, and in using these and in stating these findings, I include not only the comparison between the three-layer paint samples but also the examination of the fiberglass pieces that were found at the scene, and the association I made between the holes that were present on these ground effect pieces and how they aligned up with preexisting holes already on the vehicle, so it was my findings taken together.

Winters: I don't want to sound inartful, *but … was this to the level of at least a reasonable scientific probability.*

Kwek: *Yes, it is.*

To the level of a reasonable scientific probability in the scientific community is as strong a statement that science will make to confirm what they believe is true. Dr. Kwek had just validated Jack Holland's early assessment of the van, "Call your attorney. You have probable cause." Dr. Kwek had just validated Dr. Wiechel's findings. Dr. Kwek had just validated Judge Lisa Sadler's ruling to allow the case to go forward based on the evidence. Dr. Kwek had just validated Deputy Steve Fickenworth's belief that the Sapp van was suspect based on the matching ground effects. Another deputy, Ross Staggs wrote in a documented report, that *if the holes line up to the van, then Sapp becomes a suspect.* And each of the above people validated Dr. Kwek's conclusion that based on a reasonable scientific probability, the Sapp van was involved. No reasonable person could draw any other conclusion.

I could only imagine how the other side reacted to Dr. Kwek's testimony. His strategy was to discredit Kwek by highlighting the difference between her deposition and her court testimony. At the deposition, Kwek wasn't asked her opinion of what the paint and the ground effects taken together said to her. Attorney Gams became noticeably agitated, but Dr. Kwek stood her ground. Speaking in strong tones, she testified that based on the two findings, she had formed an opinion.

Gams:	And so, again, just so I don't want to be confused here. Based on the paint, you are not saying that the van that was once owned by Mr. Sapp is the van that was involved in this crash?
Kwek:	Based on the paint alone all I can say is that the paint is the same in layer sequence, color, microscopic appearance, and similar in chemical composition from the paint chips removed from the clothing articles. I am just saying that it is the same, those are my findings.
Gams:	Right.
Kwek:	However, taken together with the others, then I am forming an opinion.
Gams:	Within a reasonable degree of scientific probability, as opposed to what could be possible, …based upon your information, did you believe that the Sapp van was the vehicle involved in this Starinchak accident?
Kwek:	[T]here is some degree of probability.
Gams:	It has to be a reasonable degree of probability.
Kwek:	A reasonable degree of probability.

If I had been standing, I would have dropped to my knees. If I had felt comfortable showing emotion, I would have held my head in my hands and cried. A scientist, one who works for law enforcement and one who had no interest in us whatsoever but in the truth, opened the door wider for justice to enter.

Sitting in the courtroom that day, Bruce Cadwallader, courthouse reporter for the *Columbus Dispatch*, caught the gist of Dr. Kwek's testimony. In the next day's edition his article headlined, **2 EXPERTS LINK VAN TO CYCLIST'S DEATH IN '98.**

Dr. Kwek's testimony and Cadwallader's article carried us through the weekend. Surely, a person of Dr. Kwek's credentials, a scientist who authoritatively stated her professional conclusion would impact the jury. Yes, we were positive that the jury would weigh her scientific testimony against Deputy McMannis' pathetic incompetence. A man who had a scrap of personal paper on which he wrote a date—his alleged only report by the way. "Cover-up," I said to Andy. "Lies," he retorted. "Deputies were hanging around outside the courtroom in case the press showed up." Dr. Kwek had no agenda but to do her job.

The case was scheduled to go to jury deliberation the following week. We felt certain that if the jury heard and understood the facts, they would return with a verdict in our favor. The operative phrase was *understood the facts*. Our imaginations couldn't conceive that the facts would be of little importance.

The Columbus Dispatch

HIT-SKIP LAWSUIT
2 EXPERTS LINK VAN TO CYCLIST'S DEATH IN '98

Friday, March 26, 2004
NEWS   01B

By Bruce Cadwallader
THE COLUMBUS DISPATCH

Paint chips on the victim's clothing and debris found at the scene connected James O. Sapp's van to a hit-skip accident that killed a Blendon Township bicyclist, *two experts* testified yesterday.

The death of Andrew J. Starinchak, 31, on Aug. 1, 1998, remains unsolved as far as authorities are concerned.

But in July 2001, his parents found a 1993 Chevrolet Astro conversion van on Morse Road. Through their own investigation, Andrew E. and Elaine Starinchak became so convinced it was the van that killed their son on Central College Road in Plain Township that they sued Sapp, the owner at the time of the accident.

Karen Kwek, a forensic scientist for the state Bureau of Criminal Investigation and Identification, testified that she matched white paint chips found on Starinchak's clothing to paint on Sapp's van. She also said holes drilled in pieces of a running board found next to the body lined up with drill holes on the underbody of the van.

Defense attorney Mark Gams challenged Kwek's testimony, saying it differed from her vague report and a previous deposition.

"Taking the two parts together, I am forming an opinion now," Kwek responded.

John Weichel, a Columbus mechanical engineer hired by the Starinchaks, was more definite. After 75 hours of testing and analyzing evidence, Weichel said, he was sure, "This van was involved in the accident."

He said the paint chip from Starinchak's blood-soaked shirt was an 84 percent match to Sapp's van. He found 15 other forensic clues that helped him reach his conclusion.

Sapp, 56, of Reynoldsburg, has admitted he owned the van in August 1998 but denies being the hit-skip driver.

The Franklin County sheriff's office, which was looking for a conversion van because of evidence at the scene, examined Sapp's vehicle a few days after the accident and cleared him. No one has been charged.

2 Experts Link Van to Cyclist's Death in '98

66

WHEN I HAVE FLASHBACKS TO those days in the courtroom, images abound of those who came to support us, Mark and Patty, Linda, Becky, Julie, and Teresa's husband. I also see other people. One in particular—a small, elderly man, with a short-trimmed beard, dressed in tweed and carrying an umbrella. He sat in the back every day. Was he in costume? He was made to look eccentric—like a movie extra. He was a brown spot in the back. Just before the jury was sent out to deliberate, Betsey noticed that during one of the coffee breaks this little man winked and gave a thumbs up to a sheriff's deputy standing outside the courtroom. In a movie, that fleeting gesture would give the audience a hint as to the outcome of the trial. People gesture for any number of reasons. Who was this strange little man? Had he talked to a member of the jury?

Dressed in black robes, the gray-haired, stern-faced judge read without emphasis or inflection his instructions to the jury. This visiting judge wasn't a part of our community, and had about as much interest in our case as the drool on his robe. He advised the jury of his ruling to eliminate any money reward. If I had been a member of the jury, I would have been puzzled. A civil case is about money. Is this an indication that these people have no case?

I haven't done any research, but I believe the circumstances of our civil case were somewhat rare. We sued a man whose van, scientists and engineers believed based on fact, was involved in the homicide of our son. One of those experts served in the police's forensic lab. Yet, no criminal investigation resulted from her findings. The FCSO had not even questioned or investigated the owner of a van which BCI had flagged. Why? Because a deputy who kept no records said, yes *said*, that he saw the van just days after the crash. This statement made six years after the crash. His poor, faulty memory of an event six years prior trumped the facts and the physical, scientific evidence. After the FCSO confiscated the van and observed it in their garage, it was suspicious enough to have it towed to BCI. BCI's report confirmed their suspicions. Still no investigation into the owner and his vehicle. What authority was in charge of the traffic department?

Continuing, the visiting judge instructed the jury that a preponderance of evidence is the standard for the plaintiff to prevail in a civil case. He didn't explain exactly what that meant. The one juror who spoke to us after the trial said that most of the jurors didn't understand that phrase. Because her job put her in contact with offenders, this juror tried to educate other jury members. "Preponderance" means that one side of the suit has more evidence than the other side. For the jury to return a verdict for the plaintiffs, we, the plaintiffs, had to show a preponderance of evidence—at the very least 51 percent of the evidence in our favor. To Andy and me, the preponderance part had to be overwhelming to leave no doubt. And it was. The defendant had zero evidence. Zero. We strove for a moral certainty toward the accused.

Today, I can't think of one factual, verifiable piece of evidence that Gams presented—not a scrap—which would plant any kind of doubt at all that the Sapp van was not involved. We could not have gone forward if a profusion of the facts and science had not pointed precisely to the Sapp van.

Erroneously, McMannis' "*personal* log book" was allowed to masquerade as a work product, not what it actually was—a personal piece of paper which McMannis could have written at anytime, anywhere. A copy of the one page was allowed—not the entire date book.

Sitting in a juror's place, I would have had trouble figuring out why a deputy kept no official records. The FCSO couldn't run the risk of having their incompetence exposed. The ordinary parents of the victim used the evidence at the crash scene and found the van that killed their son.

Adding to the comedy of errors were the mistaken assumptions of State Farm's expert, Greg DuBois. DuBois based his testimony on glaringly wrong information—that if a ground effect is removed from a van for some reason and reinstalled, new holes are drilled. No, the existing van holes are used to reinstall the piece. We witnessed this first hand.

The testimony of Sapp's golfing buddy, a friend, was equally absurd. The buddy testified at trial in March 2004 that he met Sapp on August 3, 1998 in the parking lot of a golf course to carry Sapp's clubs, and he observed no damage to Sapp's van. He claimed that he always carried Sapp's golf clubs, but apparently couldn't remember the color of the van.

Stack up the witnesses for the defense: the personal calendar of a deputy who made no reports and kept no official log; Greg DuBois who knew nothing about ground effects; and the golfing buddy. Now recall the witnesses for the plaintiff: Dewayne Creighton, supervisor at Glaval, an expert on the design and installation of ground effects; Voss Chevrolet's service manager; Dr. Kwek, forensic scientist at BCI; Dr. Wiechel, head crash reconstructionist and Ph.D. in engineering; Deputy Fickenworth of the FCSO who acted in Sergeant Staggs place to engineer BCI's examination of the van as well as the criminal history of the van after Mr. Sapp's ownership, magnifying its suspiciousness.

The trial centered almost exclusively on the mechanical evidence and the van. Still, until the jury could see how this van was involved in injuring and killing Andrew, the human side was missing. A very small part of the trial dealt with the Coroner's autopsy and Andrew's injuries.

We had circumstantial evidence against James Sapp himself. The most obvious was his testimony that he was the only driver, except for his girl-friend's occasional trip to the grocery store. There were no stores within miles of where Andrew was killed. The girlfriend had many large chain grocery stores near her home. If the evidence pointed to the involvement of the van in a fatality and the owner testified that he was the only driver, except on rare occasions, then the probability increased tenfold that the owner of the vehicle was also the driver. Under these circumstances, Attorney Winters reasoned, the driver's identity becomes a common-sense conclusion. But this point wasn't emphasized at trial.

Adding to the circumstantial evidence was Sapp selling his van—five weeks after the crash—the day after the Crime Stoppers' tape aired on television and the article appeared in the newspaper. Coincidence? McMannis, from the same town as Sapp, spotted Sapp's van, a Glaval, and used it in the Crime Stoppers' publicity five weeks after the crash. Lo and behold, the next day Sapp sold the van. Scared? Impulsive? Records subpoenaed from Spitzer Dodge verified the date.

Several weeks into August and after Sapp returned from a five-day trip to Las Vegas on August 12, he left his neighborhood (where, he stated in his 2001 deposition, a neighbor inquired about the police being at his house) and moved in with his girlfriend who had just purchased her own house.

After the trial, a woman juror we talked with shared some stunning infor-mation about deliberations. One of the other jurors, a young man, announced that the jury should examine the physical evidence. At that point, a more senior male juror remarked that vehicle parts are never installed randomly and this same juror stated confidently that Glaval's Dewayne Creighton was the Plaintiffs' (our) paid witness. Negating the random drilling derailed the jury's examination and discussion of critical evidence. If the random drilling was not factual, then it was a waste of time to talk about the evidence. The senior juror's opinion—personal, wrong, and misguided—prevailed. Disgusted, the woman juror reported no exploration of the evidence presented at trial took place in the jury room. This jury threw out the facts of the trial. We had no knowledge of this scenario until a week after the trial. Hence, in just several hours of deliberation, most of the jury had made their decision.

To add to the injury of throwing out what was essentially the heart of scientific fact, the judge disallowed any monetary award if the jury found for us. I think that our case was a first in many instances. A civil case with no monetary award allowed? Because I testified that I wanted my son back?

When the judge said something like, "Not guilty," that's all I heard. I wasn't aware of the question the jury had to answer. I didn't gasp. We didn't break down and cry and hold each other. I didn't know what to think. What just happened here? As the jury filed out, one juror was crying—a person who sat throughout the trial with almost no expression on her face. She was not one of the sleepers—in fact, the opposite. She watched and listened with intensity. Filing out of the courtroom, this juror softly said to me, "I'm so sorry."

I knew that at least one person followed the truth.

67

THE MAN'S VAN KILLED OUR SON. The scientific fact proved that. Only a preponderance of evidence of ninety-nine per cent would ever have been enough for us. On our way to the parking garage the day before, Attorney Winters briefly mentioned that juries were unpredictable and not to get too confident. I should say that a small part of me was prepared for the unthinkable. Based on the help we got from the authorities, we learned not to expect much from the system. Mark Adams warned us that central Ohio juries are firmly on the side of law enforcement. We were, too, usually, but not in this case.

It's like getting knocked on the head. You reel, you stagger. You don't know what hit you. After the jury filed out, absently, I looked down at my tablet and pencil, picked them up and put them in my case. Betsey reached over and put her arms around me. Andy turned to put on his coat. David Winters gathered up his papers and files. No one said anything. I glanced across the aisle and people were laughing. How did Gams pull this off? Somehow, in some way, the random drilling had to be attacked and rejected. That could have been the only way.

During the time that I testified I made a concentrated effort to address my remarks to James Sapp. Every time I stared at him, he looked away. Like the deposition, he was not able to look at me.

I couldn't just leave the courthouse, knowing that this man's van had a part in our son's death and I believed that "probable cause" would put this man in the driver's seat.

As we walked toward the door of the courtroom leading out to the hall, I made the decision to speak to Mr. Sapp. I would make no scene. I would not yell—just a quiet sentence or two so that only he could hear.

Standing in the hall, but still positioned near the doorway of the jury room, I could see Attorney Gams with Sapp and his wife and another woman preparing to leave. Then, I believe one of them saw me standing at the door and the decision to leave was delayed. "Wait until she goes," I imagined someone saying, nodding in my direction. Betsey, sitting with Teresa on the bench outside the courtroom, got up and approached me. "What are you doing, Mom?" she asked.

"I have something to say to Sapp," I replied.

Just then David Winters joined us. "What's going on?"

"Would you go back into the courtroom where we were sitting and make believe you are looking for something?" I said to him. "I want to say something to Mr. Sapp."

"Sure," he said. Entering the courtroom, he walked to the bench where we were sitting and started looking around. When he did that, I moved away from the doorway, out of range. That did it. They thought I had left something behind. The party moved toward the door.

Sapp was the first to arrive at the opening. I stepped out in front of him and with contempt in every word, I said, "I believe you killed my son. *This isn't over.*"

The man took off like a scared rabbit. Like Peter when the farmer caught him nibbling on lettuce in the farmer's garden. I wasn't finished so I hurried after him with Betsey close behind. Then, unexpectedly, the woman who was with him and his wife, rushed in front of me and putting her arm out, like a crossing guard, blocked my path.

"Get out of my mother's way," Betsey said, confronting the woman.

By that time, Sapp was scurrying down the escalator as fast as he could with the fifth Mrs. Sapp close behind.

Betsey leaned over the escalator and said, "Your van hit and killed my brother."

Mrs. Sapp's words? "You just keep thinking that."

Yes, we will.

Epilogue

I CAN'T EXCUSE OR EVEN offer a reasonable explanation about why the FCSO failed to perform a most basic investigation into Andrew's death and the egregious dismissal of the BCI report on the Sapp van. It seemed that the system failed us at every turn.

I understand that we are flawed, fallible beings. We make mistakes. Decency demands reparation. And decency requires that we speak out about what happened. Silence is an enemy of justice.

At first, I was beyond angry at the jury and the visiting judge. I reported here that I witnessed at least three jurors dozing nearly every day and the judge himself napping. That was a clear sign to me that these jury members were uninterested and could not, obviously, be hearing evidence and testimony, let alone employ critical thinking as an important part of their jury duty. How could these jury members participate in an *informed* discussion? They hadn't.

We know, however, that at least one juror understood her civic duty. In a meeting with her after the trial at Attorney Winters' office, she expressed alarm to discover that most of the jury members did not understand the term, "preponderance of evidence." Struggling mightily to help those who had difficulty understanding the term and getting no results, she had yet to hear the worst. When one jury member commented, "We should look at the evidence now," another juror, older, argued to do that would be a waste of time because no part on any vehicle is ever installed randomly. He completely dismissed the custom drilling of the ground effect. He continued his argument, stating that he had worked on assembly lines and each part is precisely installed. Then he added that the guy from Glaval was the plaintiffs' (our) paid expert. That somehow we got Dewayne Creighton, an executive of Glaval Corporation, to lie for us? That evening physically sickened by the level of ignorance, she believed that she could not return. The next morning, lying in bed and wanting to have no part in what she observed, she resolved that she could not participate in the travesty she had witnessed. She decided to call in sick. Then realizing that if she was the lone voice of reason and knowledge, she had to be there to counter the inaccuracies—it was her civic duty. Despite her Herculean attempts to discuss custom installation, the jury never looked at the ground effect evidence – those pieces left at the scene of the crash. All the experts' testimony about the installation of the ground effect—the bulk and focus of this case—was dismissed by one jury member whom the other members followed blindly—*except one*. Hence, all the meticulous work, all the mechanical evidence, all the research were discarded with the swipe of one juror's opinion. The lone juror could have stopped deliberations and called for clarification, but she didn't.

I have to hand it to Attorney Gams. With not a shred of evidence to go on, he managed to get his client, State Farm vindicated. Hard evidence pointed to the Sapp van—the vehicle that killed our son. This was one case he could chalk up to pure craftiness. And maybe he can tell his own son some day, with a chuckle, about how he did it.

References

Quotation: Harry G. Frankfurt, *On Truth,* Alfred A. Knopf, New York, 2006, pp. 36, 37, 46,47, 65, 66.

Robert Browning, *Song from Pippa Passes,* Bells and Pomegranates Series, Volume I, 1841, "God's in His heaven, all's right with the world."

Obituary, Andrew J. Starinchak, *Columbus Dispatch,* August 4, 5 1998.

FCSO's Notice of Media Advisory for August 7, 1998, 3:00 p.m

Media Conference: *Columbus Dispatch;* TV Stations, Channels, 4, 6 and 10, August 7, 1998.

Liz Sidoti, "Family Pleads for Help in Son's Death," *Columbus Dispatch,* August 8, 1998, News 01B.

Reference to Deposition of Deputy David McMannis, FCSO, at Attorney M. Gams' office, Motorist Mutual Building, November, 2003.

Glaval Corporation's Van List, Brad Sherman, Service Manager, Glaval Corporation, Elkhart, Indiana, August, 1998.

Reference to Deposition of Deputy David McMannis, FCSO, May, 2000, Franklin County Prosecutor's Office.

Polaroid photos for Reward Poster, August 14, 1998, FCSO.

Reward Poster printed August 18, 1998.

Crime Stoppers, "Rewards Offered for Information in Hit-Skip Death," *Columbus Dispatch,* News 06B, September 8, 1998.

Channel WSYX, Crime Stoppers Interview with Elaine and Andy Starinchak; Deputy David McMannis, FCSO, airing September 7, 1998.

Starinchaks' Meeting with Don Corbin, Chief of Police, Johnstown Police, September, 1998.

Nancy J. Smeltzer, "Riders Stop to Recall a Fallen Bicyclist, Friend," *Columbus Dispatch,* 01A, October 19, 1998.

Yolanda Harris, *WSYX,* coverage of first Andy/24 Tournament, OSU, Beekman Field, June, 1999.

Casey, The Night Geezer, Poems, Andy/24 Tournament

Citation from Gov. Robert Taft for Andy/24 Tournament charity for Salesian Boys and Girls Club, Columbus, Ohio.

Ohio Revised Code, Hit-and-Run crashes, RC 4549.02, 4549.03, 4549.99, 4507.16.

Reference to Deposition of Deputy McMannis, FCSO, Attorney Mark Gams' office, November 14, 2003.

MADD award to retired Akron State Highway Patrolman. *Columbus Dispatch,* November, 1990.

Franklin County Sheriff Traffic Office, personal visit to Deputy David McMannis, December, 1999.

Jackson Pike Facility, January, 2000 interview of girlfriend of man named in tip.

Reference to the above man named in tip in Deputy David McMannis' deposition, May, 2000.

Sgt. Ross Staggs, FCSO, Interview of tipster, January, 2000. (no tape in machine).

Starinchaks, et al v. John Doe, unnamed driver, Case No. 99-CVC -09-7714, Franklin County Court of Common Pleas.

Email from Starinchaks' Attorney Mark Adams, April, 2000, re Deputy David McMannis' notice of deposition

Deposition of Deputy David McMannis, FCSO, Attorney Mark Adams, Franklin County Court of Common Pleas, Case No. 99-CVC-09-7719, Prosecutor's Office, Franklin County Court House, May 4, 2000. Also present: Assistant Prosecutor Harland Hale; Private Investigator Don Sonney; Retired Crash Reconstructionist for the OSHP, Jack Holland; Elaine and Andrew Starinchak.

Crash Report, FCSO, Central College Road, Plain Township, August 2, 1998.

Central Ohio Crime Stoppers Tips, August, 1998 through September, 1999

Emails to and from Attorney Adams re chain of custody of ground effect pieces by Private Investigator Don Sonney to allow Glaval Corporation's officials to examine the pieces.

Crime Stoppers, *Columbus Dispatch*, "Van Driver Sought in Bike Rider's Death," *06B*, August 9, 1999.

Conference with Glaval officials, Elkhart, Indiana, re Ground Effect, June 2000.

Reference to Tom Daniels, Sunbury Police Department; Attorney Mark Adams, Case No. 99-CVC-09-7719, Franklin County Court of Common Pleas, July 27, 2000.

Reference to Jack Daniels, Genoa Police Department; Attorney Mark Adams, Case No. 99-CVC-09-7719, Franklin County Court of Common Pleas, July 28, 2000.

Reference to depositions of three brothers; one of whom was named in Crime Stoppers.

Attorney Adams' letter to Deputy Ross Staggs, FCSO, October, 2000.

Meeting at FCSO, Mound Street, with Chief Deputy Gil Jones, Major Tom Bateson, Sgt. Ross Staggs; October, 2000. Also present: Starinchaks, Attorney Adams and Private Investigator Don Sonney.

Mark Ferenchik, "Wanted: Their Son's Killer," *Columbus Dispatch*, 01B, August 1, 2000, the second anniversary of Andrew's death

Email to Mark Ferenchik, reporter of the *Columbus Dispatch,* from Elaine Starinchak

Jack Holland, retired Crash Reconstructionist with OSHP, examination of 1993 Glaval van, Metro Chevrolet, Columbus, OH, July 10, 2001.

Daphne DuMaurier, *Rebecca,* movie directed by Alfred Hitchcock, 1935.

Deputy Steve Fickenworth, FCSO, *Investigative Summary*, July 24, 2001 of events re 1993 Glaval Astro van from Metro Chevrolet, July 12 – August 01, 2001.

Deputy Ross Staggs, FCSO, *Report* of 1993 Glaval Astro van from Metro Chevrolet, dated July 27, 2001, of events July 10, 11 and 25, 2001.

Chief Deputy Gil Jones, FCSO, letter to Attorney Benson Wolman, July 31, 2001.

Deputy Steve Fickenworth, FCSO, submitting officer to BCI, list of items and examinations requested, July 19, 2001.

Karen Kwek, Ph.D., Ohio Bureau of Criminal Investigation and Identification, *Initial report of examination* of 1993 Glaval van from Metro Chevrolet to FCSO, July 27, 2001.

WSYX, television airing of Crime Stoppers Interview, September 6, 1998, Jon Griener, reporter, Deputy David McMannis, Elaine and Andy Starinchak and daughter.

Deputy Ross Staggs, FCSO, *Report, July 27, 2001* re 1993 Glaval Astro van from Metro Chevrolet.

Mark Ferenchik and Joe Gullien, "Bicyclist's death still a mystery after 5 years; parents' civil suit...", *Columbus Dispatch,* Metro & State, August 1 2003.

Anthony Bouza, retired police chief, Bronx, New York and Minneapolis, Minnesota, *Police Unbound, Corruption, Abuse and Heroism by the Boys in Blue,* Promethus Books, New York, 2001

Franklin County Court of Common Pleas, Criminal Division, 2000; Attempted Murder by buyer of 1993 Glaval van from Spitzer Dodge, Reynoldsburg, November, 1998.

Mark Adams, email to Starinchaks re Prosecutor's permission to examine 1993 Glaval Astro van, March, 2002.

Deputy Ross Staggs, FCSO, Report stating the 1993 Glaval Astro van had been transported to SEA, May 31, 2002.

WSYX, Crime Stoppers Television interview, September 7, 1998.

"Rewards Offered for Information in Hit-Skip Death," Crime Stoppers, *Columbus Dispatch,* News 06B, September 8, 1998.

Spitzer Dodge, dealership, Columbus, OH, Sales Agreement to buy James O. Sapp's (owner) 1993 Glaval Astro van, September 9, 199

"A Slow Death in Garage: a hit-and-run case becomes a murder for a Texas woman," *Newsweek,* March 18, 2002.

Reference to Ohio Revised Code, Hit/Skip fatalities, RC 4509.02, 4509.03, 4549.99, 4507.16, 1998.

Editorial," THE LAW DOESN'T WORK- Hit-skip penalty isn't sufficient to punish wrongdoers," *Columbus Dispatch*, 14A, November 16, 2002.

Dean Narcisco, "Police Using Paint Chips to Hunt Car – Hit-and-run claimed life of officer on East Side," *Columbus Dispatch*, News, 05C, May 2, 2001.

MADD Conference, Columbus, OH, "Victims' Advocacy," July, 2002.

William Wordsworth, "My Heart Leaps Up," from *Ode: Intimations of Immortality,1807.*

Deposition, James O. Sapp, owner of 1993 van, Attorney Mark Adams, Franklin County Court of Common Pleas, 01CVD09-08815, August 28, 2002. Also present, Patty Adams, Elaine and Andrew Starinchak.

Stan B. Walters, *The Truth about Lying: How to Spot a Lie and Protect Yourself from Deception,* SourceBooks, Inc., Naperville, IL, 2000, p. 167 and p. 135.

Evelin Sullivan, *The Concise Book of Lying;* Farrar, Straus and Giroux, New York, 2001.

Ann E. Weiss, *Lies Deception and Truth,* Houghton Mifflin Company, Boston, 1988

Joe Blundo, So To Speak: "Players Endure Rain, Miss Sleep to ensure that Friend is Remembered," *Columbus Dispatch,* 01B, August 24, 2004.

Complaint, Elaine Starinchak, Plaintiff v. James O. Sapp, Franklin County Court of Common Pleas, October, 2002.

Motion for Summary Judgment, Defendant James O. Sapp, Franklin County Court of Common Pleas, Case No. 02-CVH-10-11182, February, 2003.

Attorney Mark Adams' email, "Good News" May, 2003.

Judge Lisa Sadler, *Decision & Entry Overruling Motion for Summary Judgment,* Franklin County Court of Common Pleas, Case No. 02-CVH-10-11182, May 2003.

L. Frank Baum, *The Wonderful Wizard of Oz (film: Wizard of Oz, 1939),* George M. Hill Co., Chicago, May, 1906.

Deposition, Charlie Roup, Comptroller, Frank Z. Chevrolet, Attorney Mark Adams for Plaintiffs; Attorney Danielle R. Dunn of Gallagher & Gams for Defendant, Sapp, Franklin County, Ohio, Court of Common Pleas Case No. 02-CVH-10-11182, Holiday Inn, Fairborn, Ohio, May 28, 2003. Also present Elaine and Andrew E. Starinchak.

Deposition, Pat Kowalski, Manager Voss Chevrolet, Attorney Mark Adams for Plaintiffs; Attorney Danielle R. Dunn of Gallagher & Gams for Defendant; Franklin County, Ohio Court of Common Pleas Case No. 02-CVH-10-11182, Holiday Inn, Fairborn, Ohio, May 28, 2003. Also present Elaine and Andrew E. Starinchak.

Deposition, original owner of 1993 Glaval Astro Van, Attorney Mark Adams for Plaintiffs; Attorney Danielle R. Dunn of Gallagher & Gams for Defendant, Franklin County, Ohio, Court of Common Pleas Case No. 02-CVH-10-11182, Holiday Inn, Fairborn, Ohio, May 28, 2003. Also present Elaine and Andrew E. Starinchak.

Deposition, Richard P. Masa, Manager Spitzer Dodge, Attorney Mark Adams for Plaintiffs; Attorney Danielle R. Dunn of Gallagher & Gams for Defendant, Franklin County, Ohio, Court of Common Pleas Case No. 02-CVH-10-11182, Law Offices of Attorney Adams, May 30, 2003. Also present Elaine and Andrew E. Starinchak

Deposition, Mrs. J. Sapp; Attorney David Winters for Plaintiffs; Attorney Mark Gams for Defendant, Franklin County Court of Common Pleas, Case No. 02-CVH-10-11182, August 23, 2003. Also present: Elaine and Andrew Starinchak.

Deposition, John Wiechel, Ph.D., Chief Reconstructionist with SEA and expert witness for Plaintiffs, Attorney David Winters for Plaintiffs; Attorney Mark Gams for Defendant; Franklin County Court of Common Pleas, Case No. 02-CVH-10-11182, December 12, 2003. Also present: Elaine and Andrew Starinchak.

Deposition, Greg DuBois, Engineer with CTI and expert witness for Defendant; Attorney Mark Gams for Defendant; Attorney David Winters for Plaintiffs; Franklin County Court of Common Pleas, Case No. 02-CVH-10-11182, January 9, 2004. Also present: Elaine and Andrew Starinchak.

Deposition, Karen Kwek, Ph.D., forensic scientist with Bureau of Criminal Investigation & Identification (BCI) of Ohio, expert witness; Attorney David Winters for Plaintiffs; Attorney Mark Gams for Defendant; Franklin County Court of Common Pleas, Case No. 02-CVH-10-11182, December 19, 2003. Also present: Elaine and Andrew Starinchak.

Deposition, David A. McMannis, Deputy, Franklin County Sheriff's Office; Attorney Mark Gams for Defendant; Attorney David Winters for Plaintiffs; Franklin County Court of Common Pleas, Case No. 02-CVH-10-11182, November 14, 2003. Also present: James O. Sapp and Mrs. Sapp; Elaine and Andrew Starinchak.

Bruce Cadwallader, "Van owner faces wrongful-death suit in hit-skip crash," *Columbus Dispatch,* News 03B, March 24, 2004.

Opening statements of Attorney David Winters for Plaintiffs and Attorney Mark Gams for Defendant in trial of Elaine Starinchak, Individually and as administrator for estate of Andrew J. Starinchak, deceased, et al, Plaintiff v. James O. Sapp, Defendant, Court of Common Pleas of Franklin County, Ohio, Case No. 02-CVH-10-11182, before the Honorable Judge John Martin, visiting judge from Fairfield County, Ohio; Court Room adjacent to Sheriff's office of Franklin County, Ohio, *Volume 1,* March 22, 2004.

Court Testimony at Trial, Terry Wassmuth, Deputy and partner to Deputy David McMannis, FCSO; Attorney David Winters, direct; Attorney Mark Gams, cross; Case No. 02-CVH-10-11182; *Volume 11,* pp. 8-54, March 23, 2004.

Court Testimony at Trial, David McMannis, Deputy, FCSO; Attorney Mark Gams, direct; Attorney David Winters, cross; Case No. 02-CVH-10-11182; *Volume V,* pp. 14-104, March 26, 2004.

Court Testimony at Trial, Greg DuBois, engineer and defendant's expert witness; Attorney Mark Gams, direct; Attorney David Winters, cross; Case No. 02-CVH-10-11182, *Volume V, pp. 130-202, March 26, 2004.*

Ann Fisher, *All Sides with Ann Fisher,* WOSU, NPR, May 2010.

Michael Sonney, (son of Private Investigator, Don Sonney; a victim of Hit-and-Run Crash); Obituary, *Columbus Dispatch, 06B,* July 27, 2007.

Bruce Cadwallader, "Man Sent to Prison for 2007 hit-skip," (Michael Sonney hit-skip victim), *Columbus Dispatch,* News, 04B, March 28, 2009.

Court Testimony at Trial, G. Dewayne Creighton, President, subsidiary of the Glaval Corp., former Installation Supervisor, Glaval Corp.; Attorney David Winters, direct; Attorney Mark Gams, cross; Case No. 02-CVH-10-11182, *Volume III,* pp. 123-138, March 24, 2004.

Court Testimony at Trial, John Wiechel, Ph.D., Head Crash Reconstructionist and Engineer at SEA, Worthington, Ohio, expert witness for Plaintiffs; Attorney David Winters, direct; Attorney Mark Gams, cross; Case No. 02-CVH-10-11182, *Volume IV, pp.* 90-174, March 25, 2004.

Defendant's Motion to Remove Money; Judge Martin grants motion to remove monetary award, March 25, 2004.

Court Testimony at Trial, John Wiechel, Ph.D., Head Crash Reconstructionist and Engineer at SEA, Worthington, Ohio, expert witness for Plaintiffs; Attorney David Winters, direct; Attorney Mark Gams, Cross; Volume IV, pp. 90-174, March 25, 2004.

Court Testimony at Trial, Karen Kwek, Ph.D., forensic scientist at Bureau of Criminal Investigation and Identification, Attorney David Winters, direct; Attorney Mark Gams, cross; Case No. 02-CVH-10-11182, *Volume 1V,* March 25, 2004.

Court Testimony at Trial, Employee at DSCC and golfing buddy of James Sapp; Attorney Mark Gams, direct; Attorney David Winters cross; *Volume V,* March 26, 2004.

Court Testimony at Trial, Betsey Starinchak, rebuttal witness for Plaintiffs; Attorney David Winters, direct; Attorney Mark Gams, cross; Case No. 02-CVH-10-11182, *Volume VI,* March 29, 2004.

Court Testimony at Trial, Ken Wooten, Deputy, FCSO, rebuttal witness for Plaintiffs; Attorney David Winters, direct; Attorney Mark Gams, cross; *Volume VI, March 29, 2004.*

Bruce Cadwallader, "2 Experts Link Van to Cyclist's Death in '98," *Columbus Dispatch,* News 01B, March 26, 2004.

Jury Verdict, Case No. 02-CVH-10-11182, *Volume VI,* March 29, 2004.

About the Author

ELAINE STARINCHAK taught thirty years at a suburban high school in Ohio, having earned her Master's Degree at The Ohio State University. Besides her son, Andrew, she and her husband have a daughter, son-in-law, and two grandchildren. She is an avid supporter of MADD, and also of The Compassionate Friends, a global self-help organization of families who have lost children.

Made in the USA
Columbia, SC
26 December 2017